P9-CJD-329

This Advance Reader's Edition is an uncorrected version of the book. All quotations from the text should be checked for accuracy either against a finished copy of the book or, if not available, with the Palgrave Macmillan Publicity Department.

New
Old World

Praise for *Punjabi Parmesan*

"In sum *Punjabi Parmesan* is the story of the shared journey of Europe, India and China over the last tumultuous decade. It is an enormously ambitious narrative, yet the human scale of its perspective, its unflinching honesty, its critical acuity, its humour and generosity, and the directness of the writing make it wonderfully readable as well as richly instructive."

—*Amitav Ghosh (amitavghosh.com/blog)*

"Pallavi Aiyar is the rarest of Indian writers: one who takes close and persuasive readings of societies and cultures other than her own. Turning her sharp gaze from China to Europe, she showcases brilliantly in *Punjabi Parmesan* the many advantages of broad-based experience and comparative analysis. Anyone interested in the ironies, contradictions and dilemmas of globalization should read it."

—*Pankaj Mishra*

New
Old World

**AN INDIAN JOURNALIST DISCOVERS
THE CHANGING FACE OF EUROPE**

Pallavi Aiyar

palgrave
macmillan

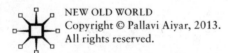

NEW OLD WORLD
Copyright © Pallavi Aiyar, 2013.
All rights reserved.

First published in 2013 by Hamish Hamilton by Penguin Books India

First published in the United States in 2015 by PALGRAVE
MACMILLAN TRADE®—a division of St. Martin's Press LLC, 175
Fifth Avenue, New York, NY 10010.

Palgrave® and Macmillan® are registered trademarks in the United
States, the United Kingdom, Europe and other countries.

The views and opinions expressed in this book are the author's own and
the facts are as reported by her which have been verified to the extent
possible, and the publishers are not in any way liable for the same.

ISBN 978-1-250-07231-3

Library of Congress Cataloging-in-Publication Data (to come)

Design by Letra Libre, Inc.

First Palgrave Macmillan Trade edition: October 2015

10 9 8 7 6 5 4 3 2 1

Printed in the United States of America.

For

My Father, Swaminathan

Contents

Preface

IT HAS BEEN ABOUT FIVE YEARS SINCE THE TERMS "EU-rope" and "crisis" came to be yoked, largely as the result of the financial troubles of governments and banks in several countries of the eurozone. Since then, the strenuous efforts of the European Central Bank have averted some of the more catastrophic potential consequences. The European Union has survived with its corporeal integrity intact, as has the euro itself. And yet, the crisis—which, as this book explains, is in fact the concatenation of several crises—continues to eat away at Europe's confidence, coherence and competitiveness.

This book focuses on the period 2009–2012, the years that I lived in Brussels as the sole Indian journalist reporting on the European Union. Yet the themes addressed are increasingly relevant. Demography and diversity, immigration and Islam, globalization and the rise of Asia remain a set of formidable challenges for Europe.

Economic growth is still stagnant, with even Germany, the region's export-oriented manufacturing powerhouse, sharply slowing. Unemployment is at record highs; measures to bring fiscal coherence to the eurozone are incomplete; and the willingness of national democracies to heed the supranational, austerity-enforcing diktats of the European Union is reaching its limits.

Across Europe, euro-scepticism is on the ascent. In European parliamentary elections last year, anti-EU parties made substantial gains, including victories in Britain and France. National elections in Sweden saw the far-right Sweden Democrats take almost 13 percent of the vote to become the third-largest party in the country, while in Germany, the anti-euro party Alternative for Germany has made inroads in regional elections.

An aging population and low birth rates in many European countries present a thorny demographic conundrum. And yet, immigration, both up and down the value chain, is resented. Most of the newly ascendant anti-EU parties, both right and left, are also stridently anti-immigrant. As Europe's cities become increasingly multicultural, the region is struggling to adapt to its new diversity.

Many of Western Europe's more recent citizens are ethnically different from, and religiously at odds with, the established majority in their adopted countries. The assumed divergence of their value system from the mainstream is provoking anxieties about what it means to be European today, concerns that are exacerbated by Islamist terrorism. The murder of 11 people in connection with an attack on the cartoonists of French satirical magazine *Charlie Hebdo* in January spotlighted these tensions.

Europe's crises are unspooling against the backdrop of a broad shift in economic power toward Asia, a long-term trend that has been accelerated by the financial troubles of many eurozone countries. It is increasingly evident that, for the old world, there is scant choice but to prepare for a new normal.

—Pallavi Aiyar
January 2015
Jakarta

Introduction

I MOVED TO BRUSSELS, THE BELGIAN CAPITAL AND
headquarters of the European Union, in the spring of 2009. My husband, Julio, a Spaniard, had recently passed a series of examinations
to qualify as a European Commission official, so the city would be
our home for much of the future. Having lived in China for the better part of the decade, it promised to be quite a disjunctive change of
scene.

Leaving Beijing had not been easy. My last few days in China were
spent in a haze of nostalgia for what I would be leaving behind. An
elderly man painting ephemeral calligraphy with brush and water on
the walkway of a park, the clatter of an intense game of mah-jongg,
the balletic swirling of steam rising from a cup of jasmine tea: every
image, scent and sound took on emotional significance as I mourned
their inevitable fading into wisps of memory.

But this didn't preclude a simultaneous state of anticipation. Seven
years was a long time to spend anywhere, and in some ways I felt I'd
had my bellyful of China. My work as a newspaper reporter had taken
me to almost every province of the vast country. I'd learned the language, made friends and had a baby during this period. And to wrap
it all up in perfect foreign-correspondent style, I'd even written a book
about it all.[1]

A new kind of life awaited in Brussels. I was aware that the Belgian capital was not renowned for excitement, but it did promise a
certain European charm: waffles and good coffee, cobblestones and
cafes. I imagined it was the antithesis of China. The calm to Beijing's
chaos, the Belgian yin to the Chinese yang.

It would be a move from the contradictions and messiness of a giant country hauling its toiling millions out of poverty to a settled, prosperous land of manicured parks and handsome fin de siècle homes. After years of being fed indigestible bits of sea slugs in remote towns in deepest Shandong, it was undeniably seductive to imagine a new diet of pralines and freshly baked baguettes.

What I would be exchanging in return for baguettes and pralines, however, was *the* story of the twenty-first century: the rise of China. For years I'd had front-row seats to the volcanic awakening of this Asian colossus, the consequences of which were leading to an epochal inversion of world power.

The China "story" had an elemental force to it. Having lived in Beijing in the years between the city's winning the bid to host the 2008 Olympic Games and the event itself, I had been witness to the visceral energy that was so characteristic of the country. In a paroxysm of growth, the city virtually vomited up entire new neighborhoods in what sometimes felt like weeks.

China's ambitions and newly resurgent position in the world were symbolized most often by superlatives relating to size: the world's biggest dam, the largest airport and museum, the longest sea bridge, the highest railway line, the most enormous IKEA store outside of Sweden itself—the list was long, with new records being added with unfailing regularity.

China's ascendancy was not limited to shiny new physical infrastructure either. Indicating one of the more startling shifts in global power relations, Beijing had also emerged as the globe's chief creditor, accumulating the world's largest foreign currency reserves and financing the spending sprees of the West, in particular, the United States.

And China was only part of the new, twenty-first century story. While Beijing might have been the showiest example among the emerging economies, my own country, India, had also transformed her hitherto lumbering economic gait to a veritable canter, achieving growth rates of 8 percent in some years.[2]

International Monetary Fund figures help to put this re-orientalization of the world in perspective. Between 1960 and 1985, advanced economies on average accounted for about three-quarters of the global gross domestic product (GDP). By 2008–9, this figure was down to 57 percent. In contrast, the share of emerging markets had risen from just about 17 percent in the 1960s to close to 40 percent by 2008–9.[3]

In short, the old world was old news. Indian newspapers had developed a Chinese obsession, alternately adulating and vilifying the country. This had worked to my advantage as a journalist, as almost every story I filed from Beijing was prominently showcased. Europe, on the other hand, barely registered a blip on the Indian media's radar. The entire continent tended to be reduced to stories of how Indian software outsourcing companies in the United Kingdom were faring. I was resigned to the fact that I'd be lucky if my dispatches from Brussels made it into the newspaper at all.

I consoled myself with philosophical reflections on my stage of life. I was, after all, no longer a footloose youngster, guzzling sea slugs with ne'er a care. I had a baby now and planned on more. Adventure for me had become equated with the contents of a diaper. Perhaps pretty, stable, pleasant Europe was exactly what I needed.

PERHAPS, BUT IT WAS NOT TO BE. The "story" found a way of chasing me. The timing of my move, in 2009, was such that before long I was once again in the eye of a news maelstrom. From the "Rise of China," I now found myself with front-row seats to the "Decline of Europe." In some ways, of course, the two were the flip side of the same coin.

But in the months leading up to my arrival in Brussels, the rebalancing of global economic power from West to East—what journalist Fareed Zakaria has called "the rise of the rest"—was unexpectedly accelerated and amplified. The 2008 financial tsunami set off by the investment bank Lehman Brothers' bankruptcy had turned conventional certainties on their head. The ensuing crisis was seminal, not only in scale, but also because of the geography of its origin. Unlike the crises of the past decades, it was not born in some poverty-stricken, developing part of the world that then needed the rich West to come to its rescue, but in the heart of global capitalism itself, the United States.

Over the next couple of years, the epicenter of the troubles would shift to Europe, with the sovereign debt troubles of the region's peripheral countries threatening a double act to the Lehman Brothers debacle. Switching on the television, I would be bemused to find the usual panel of talking heads waxing gloomily about political risk, uncertainty, lack of transparency and volatility in the context of countries like Spain, Greece and the United States, used as I was to hearing all of these labels more often applied to China, India and other emerging markets.

For much of my stay in Beijing, Western commentators had warned of the imminent implosion or explosion of the country.[4] It was growing too fast, they said, and any slowdown would cause disintegration. Given the journalistic penchant for animal-related clichés when it came to describing the changes sweeping China, the image of an elephant riding a bicycle was often invoked. With enough speed, the elephant could keep going, ran the analogy; but a single speed bump would cause the beast to lose its balance and fall off.

But the Chinese elephant was proving to be a far doughtier cyclist than assumed by many; or perhaps the image of a bicycle was the wrong one. An elephant strapped to a rocket came closer to capturing the velocity with which China had been hurtling upward and onward.

And where did that leave Europe? As a hydra whose different heads bobbed ineffectually in myriad directions? I am not a particular fan of florid bestial analogies, but it didn't take me long in Europe to realize that the region's troubles were akin to a many-headed creature.

The stories I found myself reporting as the Europe correspondent of the Indian economic daily the *Business Standard* over the next three years were filled with a surfeit of alliterative "C"s. Europe was at a *c*rossroads, facing a plethora of *c*ritical moments, its *c*redibility in question. But the most plangent "C" of all, that trilled above the cacophony of the rest, was the one in the word that came to define Europe's current state more often, yet more confusingly, than any other: "crisis."

As I wrote about Europe's crisis, or more accurately, its multiple and interrelated "crises," my reporting became an exercise in discovering just how many shades of meaning one word could have. This was a word that was abused as much as it was used, bent this way and that to serve the purposes of vested interests, populist politicians and know-it-all pundits.

Over the years I was witness to several demonstrations by disgruntled trade unionists holding up placards that read: "Say no to the crisis," as if "the crisis" were cocaine and Europe could heal itself by simply refusing it. Such ostrich-like denial was less than helpful. What was needed was a clear-eyed look at the crisis in its befuddling complexity, to peel back its sticky layers in an attempt to understand the challenges and opportunities that lay within.

There was the crisis of demographics, with the continent's already aging work force set to shrink by a million every year for the next five decades, a trend that forced the thorny issue of immigration into relief. There was the crisis of competitiveness, as large Asian challengers like China and India were changing the global rules of business. There was the knock-on crisis of Europe's famously generous welfare states, which many governments were now finding unaffordable.

And consequently, there was the crisis of social contract, as citizens and governments struggled to find democratically acceptable alternatives to replace the "deal" that had underpinned western European societies in the decades since the Second World War. Ample welfare states with beefy unemployment benefits, protected labor markets and substantial pensions had been vital to this deal, but it no longer appeared feasible without some serious reengineering.

Another aspect of the crisis of social contract had to do with the new kinds of citizens that the postcolonial states of western Europe were grappling with. These citizens were often ethnically, culturally and religiously at odds with their adopted countries of citizenship. In cities like Brussels, Amsterdam and Marseilles, Muslim immigrants, mostly from North Africa and Turkey, now accounted for over a quarter of the population. The visible differences of dress and skin color of these Muslim citizens, coupled with their ostensibly "medieval" values, provoked anxieties about what it meant to be European today. And so the region's nations were also facing a crisis of diversity.

This already dense cluster of challenges was further overlaid by a grid of crises at the level of the European Union that both affected and reflected the difficulties of its 27 member states in adapting to changing realities.

I arrived in Brussels almost a year before the euro crisis came to public view, but even then the European Union was facing something of a crisis of legitimacy, struggling to convince the world, and itself, of its continuing relevance. The original vision that had underpinned the creation of the European Union—the bringing of peace and prosperity to a warring, unstable continent—had long become normalized into a taken-for-granted fact.

That Europeans themselves were less than enthused about the "European Project" (the term commonly used to refer to the process of binding the continent in ever closer union) had hit the European Union on the head with a ballot box–shaped sledgehammer. In

2005, an attempt to bring a new European constitution into force was abruptly derailed when French and Dutch citizens voted "no" to it in referenda. Voter turnouts to the European parliamentary elections were abysmally low.

Poll after poll revealed that the European Union did not have much sex appeal for the Europeans of today, who associated Brussels with bureaucracy, waste and boredom. Moreover, despite the efforts of the Eurovision song contest, no strong European identity had emerged among the region's peoples, who continued to define themselves in national terms, as French or German or whatever the case may be, rather than as "Europeans."

The European Union was thus desperately casting about for a convincing raison d'être. The rise of Asian challengers like China and India actually played into the European Union's hand. Advocates of the European Project stridently insisted that in this shifting worldscape, only a cohesive European Union, speaking with one voice, could hope to have enough clout to maintain the region's place on the high table of global actors.

For a while, the European Union seemed to pin its colors to the mast of climate change, attempting to find relevance in its self-proclaimed role as global leader in the fight against carbon emissions. But by early 2010, details of the Greek sovereign debt crisis erupted like a thunderclap and the European Union found itself fighting, if not for its life, then certainly for its soul.

It is the euro crisis that immediately springs to mind when talking about "Europe" and "crisis" in the same sentence. This crisis refers to the fiscal and banking problems of some of the countries that use the euro—a currency shared by seventeen members of the European Union—and the contagion that continues to threaten even the relatively robust members of the group.

The euro's woes pointed to obvious design flaws in the conception of the currency, highlighting the tendency among European Project boosters to put the cart before the horse (in this case, monetary union before fiscal union), in the hope that the presence of the cart would somehow induce a horse to appear.

The crisis further drew attention to the political and economic challenges of a union that was trying to yoke together countries with sharply divergent cultures, mentalities and levels of economic development. The European Project was clearly a flawed and fragile creature.

It might have succeeded in ensuring that war between its member states was no longer a reasonable possibility. However, it had sublimated rather than eliminated the prejudices and nationalistic xenophobias that continued to lurk beneath the veneer of "union" that the European Union stood for.

Within weeks of the euro crisis coming to light, Greeks were pillorying Germans as Nazis, while northern European countries characterized southerners as lazy pigs. PIGS was in fact the unfortunate acronym by which the "peripheral" countries of Portugal, Ireland, Greece and Spain came to be referred to in the context of the currency crisis.

And finally, the eurozone's problems also brought into relief the challenge of Europe's having to contend once more with an ascendant Germany, a challenge that some historians claim has been at the heart of European history for centuries.[5] The roots of the European Union lay in devising a vehicle to contain and channel German power in the aftermath of the Second World War. But now, Germany was the only country in the European Union with deep enough pockets to lead the region out of its fiscal travails.

Seen as a whole, the euro crisis was about more than fiscal or economic problems alone. It was, in fact, an existential crisis for the European Project.

This book is an attempt to weave together the key strands of these predicaments. These are challenges that collectively present Europe (understood as both a geographical location and as a "project" that involves the weaving together of nation-states into the European Union) with a set of demanding, but momentous, choices. The stakes are high, and the direction in which these choices are made will have repercussions, not only within the region's borders and in this moment in time, but across the world and for generations to come. China's rise has been one of the great, defining stories of this century. But Europe's decline, if that is indeed what we are witnessing, is of equal import.

It's easy for this to get lost, because Europe's "crisis" is not of the same texture as the kind of crisis we normally associate with the word. Walking around Madrid's stately boulevards or Brussels's charming cobblestoned streets, little appears amiss. There is no famine here. There is no stench. And there are no tanks in the city squares.

From my Chinese-Indian perspective, Europe's crisis is a rather strange creature. It is a nice-smelling, well-dressed, bucolic kind of crisis. And that is the other objective of this book: to describe what a First World crisis looks like from an emerging country point of view.

The themes I write about in this book are wide-ranging but selective. I do not, for example, cover eastern Europe or Britain but focus on continental western Europe, where the region's stresses and strains are the most apparent. Through a mix of memoir, reportage and analysis, the chapters that follow reflect my firsthand experiences during my three years as a journalist in Europe, as well as my perceptions of Europe's multiple crises, seen through the prism of an Indian who has also lived and worked for several years in China.

RETURNING TO THE DAYS BEFORE my big move to Brussels, when I was still in Beijing, my European friends in China had been largely agreed in their envy of my departure to the "civilized" world. When I expressed any apprehensions about the change, they would rush to assure me. Things would be so much *easier* than in China, they stressed. Everything worked; you flushed the toilet and watched the toilet paper disappear instead of the water rising ominously out of the bowl; you might pay more for food and clothes, but what you got was of assured quality; people in Europe lived by their word, they were ethical; none of that lying and cheating that went on in China with its get-rich-quick culture; the air was clean, the neighborhoods green; and people queued at bus stops and didn't spit out foaming gobs of phlegm on the roads.

Efficiency, reliability, quality, cleanliness: these words had echoed in my head, taking on an almost hallucinatory allure as our plane prepared for landing in Brussels on a late April's day. The ten-hour flight had departed Beijing at the unearthly hour of two in the morning. Our son, Ishaan, had slept only fitfully and fussed for much of the journey. And we'd also been worried about our two cats, Caramel and Tofu, who were somewhere in the bowels of the plane, no doubt frightened half to death.

Random thoughts had flitted through my mind. How was I ever going to get my head around the byzantine machinations of the European Union? How would my hutong cats adjust to their new environs, which would undoubtedly lack the slinking Chinese weasels, flapping neighborhood chickens and other forms of feline-friendly entertainment they had grown up with in Beijing? How was I going to make it through the day balancing the stress of a new city and a new job with the care of my son?

I'd tried to comfort myself with visions of all that efficiency and cleanliness that I'd been told awaited me in Europe. But in fact, my multiple encounters with "crises" in the region were about to kick off a lot sooner than I could have imagined, with a personal crisis all of my own. Within an hour of landing in the Brussels airport, I would be desperately knocking at the door of a police station, wild-eyed and begging for help. I will save the details of this theatrical start to my life in Europe for Chapter One, "Adventures in Occidentalism," a somewhat tongue-in-cheek look at the culture shock that Brussels can present to someone more used to the norms of the "Orient." Although the process of starting and shaping a new life is not easy in any country, the particular challenges that western Europe poses to the newcomer offer insights into some of the wider predicaments that beset the region.

The kind of "welcome" I received in Brussels would linger with me for months. It was a constant reminder of the anxieties and dilemmas that the changing social makeup of many European societies was precipitating. Muslim immigrants had appropriated and transformed large parts of major European cities into culturally unfamiliar and potentially threatening spaces. It is these new citizens of Europe that are the subject of Chapter Three, "The Veiled Threat."

The Brussels that became my home for the next few years was not only a city of art nouveau buildings, Trappist beer and creamy chocolate but equally a city of mosques, mint tea and falafel. Almost a quarter of Brussels's current population, or some 250,000 people, are immigrants from Muslim countries, primarily Morocco and Turkey.[6] One of the complaints most often heard about Europe's new Muslim citizens was that they were a drain on the welfare state and were predisposed to unemployment or criminality. But there was also another kind of diametrically opposite charge leveled against other categories of immigrants, to which the region's Indians and Chinese belonged: that they worked too much.

In Chapter Two, "A Hall of Mirrors," I focus on these. The examples I dwell on in detail represent migrants at both the upper and lower ends of the value chain: Gujarati diamantaires in Antwerp and Punjabi agricultural laborers in Italy. Although it's likely that in the absence of the industriousness and flexibility displayed by these migrants, world-famous industries like Belgium's diamond trade and Italy's agricultural produce would be floundering to compete, these hard-working people were resented. By working "too hard" or for too little pay, they were lowering the "standard" of living that Europe's work force seemed to expect as its birthright, it was said.

As an Indian who had just moved to Europe from China, it was painfully clear to me just how entitled a generation of citizens the welfare states of western Europe had produced. In emerging countries, people were motivated by the opportunity to work. In the developed world they appeared to be motivated chiefly by the opportunity to holiday.

There was a particular conceit I often encountered that revolved around the idea that, unlike in China or India, making money was not an end in itself for Europeans, who instead prioritized other kinds of leisure activities, including time spent with family and friends. But this hierarchy of values was not some inherent consequence of an innately superior European culture. It was underpinned by enormous privileges that were increasingly unsustainable. The euro crisis would soon make it clear that Europeans were going to have to start working longer and harder, because although a Belgian plumber might still have turned up his nose at a chance to earn some extra cash, European governments were increasingly desperate for money.

Living in Brussels, I sometimes felt that life for the middle classes in emerging countries like India and China was easier than in Europe. Many of the traditional demarcations between North and South no longer applied. The ration cards for food, the years-long wait for a phone connection and the excitement engendered by visitors from abroad bearing the Toblerone chocolates and well-stitched jeans that were once unavailable at home, were already a distant memory for the millions of new consumers in Asia.

It took me a day to get a phone connection installed in Beijing, but several weeks to get one in Brussels. It took me five days to get my residence card in China when I moved there back in 2002, compared to nine weeks for the equivalent in Brussels. The cost of living in China and India is considerably lower than in Europe, making eating out and entertainment easily affordable. The same global brands available on high streets in London and Paris are oozing from the malls of Beijing's Sanlitun neighborhood and Delhi's suburb of Gurgaon.

"Life is easier for Western expatriates in China than it is for Chinese expatriates in the West," claimed the headline of one article in the *Economist* magazine, based on interviews with both varieties of expats.[7] But I was well aware that despite the inversions that the "rise of the rest" and the relative "decline of the West," were creating, it was far too premature to declare the South as the New North. This realization came home every time I took a deep breath of the clean, almost fragrant (to the Asian megacity-accustomed) air of Brussels. What really differentiated the developed and the developing world, at least from an emerging-country, middle-class perspective, was not the availability of consumer products but environmental safety and health care.

For all the enthusiastic plumbers and burgeoning shopping malls that life in China and India gave you access to, it remained impossible to turn on the tap and take a drink of water without worrying about ending up in a hospital. Indeed, the one area where Europe retained an indisputable superiority over the emerging world was the environment, something that did not go unnoticed in the corridors of power in Brussels. I arrived in Europe in the lead-up to the United Nations Climate Change meeting in Copenhagen, an event that was ubiquitously billed as humanity's great chance to agree to substantial measures to combat climate change. And the European Union had enthusiastically taken up the mantle of "leading" this fight.

In Chapter Four, "Tilting at Windmills," I focus on the hypocrisy and hubris that tinted much of Europe's climate change rhetoric. The European Union's self-styled leadership in battling global warming had much to do with attempts to give a new purpose to the European Project at a time when Europe was finding itself losing stature and influence internationally. The failure of this endeavor was demonstrated at the Copenhagen meeting, and the chapter includes an inside look at the drama and follies of what went on there.

Unfortunately for Europe's climate-change warriors, barely a month had passed since the failure at Copenhagen when the euro crisis surfaced to public attention. In the coming years, Europe's energies and resources would largely be directed toward containing the spread of fiscal contagion across the eurozone. And climate change was left dangling as a cause whose sponsors had moved on to more pressing concerns.

In Chapter Five, "The Austere New Boss," the action correspondingly shifts focus to the fiscal crisis, and in particular to the country that was subsequently propelled into the monetary union's driver's seat: Germany. Many of Europe's current predicaments have to do with the need to adjust to a global recalibration of power, as the emerging economies of Asia gain in economic and geostrategic clout. This chapter explores a different, internal dimension to the challenge of adjusting to the shifting scales of power. The euro crisis amplified the accession of Germany as the first among equals in the European Union, presenting Berlin with the challenge of leading and the rest of Europe with the challenge of adapting to this leadership.

Germany's ascendency was the result of its robust economy. But what accounted for its anomalous ability to remain a successful, high-end manufacturer and exporter, when most of the other countries of the eurozone were floundering? In order to find some answers, I paid a visit to several German *mittelstand*, the modest, yet potent, small and medium enterprises (SMEs) that comprise the backbone of Germany's economy.

The mittelstand reminded me of the kind of companies I'd encountered in the southern Chinese city of Wenzhou, arguably the most entrepreneurial place in China. But while Wenzhou's companies largely make low-value-added products like zippers and lighters, the mittelstand are strong in the high-end electrical engineering and industrial product sectors. Within the world of industrial components, the mittelstand's offerings are the haute couture to China's prêt-à-porter.

But the question remains, for how long? German SMEs had certainly proved impressively resilient, yet my interaction with mittelstand management left me convinced that they were dangerously smug. They seemed to believe that their firms' sound economic health was linked to an essential German superiority and was consequently impervious to external shocks. And while I found it to the mittelstand's credit that they tended to treat the rise of emerging economies like China as an opportunity rather than a threat, I also felt they could be too easily dismissive of their potential as serious rivals.

For the moment, China provided the market that Germany needed while Germany supplied the technology that China was still lacking. But in China nothing was ever static. Through the period covered in this book, the Chinese challenge to Europe, including Germany, was becoming increasingly intricate. Chinese companies had begun buying top-quality European assets, including some of Germany's prized mittelstand. Chinese manufacturing plants were now being set up in Europe, even as Beijing poured money into developing China's indigenous high-tech industries. Chinese tourists had emerged as the knights in shining armor for Europe's travel industry, while Chinese consumers were propping up prices for all manner of European products, from luxury handbags to French wine. Chapter Six, "Chateau Chongqing," explores in detail the perils and promise of the Europe-China relationship from a variety of vantage points, including that of a group of ten-year-old Little Emperors on a tour of the continent.

The next chapter, "The Global Gherkin," highlights Europe's dealings with the world's other major emerging economy: India. India does not pose an economic or strategic conundrum for Europe on par with that of China. However, the presence and trajectories of Indian companies on the continent encapsulate many of the ironies, benefits and difficulties of globalization, shedding light on some of the changed circumstances that countries in Europe are struggling to accommodate to. From the iron and steel empire of the mighty Lakshmi Mittal, to the humble gherkins of southern India, Chapter Seven takes a wide-ranging look at Indian businesses in continental Europe, a relatively new region of operations for them.

I was the only journalist representing Indian media in Brussels through the period I lived there. It didn't take me long to realize that European and Indian officials charge each other with almost exactly the same faults: the inability to focus on results and the lack of clear negotiating mandates.

Cue an epiphany: the Chinese were the Americans of Asia, and the Indians were the Europeans. After all, the United States and China were both oriented toward outcomes, even as the European Union and India valorized process. The United States and China were, moreover, able to act decisively in their national interests on the global stage, while the European Union and India struggled to find a strong and unified voice amid the clamor of their fractured coalitions and mind-boggling plurality. Yet it was precisely these similarities that fueled the disdain with which Brussels and New Delhi treated each other.

I believe that failing to engage with India will be to Europe's detriment. After all, in some ways, India is a proto–European Union, having successfully knitted a diverse geography comprising a multitude of social and cultural norms into a political and economic union. India stands as testament to the fact that despite some outsized challenges, projects like the European Union are not inevitably doomed to failure.

The somewhat unlikely subject of Chapter Eight, "Disunity in Diversity," is the rarely-featured-in-the-global-imagination country of Belgium. Belgium is not a European behemoth like France or Germany. Neither is it one of the PIGS nations, facing ruin as a result of the euro crisis. It is instead small and prosperous and commonly thought of as dull. But as this chapter will show, Belgium is in fact far from unremarkable and has always been a reliable barometer of the broader inclinations and mood of Europe.

Like the European Union, it is a nation deeply divided along a North–South axis, by language, culture, mentalities and economic development. Flanders is the rich, Dutch-speaking, fiscally conservative northern half of the country that reluctantly subsidizes the social security benefits of Wallonia, the economically backward, francophone, socialist south.

A set of complex, arguably Kafkaesque, institutional arrangements cobbled together over the years has prevented the country from tearing apart despite the visceral divisions that plagued it. Like the European Union, Belgium has been unable to resolve its problems yet manages to keep muddling along, averting collapse.

Despite all the sound and fury surrounding Europe's crises, these could come across as overblown First World problems, from a Chinese-Indian standpoint. In Brussels, furious protests outside the EU headquarters were pretty much part of the scenery.

At first, I found these curiously exhilarating. After all, while there was much to admire in the dynamism and entrepreneurial spirit of the Chinese people, life in Beijing for someone used to the raucous arguments that formed the bedrock of social and political life in India, could be stifling.[8] Given the massive dislocations—economic, social and environmental—caused in China by its embrace of state capitalism over the last three decades, the lack of audible dissent on Beijing's streets was a deafening silence.

In Brussels, the pageantry of cows mooing at cops and the anarchy of fishermen throwing their daily catch at eurocrats, held an allure to China-habituated eyes. But once the initial luster wore off, I no longer saw these protests as potent examples of people power, but as blackmail by the elite of rich Europe's work force.

These were not malnourished coal miners from northeast China whose families were dying from lung cancer. These were not subsistence peasants from Sichuan whose land had been arbitrarily appropriated by corrupt local government officials. These were not tribals from India's forests whose women had been raped and leaders murdered by mining company bosses.

They were usually trade-union-protected workers fighting against any loss of their substantial entitlements, no matter the cost to their countries as a whole. Striking dockworkers, refuse collectors, pharmacists, newspaper vendors, taxi drivers: everyone was in on the euroballoo. But while these strikers got all hot under the collar shouting about their ostensibly dire circumstances, I wondered if they realized just how elite they were.

Was it all that much of a crisis if Europeans had to retire a few years later than they had become used to doing? If they had to forgo their thirteenth month of pay every year? If they had to learn a language to find employment a bit further away from their hometowns than they would have ideally preferred?

A lot of the talk of the "Decline of Europe" variety was in fact about a relative decline, a gradual process by which other parts of the world were beginning to claim fairer and larger portions of the global economic pie.

If Europe were no longer as dominant in the world because other nations, long denied a fraction of the wealth and comfort of western European nations, were finally catching up, shouldn't this, in fact, be celebrated, rather than bemoaned?

In Chapter Nine, "Celebrating the Decline of Europe," I take a stab at answering this question. Is Europe's "crisis" merely the problem of a poor little rich boy, offset from a global standpoint by the great gains being made by the rest of the world? Or is everyone a loser if Europe fails?

Without giving away my answer to that vital question, let me confess upfront that I don't claim to know the outcome of the churnings that are roiling the region. The euro crisis remained unresolved through the writing of this book, and I lack the crystal ball that would let me either reassure or commiserate regarding the ultimate fate of Europe.

The legacy of Europe's contemporary crises could turn either way. We might conceivably find a more united and coherent Europe with greater policy coordination and a renewed sense of purpose emerging at the end of the tunnel. Contrarily, we might also find a Europe where the democratic deficit of an unelected technocracy, amplified by the hard times, leads people to reject the very idea of the European Project, seeking comfort in the sense of control and familiarity of the nation-state instead.

But clearly, while the choices that European leaders and citizens make in the coming years will calibrate the degree and temper of Europe's decline, there will be no simple return to "how it used to be." A cold fact that this once-imperious region of the world needs to come to terms with.

ONE

Adventures in Occidentalism

THE PLANE HICCUPPED ITS WAY DOWN TOWARD THE runway. I wiggled my ankles, stiff from the long ride from Beijing to Brussels. Another journey; another country. Seven years had passed since I had first landed in China, and now this new moment of arrival, with its attendant anxieties and anticipations.

Once inside the airport building, I looked on enviously as Julio and Ishaan sailed through immigration, their smart maroon Spanish passports in hand. As usual, I was left alone in the people-with-potentially-suspect-motives line, an unavoidable consequence of my Indian nationality. A salty whiff of nervousness wafted about the inhabitants of my queue.

We were the headscarved, the brown-faced; the wrong religion, the wrong smell. We tried to look confident, even nonchalant, as we approached the dispassionate scrutiny of the uniformed immigration officials ahead. But no matter if we were Indian or Moroccan, Chinese or Turkish, our hearts beat a tad faster as we moved forward. No matter if we were cash-rich tourists or scholarship-winning students, we were diminished to supplicants.

I hated the feeling, even more so because those closest to me—my husband and friends—were such strangers to it. As a Western-educated Indian I occupied a peculiar kind of space from their perspective, somewhere in the fuzzy middle ground between "us" and "them." In this I mirrored the predicament of emerging countries like India more broadly, the perception of which pinged between the poles of embryonic great powers and hopeless hellholes.

How could China and India, veritable superpowers, claim the sham titles of "developing countries" anymore, I would be asked repeatedly in the months that followed. In the run-up to the United Nations' talks on climate change in Copenhagen that December, there was much indignation at the defiance of emerging Asian countries that refused to commit to carbon cuts on the "spurious" grounds of equity.

Admittedly, the connection between carbon emissions and visas is not statistically robust, but there was an unreflexive hypocrisy in the way that the developing/emerging world was treated in Europe that was irksome. We were firmly of the Third World when it came to the granting, or not, of visas but morphed into superpowers on a level playing field with the West when it was a question of taking the economic hit for climate change mitigation.

Of course, this did not preclude my having my own brand of visa-related hypocrisy. I often oscillated between the desire to distance myself from the unmannered poor of the developing world and a more "noble" feeling of solidarity with the visa-hungry. Sometimes I was upset because it was I, the Oxford-educated sophisticate, who was being treated on par with the illiterate Punjabi peasantry. But at other times, I felt full of indignation on behalf of the illiterate Punjabi peasantry who were so regularly humiliated by the whole visa process.

But on that day, I was preoccupied by thoughts of a more prosaic nature—how to get us all out of the airport and into our serviced apartment with the minimum of stress. Luckily we bumped into Dimitri, a Dutch friend who worked for the United Nations in Beijing, as we exited the flight, and he offered to help us with our luggage: several large suitcases, car seat, stroller, travel cot, two cat carriers with cats, in addition to an assortment of backpacks and laptop bags.

Dimitri had also long crossed over to the other side of freedom and baggage claim as I continued my slow shuffle along the queue, sandwiched between an elderly Chinese couple in polyester suits and a large, turbaned African woman with a sleeping baby tied to her back. By the time I made it through, Julio and Dimitri had unloaded our bags from the carousel and rescued the cats.

We walked through customs, our expensive and hard-won pet paperwork at hand. It had taken three months to have Caramel and

Tofu certified EU-worthy, including sending blood samples to a lab in Europe and injecting them with microchips that effectively functioned as their visas. But it had turned out that a cat could gain easier entry into Belgium than an Indian: no one stopped us to scan the cats or check their paperwork because no one was in fact manning customs.[1]

On emerging into the arrivals area, we were introduced to Dimitri's father, who'd come to pick him up. Hands were shaken, and Ishaan dutifully cooed at. Then Julio went off to explore the cab situation, anxious to find one commodious enough for our effects.

Dimitri, his father and I stood in front of Ishaan's stroller, chitchatting about nothing in particular. The cats lay curled up in their cages, panting in exhaustion. Behind us a uniformed officer yawned lazily as he reclined in his seat within the cocoon of the security booth located at the exit of the customs area.

Despite the early hour, the airport was swarming with people reuniting, kissing, weeping, backslapping. I felt a light tap on my shoulder and turned to face a tall young man who spoke to me in rapid-fire French. I picked out *"excusez-moi," "ici," "arrivees"* and *"departs."* He was asking me whether this was arrivals or departures, I divined. "Arrivals," I replied triumphantly, my hand making what I hoped looked like plane-landing motions, and felt most clever at being able to understand French without ever having learnt it.

The man looked gratified and strode off into the crowds with a *"merci,"* and I turned to Dimitri, smirking. "Not bad, my French, huh?"

"What the fxxx!" he snarled in response and began to run manically away. I was a bit put out. This wasn't quite the reaction I'd been expecting. I turned in bewilderment to his father who appeared equally deranged, rummaging wildly through the bags that we had stacked up on the trolleys parked next to us.

Only then did it dawn on me that various items were missing: my handbag, our computer case. We'd been robbed. On our first morning in Brussels. Bang in front of the security booth. Dimitri had put it so well: "What the fxxx!"

Dimitri's father explained the mechanics of the trick we'd fallen so hard for. The man had asked me a question, not in order to ascertain whether this was arrivals or departures (come to think of it, there was a large sign indicating "arrivals" right above us), but to distract all of us for the few seconds it took for his accomplice to help himself to the choicest pickings among our belongings and disappear.

My wallet had gone and with it my credit cards and cash. Our laptop had been taken and with it the external hard drive on which we had so carefully backed up all our pictures and important documents from sundry computers we'd used in Beijing over the years. And our hard-won documentation for the cats had been in the laptop case as well. In an instant, Caramel and Tofu had been transformed from EU-certified, high-quality felines to paperless potential bearers of fleas.

And so, instead of making our way to the nice serviced apartment we had booked for some well-deserved rest, I spent the next hour at the airport police station getting my first glimpse into the kind of predicaments that were confounding Europe.

"So," the balding, thickset policeman in charge of interviewing me began laconically, "welcome to Brussels." I launched into the story of what had happened, as animated as the cop was phlegmatic. "What did he look like, the man who talked to you?" he asked, once I'd finished describing the exact contents of my handbag. "Um, he was tall, quite thin," I answered. The cop looked unimpressed. "He had wavy hair," I continued, trying to do better. The policeman sighed and put his pen down.

"Did he look North African?" Wow! That cut to the chase. "I suppose he might have been," I replied lamely. "Yes," he thundered, suddenly a lot livelier than before. "They always are North African. What can we do? They come here, they rob, they return to Morocco."

"Does this happen often?" I ventured. "Oh yes," he replied, "several times a day. In fact, you're lucky you only lost a wallet and laptop. The other day, a Chinese lady lost everything, even her passport. And she didn't speak English. It was terrible for her." He began chuckling most ghoulishly.

"Are you from India?" he asked, when the tide of mirth appeared to have passed. I nodded, hoping to wrap up the conversation, but the cop's loquaciousness was boundless by then. "I really like Indian food," he continued rubbing his ample belly unappetizingly. "It's strange, because Mexican food always gives me an upset stomach, but Indian is just fine."

He handed me a typed-up copy of the police report. "Well, hope you settle in soon. Brussels has some good Indian restaurants." It was obvious I was being dismissed.

"Um, wouldn't you like some contact information for me?" I asked, taken aback at the abrupt conclusion to our interview. "Why would I need that?" he queried, looking genuinely perplexed. "So that you can let me know if you find anything?" He looked at me as though I were a particularly exotic Indian insect. "You can phone the airport's lost-and-found department in a few days. If we find anything, we'll deposit it there."

IT WAS TURNING OUT TO BE quite a first morning in Brussels, "the heart of Europe" as it liked to boast of itself. "Ah! You fell for the question trick," clucked the taxi driver when we were finally on our way into town along with the recently filed police report and what remained of our baggage. "In Brussels you should remember to never answer a question from a stranger."[2]

I thought back to the numerous times in Beijing when I'd turned to passersby for help. Despite my imperfect Chinese, I had always met with kind, helpful responses that involved neither violence nor silence. But of course that was in the developing world, I thought to myself bitterly.

Of course, being careful when approached by strangers is something that every mother teaches her babe around the world. But in the vast megalopolises of the developing world, a sense of familial connectedness, an anachronistic spillover from village to city life persists, even in cities like Beijing and Delhi, which are home to upward of 17 million people.[3] This is evident in the way that one addresses strangers: not an impersonal "madame" or "monsieur" but "brother" and "sister," "auntie" and "uncle," appellations that instantly transform unknown and potentially threatening strangers into presumed allies who can be called upon for help.

Beggars and traffic-intersection hawkers make particularly good use of this tradition. In Delhi, gangly adolescents trying to sell trinkets to motorists at red lights had been a constant in my life. Nothing quite drove home one's arrival in middle age with the same punch as when these youth switched from calling out to me as "didi," or sister, to "auntieji."

Ishaan suffered his first experience of culture shock when a year into our stay in Brussels, he greeted a neighbor with a "hi, auntie." The lady, a kindly schoolteacher, shook her head and clarified, "I'm not your auntie, dear." She wasn't being rude, merely factual. But the manner in which we address each other can push us apart, emphasizing our separateness, just as it can draw us closer, underlying our connections. And in moving to Europe I sometimes felt adrift, isolated from those I lived among, in a way that I'd never experienced in China.

The developed world's stranger anxiety has its roots in textbook sociological catchphrases: urbanization, atomization, anomie, mechanization, individualism. There is a teleological feel to these theories. Societies when poor are largely agrarian and characterized by dense networks of family and clan that provide traditional welfare nets. With industrialization and increasing urbanization, in short "modernity," traditional social networks lose their potency. Extended families are replaced by the nuclear family. The individual's choices gain precedence over the community's ways. Traditional values rooted in religion are replaced by consumerism. Even as people come to live in ever more populous urban conglomerations, there is a breakdown of trust between people who have no shared history.

There are certainly aspects of this trajectory to be spied in both China and India. But the crucial difference between Europe and these Asian behemoths is in the sheer number of people that Chindia is home to, which makes the demarcations between public and private, mine and yours, a lot fuzzier than in the West.

In Delhi and Beijing, to live is to jostle. The idea of some kind of sacrosanct personal space is impossible to achieve in any sustained way, although the elite certainly strive to realize it. But even the plushest of air-conditioned cars bear the telltale bruises other vehicles invariably inflict on them in the frenzied crush of parking spaces. The grimy fingerprints of street urchins adorn their tinted windows, mementos of the tap-tapping of hungry children demanding money at stoplights.

I had grown up with what to a Westerner would seem a very lax consciousness of private property. I'd thought nothing of stopping by a parked car to hitch my foot up onto the hood and tie a shoelace. I got the shock of my life the first time I tried this on a car in England back in my student days and set a car alarm off.

I still smart with embarrassment remembering the sharp reaction I provoked in a German college mate at Oxford when I unself-consciously helped myself to his open packet of chips while we sat chatting in the common room one afternoon. In China, even the poorest peasants share their boiled eggs and oranges with whoever happens to be seated next to them on a bus or train.

In the shabbier addresses of Beijing and Delhi, cramped quarters and an unreliable electricity supply force people out onto the streets; so, much of private life is lived in public. But even in the posh, gated communities of south Delhi and Beijing's Central Business District, one's aural space is anything but private, constantly intruded upon by a variable mixture of honking cars, tinkling cycle bells, barking stray dogs, belching cows, itinerant knife sharpeners, the local temple's devotional songs, the jack-hammering of construction sites, and the neighbor's mobile phone conversations.

Would this physical and aural jostle for space gradually disappear as India and China grew richer? So far, it had only gotten worse, as ever more people poured into the upwardly mobile cities from the poorer countryside.

Regardless, avoiding strangers and their questions in Europe was advice that was not solely rooted in the region's high level of urbanization. It also had to do with the insecurities provoked by the millions of immigrants who had transformed swaths of many European cities into culturally unfamiliar and potentially menacing spaces. A few months into my first year in Brussels, I met for lunch with a young Taiwanese academic who was spending a few months in the city to research EU-China relations. His wife, who had recently joined him from Taipei, had come along as well. As we took a post-lunch stroll in the streets that criss-crossed their largely immigrant neighborhood, she told me that Brussels was not quite what she had expected. I asked her what she meant.

"Where do Brussels people come from?" she queried in response. I spent the next ten minutes trying to explain the complex divisions between Dutch-speaking Flanders and French-speaking Wallonia, and Brussels's unique position as a francophone enclave in Flanders. "So, although historically Brussels folk were Flemish, the city became majority French-speaking under King Leopold II; and although genuine Bruxellois don't identify themselves as either Flemish or Walloon, they are a dying breed," I concluded my lengthy discourse. She looked at me clearly dazed. There was a brief pause before she shrugged and said, "Really? It feels to me they mostly come from Turkey."

It was a comical moment, but her comment highlighted the fact that almost a quarter of Brussels's population, or some 250,000 people, are immigrants from Muslim countries, primarily Morocco and Turkey.[4] In many schools in certain Brussels municipalities like Anderlecht and Schaerbeek, over 90 percent of pupils are Muslim.

As an Indian I was used to streets as arenas of extreme, visible eclecticism. Delhi is a city where miniskirts and burkas, camel carts and BMWs, ash-smeared ascetics and multinational executives bob alongside each other. The city's polyphonic cacophony comprises Hindi, Punjabi, English and Hinglish along with lashes of all the rest of India's more than 20 official languages. Almost nothing looks or sounds out of place there.

But Europe is different. The creation of the modern nation-state, predicated as it was on the idea of a "nation" comprising one ethnicity, one religion and one language, had bleached the diversity out of many European countries long ago. The retreat of overt religiosity to the private sphere, coupled with the spread of homogenized, mass-produced goods for consumption, only added to the relative uniformity that Europeans associated with themselves.

To be Belgian meant being white, culturally Catholic, eating speculoos[5] biscuits with afternoon coffee and going to the seaside in the summer, come drizzle or high water. To be Spanish meant being white (defined generously), worshipping the pig by eating it in every possible form, and smoking Fortuna cigarettes under no-smoking signs with insouciance.

Being neither Belgian nor Spanish was easily equated with wearing headscarves, molding your actions to the Koran's diktats, or being called Mohammed. Yet, since 2008, Mohammed has in fact become the most popular name for baby boys born in Brussels.[6]

In countries like India, the premodern, modern and postmodern are interlaced and co-temporal, recalling the idea of *tiempos mixtos,* or mixed time, elaborated by Latin American sociologists in the 1980s.[7] But time in Europe is less of a hybrid, or at least had become less so, over the course of the nineteenth century, making the visible "otherness" of some of the region's recent immigrants problematically dissonant.

And, of course, the situation is further muddied by the fact that some immigrants are indeed disproportionately involved in criminal activity. While Belgium does not collect data that directly correlates ethnicity with crime, statistics linking nationality and crime are available. Moroccan nationals, for example, comprise only 7.6 percent of the foreign population in Belgium but constitute 26.3 percent of the foreign population in prison.[8] Moreover, since only 20 percent of those with Moroccan roots who reside in Belgium are not Belgian nationals, the actual proportion of those in prison with a Moroccan background could be considerably higher.

In Belgium, it is Moroccans rather than Turks or Congolese or Chinese who are perceived as the most likely to be involved in crime—something I didn't know when the airport policeman had baldly asked me whether the man who'd engaged me in conversation had looked North African.

Still, the cop's attitude was rather spurious.

North Africans are thieves; there are many North Africans in Belgium: so there is not much we can do to prevent theft.

It wasn't the strongest of syllogisms. Even aside from the frightening racism embedded in such an argument, surely regular theft at Brussels's international airport must have as much to do with the incompetence of the police as with the presence of North Africans.

In any event, I had scant time to recover from the shock of being robbed at the airport, given the paramount demands of setting up a house and shaping new lives for my family. The latter was to prove a lot more complicated than I had imagined. After all, although I didn't recognize it as such at the time, I was in a country in the throes of a crisis. And nothing goes smoothly in a crisis, even one of the First World variety.

WE BEGAN OUR EUROPEAN LIVES just as continental Europe was gearing up for what the Belgians (or at least the French-speaking among them) called "*Les Grand Vacances*." This was a staggeringly long period between July and August when large parts of the continent, and certainly Brussels, came to a halt, with everyone from EU civil servants to primary schoolteachers heading off on a grand vacation, clasping suntan lotion and beach towels.

It was not a good time to be attempting to settle in. Every time I tried to get hold of a gardener, plumber, or *chauffagiste,* to lure them to our newly rented home with offers of large sums of money, my efforts would meet with a hollow laugh.

Me calling a gardener recommended by a friend: "*Hello, any chance you could come over tomorrow to take a look at our garden? It needs mowing and weeding, and the hedge needs urgent pruning.*"

The gardener, cackling in amusement: "*Tomorrow? No, madame, it is impossible.*"

Me making a second, less ambitious, attempt: "OK, *how about next week?*"

The gardener with a sniffy mix of pity and contempt: "*But, madame, I am fully booked for the next month. If you still wish it, I can try and make it after the* vacances. *I think I have a vacancy on September 24.*"

We were speaking in May.

And so it went. It took us four months to buy a car—the sales staff we made initial contact with at various car dealerships invariably having vanished on vacation when we tried to call them a second time. This was more problematic than one might imagine as it became tougher and tougher to get around the city, with public buses having halved their frequency following a special grand *vacances* schedule as we approached July.

In Julio's European Commission dining hall, we were bemused to see a little tableaux of a beach scene set up in the center of the cafeteria, complete with an inviting-looking cocktail glass decked out with a pair of sunglasses. It was like a shrine to the God of *vacances*. Indeed, I was increasingly convinced of the religious overtones to vacations in Belgium, where many seemed to hold holidays as the raison d'être for work, and even life itself.

Several years into living in Belgium, my initial frustration with the European summer vacation felt a tad churlish. It is the promise of the sun and sea to follow that makes the endless damp, crepuscular winter of northern Europe bearable. And as the light begins to stay golden late into the evenings, everything from the *guttur-goos* of wood pigeons fat from gorging on cherry trees to the spicy charcoal scent of neighborhood barbeques does seem to seductively suck one into a vacation-desiring haze.

But my first reactions were conditioned by seven years in China—a throbbing, driven world on the go, 24/7. Beijing is a city where 1,000-bed hospitals had been set up in seven days.[9] Factories along the country's long coast buzzed night and day producing the cameras, clothes, sex toys, cheese graters, car jacks and electrical equipment that stocked the world's shops. Cargo ships leaving from the ports of Hong Kong and Shenzhen alone carried upward of 40 million standard 20-foot-long containers annually, or one per second, round the clock and year-round.[10]

Imagine, then, my disorientation in having landed from China in Brussels, a city that not only shut shop for *les grand vacances* but every Sunday as well. When I tried to impress people by telling them how China was pretty much open for business twenty-four hours a day, seven days a week, they would shake their head sadly, exclaiming, "Yes, isn't it terrible?!" Not quite the reaction I was hoping for.

In China, as in India, money definitely made the world go round. Even the Chinese Communist Party had turned blatantly capitalist. The opportunity to find better work, make more money, and improve one's lot in life is what drove everyone, from migrant workers in assembly lines to university students sitting exams and business executives putting in extra hours.

Following the 1949 Communist accession, a concerted effort had been made in China to root out religious belief, which was equated with superstition. People were taught to believe in the Communist Party instead of God. Over the last few decades the belief structures of the country had once again metamorphosed and money had emerged as the new God.

But China's arguably excessive focus on the material is understandable, given its twentieth-century past. The ability to make money had been a hard-earned right, one that couldn't be taken for granted. What I found more difficult to understand was the strange disconnect between the offer of money and the provision of services I so regularly encountered in Brussels. Plumbers were simply not interested in interrupting their weekends in order to come and help you out with a leaking faucet, even at 50–100 euros a pop. It just didn't seem to be worth it to them.

Anecdotes to support this point were bountiful. A British friend told me of the time he offered a delivery man from an IKEA store an extra 50 euros to help carry some furniture into his home. Initially reluctant, the man eventually agreed and told my friend to go inside the house to wait. My friend obliged. When several minutes had passed with no sign of the furniture, he went back out to discover that the delivery man had driven off, leaving all the furniture on the road, and so without the extra 50 euros.

Many Europeans I talked to about what, to me, was a peculiar lack of interest in making more money when the opportunity presented itself, confirmed my observation with pride. "Yes," they would say smugly. "Money is not everything to us." Time spent with family, eating a hearty lunch, indulging in hobbies like gardening, and of course enjoying vacations: these were the important things in life, I was instructed. Not just making money.

Of course, homes with gardens, lip-smacking meals, and relaxing vacations did not materialize for free, but I understood their meaning. Their conceit revolved around the idea that, unlike in China, making money was not an end in itself in continental, western (for, this patently did not apply to the Romanians, Bulgarians et al. of the east) Europe.

What they did not acknowledge was how this hierarchy of values is not the result of innately refined European culture but in fact underpinned by enormous benefits that were increasingly unsustainable. But this was back in 2009, several months before years of dodgy book-keeping in Greece came to light, sparking the fiscal fires that would blaze across the eurozone for the next few years, forcing governments to break the news to their uncomprehending publics that these privileges could no longer be protected. It was no longer business as usual.

THIS SHOULD HAVE BEEN UNSURPRISING because much of what passed as "business" in some European countries hardly deserved that label. There were times I felt the world had got its labeling mixed up, and I had not left communist China for capitalist Europe but capitalist China for a very socialist Europe.

Now, the lack of interest in selling something is one of the more obvious hallmarks of a non-capitalist society. Old China hands are full of hoary stories from the 1980s when the classic response to any request at a store or a restaurant in Beijing was "*mei you*," or "we don't have it." The enduring image of old-style China is thus of listless sales staff who equate customers with annoying intruders to be dispatched as quickly as possible, preferably empty-handed.

Fast-forward to the present day, and the shopping experience in Beijing usually begins with salespersons accosting you on the road outside, herding you into their shop with a mixture of begging ("please, I have made no money today"), bribing ("I will give you cheaper") and, if all else fails, yanking and pulling at your clothes.

And it is in Brussels that one is far more likely to encounter the dreaded "mei you." In our first week in the city, Julio set off to the neighborhood supermarket to procure a pair of house slippers. Having failed to locate any, he looked around for store staff who might be able to help. Finding human beings to talk to in Europe was never easy in these circumstances, with customers being furnished with their own portable scanners with which to total up their bills, and fully automated checkout counters fast replacing people. But with some persistence, he finally tracked down a lone, uniformed youth limply stacking boxes in a corner.

"Excuse me, but do you know where I can find some slippers?" Julio asked, instinctively adopting an apologetic tone, given the youth's less-than-enthusiastic expression. "But, monsieur, it is June," came the mystifying reply. "Um, that's true," agreed Julio, miffed but still hopeful. The box stacker sighed in despair and shook his head with irritation at being expected to provide further explanation. "But this is not the season. Slippers are only available from September."

The bizarre seasonality of slippers aside, it was the attitude of the salesman that was the real jolt for someone newly moved from China. And there seemed to be no escape from it. A few days later, we went shopping for a stroller for Ishaan in one of Brussels's more upscale baby shops. When we asked a sales assistant to explain the relative merits of the final two models we had narrowed down our choice to, she told us it was a quarter to six in the evening and the store was closing. The store, in fact, closed at six. She could have helped sell a 600-euro stroller. We were in culture shock.

Perhaps I shouldn't have been that surprised. I'd already got an inkling of the attitude to customers common in Belgium from my very first French lesson. Chapter One of my newly acquired textbook ended with a "dialogue" titled "*Une cliente difficile*," a difficult customer. Here is a translation in English:

THE WAITER: Bonjour, madame. Your menu! Let me suggest the
   rabbit in mustard.

VIRGINIE (THE EPONYMOUS DIFFICULT CUSTOMER): No, thank
   you, I am a vegetarian.

THE WAITER: Ah . . . *Alors*, we also have grilled salmon with rice.

VIRGINIE: Ah, *non!* I would like only vegetables.

THE WAITER: Only vegetables? Fine, here's a plate of crudités
(sliced raw vegetables).

VIRGINIE: Actually, I'd like some cooked vegetables.

THE WAITER: Cooked vegetables? Here are some French fries.

VIRGINIE: But, those are awful!

THE WAITER: Ah, *bon* . . . a plate of rice with green beans?

VIRGINIE: Yes, that's great. But please no butter on the vegetables.

THE WAITER: No butter? I see . . . Ah, difficult customers!

My French book was to prove an excellent preparation for life in Europe, in more ways than one.[11] The bit about the *cliente difficile* was followed by a lengthy section on *vacances,* teaching me valuable vocabulary like *"le pont,"* literally "the bridge," which referred to the practice of taking an extra day off to make a truly long weekend in the event of a public holiday falling on a Thursday or a Tuesday, that is, "bridging" the gap between the public holiday and the weekend.

And before long I was on Chapter Five where a dialogue entitled *"Une greve de train,"* or a train strike, involved a hapless chap called Antoine beseeching *L'employee* at the train station to change his ticket for Toulon on account of a train strike having been announced on the day of his scheduled departure.

"I need to be in Toulon to pick up my eighty-five-year-old sick mother. Please, can I change the ticket to an earlier date?" Antoine begs. "Ah, non, monsieur," replies *L'employee* implacably, "it is impossible. Your ticket is non-changeable and non-reimbursable."

It didn't take long in Brussels before one became rather intimate with strikes. Public transport officials in particular seemed to enjoy going on strike every so often for reasons that were often obscure. One particularly disruptive wildcat strike was eventually explained as a response to an attack on a metro driver by a passenger the night before. It later transpired that it was in fact the driver who had begun the fistfight because he hadn't liked the "aggressive" tone in which the passenger had asked him a question.[12] So, it wasn't only waiters who found their customers *difficile.*

STRIKES WERE A DEFINING FEATURE of the years I spent in Europe. Everyone from taxi drivers to dairy farmers was up in arms "against" the crisis, quivering with talk of injustice. But I couldn't help notice that these strikers were, in fact, part of the global labor elite. For workers in most other parts of the world, the injustice was how unfairly advantaged their European counterparts were.

The European dairy protests in the fall of 2009, for example, were held against the European Union's plan to gradually abolish milk quotas. Dairy prices had plummeted that year, but in response the European Union had enacted a range of short-term aid measures, including export subsidies (which hurt dairy producers in poorer parts of the world) and the direct procurement of butter and skimmed milk from producers at higher than the market prices.[13]

Not satisfied, dairy farmers in Belgium alone spilled around 3 million liters of milk on fields in September,[14] joined by farmers in France and Germany dumping equally egregious quantities. There was something deeply amoral about these rivers of wasted milk to me. But then I came from a country that was home to more than a third of the world's 150 million malnourished children under the age of five.[15]

The privileges of this global elite among the working classes were sometimes protected at absurd lengths. In France, thanks to union pressure, the number of taxi operating licenses that the state grants per year had actually diminished since 1931, despite the population having grown by more than 50 percent. There were 20,155 taxis in Paris in 1931, 14,300 in 1967, 14,900 in 2003 and 15,300 in 2007.[16]

Following large-scale protests in Marseilles in 2011 against attempts by the government to change some of the port's uncompetitive practices, an advertisement was placed in a national French newspaper for "the best job in the world." "Become a crane operator at the port of Marseilles for 4,000 euro a month, work eighteen hours a week, enjoy eight weeks' holiday a year, and savour a job for life," read the ad, placed by a local business federation.[17] This was satire, yes, but with a kernel of truth. Industrial action in Marseilles cost it 210 ship calls in 2011, representing 1.4 million tons of traffic and 4.5 million euros in revenues.[18]

The euro crisis that surfaced in 2010 was a symptom of the lack of competitiveness of many European economies, at the heart of which lay bloated pension systems, inflexible labor markets leading to sky-high youth unemployment and a range of entitlements and handouts that the states concerned could no longer afford to pay. For example, in Spain, one of the countries that was to become part of the epicenter of the eurozone crisis, trade unions resolutely opposed any changes to the two-tier job market that protected cosseted "insiders" with permanent jobs while exposing those on the outside to abuse and very little protection. Those on the outside tended to be migrants and youngsters. By the end of 2012, unemployment among Spain's youth had reached 55.6 percent (against an overall unemployment rate of 26.1 percent).[19]

But for me, nothing seemed to exemplify European socialism more than the regulations governing retail in Belgium. These were the most complicated in Europe, even beating France to the post. Julio being scolded for asking for slippers in June was something of a tip-off, but nothing quite prepared me for my voyage of discovery into the world of Belgian markets.

I began by dashing off an e-mail to the Directorate-General for Regulation and Organization of the Market (no, I am not making up the name), asking for an opportunity to learn more about all the regulating and organizing of the market they did. "It would be useful for an Indian audience, where many changes in the retail sector are currently taking place, to learn from the Belgian experience," I wrote somewhat disingenuously.

My tactic seemed to work. A week later I was seated in the aforementioned directorate before a panel of five earnest young government officials armed with pages of notes. This is what I learned: In Belgium, shops can only legally go on "sale" twice a year, in January and July; it is only during these periods that shops may sell goods at below cost or "extremely reduced" profit; and for six weeks before the sales period, shops may not advertise price reductions.[20]

Although offering discounts (as long as these do not amount to a loss) was legal at other times of the year, for a month before the biannual sales, textiles, shoes and leather products were not to be discounted at all. Moreover, the sales were reserved for the "seasonal renewal" of stock, so products deemed non-seasonal could not be included in the sale. Sofas, for example, were considered seasonal, but antiques were not.

To implement all of this, 200-odd inspectors from the directorate wandered around the country inspecting, while "many" complaints regarding non-compliance were also phoned in.

The rationale behind this mountain of red tape was the protection of SMEs, which it was believed would go bankrupt were big retail allowed to dump in an unrestrained manner.

But the officials admitted that the sales were in fact the most profitable time of the year for SMEs. Rather than cause loss of money as a result of the sale of stock at prices that were below cost, the sales had been found to unleash a consumer frenzy that set their cash registers ringing.

Decades of zealous regulation were, however, drawing to a partial close, thanks to the diktats of the European Union. In April 2009, the European Court of Justice ruled that the Belgian prohibition on "combined offers" was incompatible with European directives and must be changed.

A "combined offer" is one where the acquisition of products or services is tied to the acquisition of another product or service, for example, the common ploy of "buy one and get one free."

"Now because of the EU we must allow this," sighed one young bureaucrat, visibly distraught. But she collected herself quickly and moved on to detailing the next regulation pertaining to the operation of public phone booths and cyber cafes. "We are quite strict about their opening hours. They must shut at 8 p.m." "Er, why?" I asked, although by now nothing much surprised me. "Why? Well, to protect the public tranquility," she answered eyebrows knitted into a frown at my lack of perspicacity.

TWO

A Hall of Mirrors

THE CLARION CALL OF CONCH SHELLS BATTLED WITH THE shrill ringing of brass bells. Wizened men in masks, scantily wrapped in white robes, clutched outsized marble statues atop a chariot festooned in flowers and fluttering silk. As a pair of horses drew the vehicle through the usually muted streets of Wilrijk, an unremarkable Antwerp suburb, thousands of Indians dressed in heavy brocades and shimmering shot silk danced alongside. The colors were bruising, the clamor assertive.

Antwerp, a medieval port north of Brussels, was a city of trams and docks, and home to one of Europe's largest orthodox Jewish communities. While walking through the city's lanes it was possible sometimes to reach back into time and happen upon a perfectly framed moment of interwar life. The procession through Wilrijk was a twenty-first-century Technicolored rupture of Antwerp's sepia-tinted serenity. Local onlookers stared in bemusement, pulling their clothes more closely to themselves, as if trying to hold on to sureties that no longer existed.

The parade ended at the steps of an enormous confection of white marble: the largest Jain temple outside of India. Built at a rumored cost of 25 million euros, it had florid carvings that filled its every crevice—the work of hundreds of craftsmen that had been imported from India over a period of several years.[1] As various venerable acharyas, propped up by temple committee members, walked up the stairs carrying statues of Jain tirthankaras, a helicopter showered flower petals from above.

The hundreds of watching devotees were jubilant. The morning's *pranpratishta* ceremony marked the formal opening of a temple for which many had waited decades. As the day waned into the afternoon, a massive lunch service got underway in a purpose-built tent adjacent to the temple. The food had been prepared by Jain cooks specially flown to Belgium for the occasion, and great waves of hungry Indians spilled into the tent. Unperturbed by the crowds and the crush, the devotees navigated the swirling chaos with ease, finding tables and empty chairs, scarfing down Jain delicacies heaped high on plates.

The only faces betraying utter confusion were those of the handful of white waiters that dotted the tent-scape, bobbing around like lost souls in an utterly foreign land. Ironic, given that they were probably among the very few present who were actually native to Antwerp.

I found myself sitting next to a rotund middle-aged lady who beamed at me through mouthfuls of paneer. On ascertaining that I was a journalist she began to babble about the various recent "bulgaris." My mystified look prompted her to explain further. "It's why we no longer wear much jewelry," she said, her eyes as round as her belly.

I took in the sparkling diamonds on her ears and fingers and wondered what her definition of "much jewelry" was, exactly. Did the "bulgaris" she'd mentioned refer to the Italian luxury brand?

We were joined by one of the temple committee members, a post that seemed to elicit some respect, going by the reaction of the others at our table. Ingratiating grins were suddenly on full display as space was hurriedly made for the new arrival.

"Yes, we are all learning the necessity of being discreet," the committee member pronounced, to much exaggerated nodding from around the table. "The robbers wait for any opportunity."

The conversation finally began to make sense to me. My podgy neighbor had in fact been telling me about the recent spate of burglaries that had the Antwerp Indian community in a flap.[2] "Actually, please don't write about this temple either," the committee member continued, addressing me directly. "We really want to be discreet."

I wasn't sure that creating a mammoth, ornate marble temple was the best path to discretion. If anything the temple was a palpable, in-your-face statement of the Indian presence in the city. It laid claim on Antwerp. It planted a temple-shaped flag of arrival on it.

IT WAS ALL RATHER APPOSITE. Antwerp had been a key facilitator of European colonialism, for centuries serving as the entry point to the continent for silver from the Americas, diamonds from the Congo and spices from India. But in recent decades, the city had undergone a flip of fortunes, from erstwhile colonizer to a colony of sorts itself. Merchants had been at the forefront of European expansionism and so too were they at the vanguard of the modern-day conquest of Antwerp. However, the traders in question this time round were not Europeans but Gujarati diamond entrepreneurs who had gradually come to control up to 70 percent of the city's lucrative diamond trade.

I had first met with some of these diamantaires a year before the temple opening, only a few weeks after I'd moved to Brussels. I'd been curious about how it was that the Gujaratis had come to be so successful, and also the tensions that their ascent must undoubtedly have generated. It was one of my first assignments for the *Business Standard*.

My initial impression of Hoveniersstraat, an L-shaped lane by Antwerp's main train station, had been one of unrelenting greyness. The typically dull Belgian sky had accentuated the drabness of the slab-like buildings that flanked the street. There had been scant indication of the mounds of glittering treasure that lay behind the anonymous walls of these office blocks. For this unimposing pathway was the pulsating heart of the global trade in diamonds.[3]

Diamonds that make it to jewelry almost always travel a criss-crossing road from the mines of war-torn Africa to the luxury stores of New York. But whatever the route of the road, the odds of them having passed through Antwerp remain overwhelming. Despite, or possibly because, of the Indian takeover, 80 percent of the world's rough diamonds and half of all polished stones still change hands in this city.

The business conducted by the four diamond exchanges and 1,500-odd, family-owned diamond companies in and around Hoveniersstraat is worth tens of billions of euros. The trade accounts for almost 10 percent of Belgium's exports.

Antwerp's diamond business had long been controlled by its orthodox, largely Hasidic Jewish community. Although 65 percent of the Jewish population of the city was exterminated during the Second World War, those who had remained, their ranks swelled by others fleeing former Nazi-occupied countries in Eastern Europe, had been able to regain control of the centuries-old diamond trade.

In the popular European imagination, diamonds remain inextricably linked with the Jews. When I'd told a group of Julio's colleagues in Brussels my plans for a story on the Indian community's role in the trade, they'd expressed surprise. Diamonds? Wasn't that a Jewish fiefdom?

Once upon a time, it had been. But today, it is the Mehtas and the Shahs rather than the Epsteins and Finkelszteins who rule Hoveniersstraat. Indians have come to control almost three-quarters of Antwerp's diamond industry, a figure associated with the Jews only a few decades ago.

The first wave of Indians began to wash up on Antwerp's shores in the 1960s. They started at the bottom of the business with low-quality roughs, which offered very small margins of profit and were of little interest to the established Jewish diamantaire houses. These stones were sent to family members back in India for cutting and polishing, where labor costs were a fraction of those of Antwerp's.

Three decades on, the Indian community in Antwerp consists of around 400 families, a majority from the single town of Palanpur in Gujarat. Today, companies that had begun as one-man operations, dealing with a handful of diamonds at a time, have been transformed into billion-dollar global enterprises, employing thousands of workers, with factories and offices dotted across the world.

There are three main ingredients to this Indian success story: cheap labor, large families and a willingness to work harder than the competition.

The cost of polishing and cutting diamonds in factories in Surat, the main diamond-processing center in India, is as little as a tenth of the equivalent price in Europe. The inexorable logic of costs and demographics has meant that over the years the cutting-and-polishing business has almost disappeared into oblivion in European cities like Antwerp and relocated to Asia, in particular India. In the 1970s, Antwerp had boasted a skilled diamond-processing labor force of between 25,000 and 30,000. This number is now down to fewer than 1,000. In contrast, Surat employs some 450,000 people in the business, and over 80 percent of the world's rough diamonds are now processed in India.

For Indian diamantaires in Antwerp, the familiarity with Surat and other manufacturing centers in India is a big advantage. "For us, sending rough diamonds to India for processing isn't outsourcing as much as 'homesourcing,'" Santosh Kedia, owner of the jewelry company Indigems, quipped over lunch.

We were eating in the functional environs of the Antwerp Indian Association's dining room, also on Hoveniersstraat. Kedia served as chairman of the association, a social club with more than 2,000 members, virtually all in the diamond business. Three other board members of the association joined us for the meal, two of whom had lived in the city since they'd been toddlers back in the 1960s.

Kedia explained that when Indians first started to operate out of Antwerp they were bit players in the trade. "Most of us [Indians] had very little money in the sixties, but we created a new business area for small stones and low quality roughs." Building on this virgin territory, by the 1980s many Indian traders had made substantial profits and begun the move up the value chain.

The food was delicious: aromatic, steaming bowls of *rajma* and *kadhi*. Antwerp's Indian diamantaires are almost without exception Jains, and given the religious restrictions on their diet, tend to import personal cooks from India who are familiar with their particular culinary needs.

In China, I'd had the occasion to try to explain to a Chinese host the details of this diet in preparation for a dinner party where a few Jains would be in attendance. The Chinese already struggled with Indian pickiness when it came to food. Indians, especially upper-caste/class ones, delineated their status by increasingly finicky choices: no meat, no garlic, no onions. Many, including most Jains, wouldn't even tolerate a non-vegetarian in the kitchen.

And "non-veg" Indians would eat chicken, but not chicken feet; lamb, but not the intestines; prawns, but not octopus. To the average Chinese for whom status was flagged by the ability to afford as large a variety of food—the meatier the better—such discriminations were deeply mystifying.

When I informed the Chinese host that his Jain guests were not only vegetarian but didn't eat onions or indeed any kind of root vegetable at all, the gentleman in question gasped as if in the throes of a painful bout of indigestion. And I hadn't even got to the part about the prohibition on green-colored vegetables on certain days of the religious calendar.

Happily tucking into that steaming-hot rajma in Antwerp, I'd wondered aloud about how difficult it must be living in Belgium, given Jain dietary strictures. I could only imagine the apoplectic reaction of the typical Belgian waiter to a customer demanding a vegetarian meal, but one without any carrots, potatoes, garlic or onions.

Aditya Jasani, a sharply dressed youngster in his twenties, whose father had moved to Antwerp in the 1970s, shook his head. It wasn't that bad, he said in his generic, international-school accent. "Many of us aren't very strict any more. Some people even eat eggs."

I'd tried to look suitably impressed at this radical declaration. But unsure about how to respond appropriately ("Wow! Even eggs?!" felt rather disingenuous), had swiftly moved to change the subject. What about the other reasons for the Gujarati's success in Antwerp, I asked, steering the conversation back to where it had started.

"It's our joint families," Kedia replied. Joint families refer to the convention of many family members living together in one house. But what Kedia meant was the propensity among Gujarati Jains to have large, closely knit families.

Dilip Mehta, the CEO of Rosy Blue, an Antwerp-headquartered company that bills itself as the world's largest diamond manufacturer, agreed when I met him at his office on Hoveniersstraat later in the afternoon. "We always have the possibility of global distribution because a cousin or nephew who can blindly be trusted can always be sent to any country to set up operations," he explained, leaning into a high-backed leather swivel chair.

That the Jews lacked similar extended families was a major disadvantage for them, in Mehta's opinion. Given the global nature of the trade, he argued that it was necessary for successful diamantaires to have a reach that extended from the African countries where the diamond mines were located, to Antwerp where the stones were traded, to India and increasingly to China, where cutting and polishing was centered, and finally to the jewelry centers of the world like New York, Hong Kong and Dubai.

Rosy Blue earns annual revenues of well over $1 billion and has a presence in 14 countries, including factories in India, China, Thailand, Sri Lanka and Armenia. "We employ over 10,000 people globally, but a member of the Mehta family heads every operation," he said, his eyes crinkling above his beak-like nose.

Dilip Mehta had been given the honorific title of "Baron" by the Belgian king in 2006 for services rendered to the country—a fact he was coyly proud of. He spent some time reminiscing about his youth to illustrate how far he'd come from his modest beginnings. Having dropped out of college, he'd been dispatched by his family to Surat, then an up-and-coming polishing center, to work on the factory floors. "I had no car, just a bicycle, and would cook for myself every night," he said, absently stroking his balding head.

Mehta moved to Antwerp in 1973, following his father and brother who had set up shop in the port city a few years earlier. Theirs was a typical story. They'd made a living buying cheap, low-quality roughs, which they sent to Surat for polishing and finally sold at a small profit back in Antwerp again.

"It was just me and a cousin in a two-room office," recalled Mehta. "We would go door to door with our stones. I've always held that no matter how big you are in this business, you are still a sales-man and a salesman should have no ego."

Fast-forward a decade or two and Baron Mehta's name commands instant respect on Hoveniersstraat. The cheap labor and extended family had helped. But it was the third ingredient to the Indian story that was really the key, according to Mehta: a willingness to work harder and longer hours than the competition.

"The Jews just couldn't withstand our competitiveness," he said with a matter-of-fact shrug of the shoulders. "We are married to our businesses. We will work at night. We will work on the weekends. We will do whatever it takes to get a client. And we are willing to work this hard even for small margins."

The baron sighed. "Of course, sometimes I feel guilty that I'm such a company-driven person. My family always comes second to the business. But that's just the way it is."

How integrated into broader Belgian society were the Indians, I asked him. Did his kids go to a Belgian school? Was there any inter-marrying? The Jains were a notoriously conservative community back in India, and I was curious about how the decades of living in Belgium had impacted their mores.

"I think our challenge is really to learn how to keep some dis-tance between ourselves and the Belgians on the one hand, and learn from them on friendly terms, on the other," opined Mehta. Most Indians lived in ghettos, he said, because nothing in their education back home had equipped them to deal with living among Europeans. They avoided contact with locals because they were nervous about coming across as unmannered and incompetent.

Mehta was an advocate of "greater mixing." But it was important to remember your own identity at the same time, he warned. "You can go to a cocktail party if it's necessary for business. But that doesn't mean you should yourself drink. Never be ashamed of who you are." Jains are forbidden from alcohol by religious strictures.

But what about the second generation who were born and schooled in Antwerp? Mehta said most families sent their kids to English-speaking international schools, so only a handful of youngsters had learnt Flemish, the variant of Dutch spoken in northern Belgium. Inter-marrying was almost unknown.

Aditya Jasani, the youngster I'd met at lunch earlier, confirmed this. "Most of us still live like expats," he'd said. "We have one foot here, but another foot in India. Belgium is for business only. It's not our home."

I remembered these words a few months later when I was on the trail of a story about the sport of cricket's alleged Flemish origins.[4] The evidence for this claim involves a medieval English poem and a painting by the Flemish master, Pieter Brueghel the Elder. But in order to avoid bewildering the reader with a lengthy digression, I will skip the details and go straight to a meeting I had a few months later with Charles Blommaert, an earnest-faced Belgian cricket lover.

Blommaert had founded a cricket club in the Flemish city of Ghent and was a driving force behind the country's fledgling cricket league. The game was completely new to Belgium, its possible Flemish origins notwithstanding, and it was usually Indian and Pakistani expats who taught interested Belgians the finer points of the notoriously complicated sport.

The best-financed cricket club in Belgium, Blommaert revealed, was the Antwerp Indians, whose members comprised the prosperous Gujarati diamond traders. But instead of using their resources to popularize the sport within the wider community, the Antwerp Indians didn't permit anyone not of Indian origin to join their club. Clearly, promoting integration, even of the innocent sporting kind, was not a priority for them.

This fact was driven home at the opening ceremony of the Jain temple, where despite the community's public statements about the temple's value to Belgian society (publicity material claimed it enhanced "the glory of Belgium" and was intended as a "return gift to the country" from the Jain community), the only "natives" visible among the celebrating hordes were a clutch of waiters.[5]

BACK ON HOVENIERSSTRAAT, I'd visited the offices of one of the larger Jewish diamond merchants still in business, Abraham Pinkusewitz. His company employed 3,500 people in operations that stretched from Antwerp to Russia and China. Pinkusewitz had chosen China over India as the base for his diamond-manufacturing operations because, despite having come to the polishing game late, Chinese labor was "more efficient and reliable."

Pinkusewitz was a Hasidic Jew with a great white beard and deep-set eyes that burned intensely. His own children no longer lived in the city, having moved to Israel. I asked him why they had moved out.

"It's not a question of moving out," he replied shortly. "It's about others moving in. With cheaper labor." It was obvious whom he was referring to, but he did not spell it out. Pinkusewitz avoided my eyes, and a short but loud silence followed.

"Would you like a cup of coffee?" Eli Finkelsztein, the company's public relations manager, interjected in an obvious bid to move the conversation forward. But Pinkusewitz was boiling over with an anger that proved difficult to stem.

The Jews had always laid an emphasis on trade and business, he continued. This was because agriculture and other professions had been closed to them. But although business was important, it was not the "most important thing in life."

"We must adhere to certain rules," he growled. "We must keep the Sabbath, we must pray at least two hours every day. We have our religion. Our family. Our studies. So, we cannot be open at night and on the weekends or whenever, unlike the Indians."

Finkelsztein had begun sniffing nervously by now, putting an occasional restraining hand on Pinkusewitz's arm. But the old man shrugged him off.

"The Indians work too hard," he spat. It was the first time I'd ever heard "work" made to sound like a dirty word. "That's all they talk about, 'diamonds.' It's their life and they won't stop at anything to grab customers. Even if it means selling at a loss."

The bitterness was sharp. Pinkusewitz talked about his father, "an aristocratic, clever, respected man." A diamond broker of impeccable honesty with a reputation that opened all doors in Antwerp. "If I said I was the son of Pinkusewitz, I was welcomed without question. The name meant something special. Once," he said.

But over the last few decades, the competition posed by the Indians had proved unassailable. "In Antwerp, there is nothing for us [Jews] but diamonds. If we cannot work in diamonds, we must leave," he went on. "Without family, this business cannot continue."

Pinkusewitz was planning on making a last-ditch effort at persuading one of his sons to come back from Israel and take over the business. If he failed, it would be the end of the family's long history in Antwerp.

I felt uncomfortable. Pinkusewitz had not raised his voice, but when he spoke his words crackled with slow-baked emotion. Like so many of his community, it was apparent that Pinkusewitz was handcuffed to the painful history of the Jews, which cast their present-day plight in particularly sharp relief. How many times had they been hounded out of the professions they had carefully staked out as their own with hard work and forbearance? And over how many centuries?

But their latest ousting at the hands of the Gujarati Indians was far from a pogrom. It was rather a clash between the old order and the new: a collision that was being mirrored across Europe in diverse ways as once-settled power equations were re-adjusted and re-orientalized. This was a world of intense economic competition from the mammoth old-new challengers of Asia. It was a world of interconnectedness, new technologies, new identities and new fluidity. It was a world in which you had to run to stand still.

For Antwerp's orthodox Jews, adjusting to these times has proved wrenching. It is not inconceivable that a decade down the line all that may remain of their rich legacy in the city's diamond business will be the word "*mazel*," the Hebrew term for "luck" and one with which all sellers irrespective of nationality continue to seal a sale.

As I walked back to the train station that evening, the Jewish presence on Hoveniersstraat was very visible. They stood clustered in little groups outside the diamond exchange in long, dark frock coats and broad-brimmed black hats. Some twirled their earlocks, most sported full beards. But an anachronistic feel, and not just one to do with their dress, clung to them. A closer look revealed faces lined with age. The Indians, conversely, were bubbling with youth, dashing up and down between offices and making swift telephone calls.

The allegations Pinkusewitz had made against the Indians—the "unfair" competition they posed because of their willingness to work too hard and their desire to "grab" business at any cost—are charges that have been leveled time and again, over centuries, against the Jews themselves. But in post–World War II Europe, Jews are no longer the demonized "other" that they had once been. Although still a distinct community (in Antwerp, it is common to refer to Indians, Jews and Belgians as three distinct categories), the Antwerp Jews of today appeared, somewhat unreflexively, to espouse a common European sentiment toward the continent's new immigrants: they worked too hard for too little.

THE ARGUMENT IS MADE both up and down the economic scale, against Indian diamond merchants as much as Chinese factory workers. Having spent my life in India and China where "eating bitterness," as the Chinese call it, is an unquestioned virtue, this antipathy toward hard work was startling to me. The harder the immigrants worked, the worse the criticism they had to face.

I had first come across this in newspaper reports I'd read with some bemusement while still in Beijing. Back in 2004, shoe warehouses owned by the Chinese in the Spanish town of Elche were set on fire after the Chinese immigrants were accused of working beyond the stipulated number of work hours, for "unacceptably" low levels of pay. Presumably, the pay was perfectly acceptable to the workers in question; it was unacceptable only to their Spanish competitors.

In Elche, a traditional bastion of the Spanish shoe industry, the Chinese had come to control 10 percent of the business within a few years. Their business was flourishing even as Spanish manufacturers faced a drop in production. The reports I read had Spanish businessmen spluttering in indignation about the non-stop work ethic of the Chinese.

An article in the *Christian Science Monitor* blamed the outburst against the Chinese in Elche on the feeling among Spaniards that the economic practices of the Chinese "threaten age-old social customs, employment norms, and labor relations."[6] Their single-minded desire to make money "clashes with traditional values that privilege family, friends, and leisure over moneymaking."[7]

Given that only 40 or 50 years ago poverty regularly forced Spaniards and Italians to emigrate, I wondered how "traditional" and "age-old" these social customs and values were.

Elio di Rupo, the socialist politician who took over as Belgium's prime minister at the end of 2011, for example, had been born in 1951 in a squatters' camp for Italian immigrants in the Walloon municipality of Morlanwelz, after his mother and father, landless peasants with six other children, had headed north to find work. After his father was killed by a truck when Elio was one year old, three of his brothers were placed in an orphanage while his mother raised him and his three sisters on the equivalent of less than ten euros a month.

Had Rupo's mother privileged leisure over moneymaking, as was ostensibly the "traditional" culture in socialist Wallonia? The more I read about the relatively recent past in Europe, the more amazed I was at what shallow memories people had. Prosperity had been a potent amnesiac. The slow, brutal slog of the labor movement in Europe had taken centuries to accumulate and crystallize into present-day entitlements but had taken only a single generation to be internalized as "normal."

This occurred to me forcefully as I read the Belgian-American writer Luc Sante's eclectic memoir, *The Factory of Facts*. Sante described his father, a factory worker in the southern Belgian town of Vervires, as having an "antlike capacity for labour" that was a mixture of "duty, stubbornness, pride and fatalism. A nearly biological imperative of bending to the task."[8] When his father made the decision to immigrate to the United States following the closure of the iron foundry he had worked in, Sante wondered at this "ability to cast off into the trackless unknown."

Fast-forward some 50 years, and the Belgium I lived in was one where, far from the "unknown," it was rare for a Walloon to migrate a few kilometers to the north into Flanders in search of a job.

During the course of the 1950s and 1960s, Wallonia's economy had become depressed as heavy industries like iron, steel and coal slid into terminal decline. But at the same time, the present contours of the welfare state were being constructed, making it easier for people to choose not to work. By the time I moved to Belgium, Wallonia's unemployment rate at near 12 percent was twice that of rich Flanders in the north. Jobs were available in Flanders, but Walloons rarely spoke the Dutch necessary to work up north.

By late 2011, a sustained economic downturn had forced Belgium to investigate the possibility of modifying its labor market and social welfare system. Elio Di Rupo, the socialist prime minister whose own parents had emigrated from Italy, found himself reluctantly agreeing to a series of reforms.

Among these was disqualifying a person for the country's generous unemployment benefits if a suitable job was available within 60 kilometers of that person's residence, a distance that was less than an hour by car on Belgian roads. Pre-reform people had only been obliged to take a job if it existed within 25 kilometers of their residence.

Displaying absolutely none of the "antlike capacity for labour" that had been part of the makeup of their compatriots only a generation or two ago, Belgian workers reacted with a general strike. Some of the strikers passed through Avenue de L'Opale, the tree-lined road where we lived in Brussels.

I was struck by how celebratory they looked as they walked past my living room window. It was barely 8:30 in the morning, and some of the strikers were drinking Jupiler beer. Others were beating drums. A few couples were strolling arm in arm. It was a relaxed, festive atmosphere. Later, the newspapers reported the strikers as having a single message: NO; no to austerity, no to cuts in wages and pensions, no to insecurity and unemployment, no to deregulation of labor standards.

What they were actually saying was "no" to having their unemployment benefits contingent on the availability of a suitable job within a 60-kilometer radius, "no" to unemployment benefits being adjusted to career length and a number of other similarly mild proposals that would still leave them with some of the world's most elaborate entitlements, as the global labor elite.

What no one ever seemed to suggest was that rather than immigrants working too hard for too little, perhaps it was the locals who were working too little for too much. This was certainly the case from an Indian or Chinese immigrant perspective. Of course, it is always harder to give up something one already had than to make do without what one had never possessed. Giving up the entitlements that Europeans had come to take for granted was always going to be a more dislocating experience than making do without the entitlements that the immigrants had never had.

Securing rights for labor and the creation of the welfare state in Europe had come at the end of centuries of often bloody battle. The continent's industrialization took off on the back of a work force that was used hard and paid little, suffering from high rates of malnutrition and poor housing—conditions familiar to anyone in modern-day India or China.

In his book, Sante describes how salaries for workers were often frozen for very long periods of time, like during the entire eighteenth century, cutting out workers from a share in rising prosperity. For centuries, the industrialists had held all the cards, given their ability to fire entire work forces, if pushed. In the mid-nineteenth century, for a twelve-and-a-half-hour day of work, a woman's salary could buy a loaf of rye bread, and a child's wage a loaf of black bread. The first legal trade union in Sante's hometown of Verviers was established only in 1905 following a decade of bloody walkouts and lockouts.[9]

"Crumbs of reforms" were slowly aggregated "at a staggering price in privation, beatings, killings and prison time." The cycle recurred in the 1930s until the Second World War calmed the class rage. "Verviers continued to be a one-industry town until the 1950s, when it began turning into a no-industry town."[10]

Reading about the pain, rage and idealism that underpinned the labor movement in different parts of Europe helped give some sympathetic context to the widespread reluctance to labor reforms in modern-day Europe. And also went some way in explaining the fear engendered by immigrants and their willingness to accept harsher conditions of work.

Across Europe, the 1970s and 1980s had seen a change in the region's mainstream work culture, with the dream of upward mobility for all becoming widely promised and expected. The current combination of immigration, globalization and economic slowdown in the West may have created a new reality for workers, but the belief in the "right" to this upward mobility persisted. Europeans had come to resent having to do work lower down the economic scale even if their skills and education levels did not qualify them for other work.

A 2010 BBC documentary I saw conducted an experiment where 12 unemployed Brits were offered the chance of temporary employment in place of immigrants in the once-prosperous market town of Wisbech in Cambridgeshire.[11] The Brits were all of one opinion in believing that the immigrants were "stealing" British jobs.

As it turned out, several among those given the chance to work did not even show up at their new jobs, texting in sick or offering excuses like having to take a girlfriend to the hospital. Those who did make it through the few days of work clearly looked overwhelmed by how hard it was, lending weight to the idea that the willingness for hard work had somehow exited British work culture.

Professor of sociology Richard Sennett, the expert interviewed on the program, agreed that there was some truth in the notion that the "British unemployed were simply unwilling to knuckle down to hard work." But he also pointed out that it was unfair to compare them to immigrants who were often young and worked hard to put aside cash for a better future back home. Immigrants, he said, saw these jobs as temporary, so they were "willing to put up with the crap," because they were not planning to do such work for the rest of their lives.

But, in fact, there is often nothing temporary about the move made by immigrants, at grave personal risk, from a home thousands of kilometers away.

THIS WAS THE CASE with 41-year-old Harbhajan Singh. The Punjabi Sikh had spent more than ten years cutting down trees in the central Italian countryside for Trulli Vittorio, a timber company. I had scrambled up a low hill over thick, thorny brambles to get to the clearing where Harbhajan and two other Punjabis were felling trees on a Saturday afternoon.

It was a bright day in late February 2012. Harbhajan attacked the trees like a demon, his chainsaw cutting great bloodless gashes into the trunks. The noise was violent. Wood chips sprayed high into the air as the trees lurched drunkenly. Other than his blue turban, Harbhajan wore no protective gear.

As a tree came down, I squealed and scampered away to safety. Harbhajan and his friends stood their ground, confident, smiling at my fear. Angelino, a short, stocky Italian who was the Punjabi workers' overseer, called a rest stop.

Harbhajan had been working from seven in the morning. It was close to four in the evening by then. Usually, Saturday was a lighter day with work finishing just past noon. But the economic situation was tough. The bosses needed their workers to put in a few more hours than stipulated in their contracts. Harbhajan didn't get paid extra for the additional hours. "With the economy like this, we've all got to work a bit harder. It's normal. I don't mind," he said with a shrug of the shoulders.

Harbhajan was in the business for the long haul. "I've been here ten years and I'll still be here for as long as I can work." He'd been lucky. Not only had he secured a kosher Italian residence permit during one of the periodic legalization initiatives that Rome undertook every few years, but he also had a permanent work contract with his company.

He was paid 65 euros for an eight-hour day (plus the occasional extra hours). "We're cheaper than most other immigrants," he boasted. Even the Romanians and Armenians wanted at least 80 euros for a day's work. The illegals among the Indians often worked for as little as 3 or 4 euros an hour.

Harbhajan and his co-workers, all of whom had lived in Italy for at least a decade, spoke of their work with pride. They claimed the Punjabis had transformed Latina, the Italian province just south of Rome that I was visiting to learn more about these immigrants.

"Italians don't like to work too much," said Sartaj Singh, a clean-shaven Sikh who was working alongside Harbhajan on that day. "They keep going on holiday and make life difficult for the bosses." He lowered his voice even though we were talking in Punjabi and indicated Angelino, his overseer, with a quick sideways motion. "He never gets to work before ten in the morning, even though we start at dawn."

"Before we [Punjabis] got here, the fields were barren," chipped in Harbhajan. "There was no one to work in the fields. If there is agriculture in Latina today, it's all because of us," he beamed.

This was not an empty boast. Punjabi agricultural immigrants in Italy constitute the second largest Indian diaspora in Europe, after the United Kingdom.[12] Official Italian government figures put the total number of workers from India in Italy at around 121,000. But given the high number of illegals, the real figure is probably closer to 200,000, according to Marco Omizzolo, an Italian sociologist at the University of Florence, who studies the community.[13]

In the Lazio region, an area that includes Latina and the city of Rome, government estimates put the number of Indians at some 14,500, but in regions like Lombardia in Italy's northwest this figure rises to 46,372. The vast majority of the Indians in the country are Punjabi Sikhs who have immigrated over the last 20 years, and most of them work on vegetable and dairy farms.

Tucked away in the remote Italian countryside, their presence has gone largely unnoticed in Italian society and is only rarely reported in the media. But it is nonetheless said by those in the know that were the Indians to go on strike, the country's production of cheeses like Parmesan and Grana Padano would shut down.[14]

"You know, Italians don't like to work in the fields," explained the First Secretary in charge of information at the Indian embassy in Rome expansively. "Italy needed labor, and since the late 1980s Indians have been providing it. It's worked well because they [the Italians] see the Indians as reliable, enterprising and quite docile. They work hard and don't demand things like some of these others. . . ." The First Secretary left the rest of the sentence dangling complicitly between us.

Indeed, their "docility" and willingness to work hard while staying out of sight has meant that Italian authorities usually turn a blind eye to the illegal status of many of these workers. They are rarely detained. If they happen to literally run into the local police, they are fingerprinted and let off. Deportations are extremely rare.

The immigrants I spoke to over a three-day period in Latina were remarkably positive in their assessment of the Italian police. "They're friendly and quite polite," said Gurtej Singh, a hulking 40-year-old dressed in a white turban and spotless kurta pajama and sporting gold-rimmed dark glasses. "Not like in India where they treat you like dirt and want bribes for everything."

Gurtej Singh had arrived in Italy in 2001 but had waited nine years before getting legal documentation. He'd been caught and let off by the police more than a few times in the intervening years.

Gurtej told me about the fraught overland journey he had made from Punjab to Europe after paying an "agent" in India three lakh rupees (4,500 euros). The agent had convinced Gurtej and seven others from his village that the trip would be a cinch. They'd be taken from Delhi to Moscow by plane, before being whisked off straight to Germany in a taxi, they were assured.

The reality proved starkly different. The first leg of the trip was indeed by plane to Moscow, but once in Russia they were kept isolated in a windowless room for over a week with little food and no information. Eventually, they were joined by small groups of illegals from Vietnam, China, Bangladesh, Sri Lanka and Afghanistan.

They were then taken on foot through Ukraine and the Czech Republic. "Madam, it was winter and there was so much snow, sometimes till our knees," Gurtej told me, his voice flat and eyes invisible behind his dark glasses. "There was a man in our group who got frostbite and he collapsed. He couldn't walk any more. The agent just left him there to die."

Gurtej and several in his group were arrested near Prague after being abandoned to fend for themselves on a winter's night in a "house" without a roof, somewhere deep in the countryside. "The agent just took off and said he'd come back for us the next day. But we realized if we stayed we'd die in the cold, so we began to walk even though it was dark and we didn't know where we were going."

A few hours later, their group was arrested and held in a detention center for around a month. They were eventually issued permits that allowed for short, unsupervised trips into town. On one of these outings, their agent showed up again and spirited them away. Gurtej eventually reached Germany, his intended destination in Europe, two and a half months after he'd left Punjab.

In Germany, there were jobs available in the horticulture sector, but prospective employers asked him to shave his beard and take off his turban. "They thought I looked like a terrorist. But for me, my religion is everything," said Gurtej, "and I refused. Then I heard in Italy they were less strict about these things, so I came here instead."

We were standing outside a gurdwara near the seaside town of Sabaudia. The building that housed the gurdwara had been a warehouse for stocking agricultural produce, and despite the obvious care that had gone into maintaining it, retained a makeshift air. Outside, the yard was little more than an unpaved dirt track.

Motorbikes, bicycles and a few cars crowded the yard. I reckoned 400-odd devotees had come in that morning from the surrounding farms for the Sunday prayers. Gurtej said the numbers could swell to 800. In all, there were 35 gurdwaras in Italy, including some of the largest outside of India. But the one in Sabaudia was unimposing.

It had been inaugurated only a few days before the attacks on the World Trade Center in New York on September 9, 2001. When neighbors heard the gathered Sikhs shouting out "*Bole So Nihal, Sat Sri Akal,*" the traditional *jaikara,* or "shout of exaltation," which the Sikhs use to express religious joy, they called the police, convinced that they were "terrorists" celebrating the attacks.

"We've had a tough time since then, trying to explain to people we are not terrorists," said Gurtej, "and they mostly get it now."

But it wasn't uncommon for workers returning home on bikes after a ten-hour shift in the fields to be pelted with lemons and stones by Italian kids.

Why, I asked. "Because we look different," replied Gurtej serenely. "They don't really understand what they are doing." How do you put up with that kind of humiliation, I persisted. Harbhajan joined in. "The money is better and it's not like life is without humiliations back in India. At least here, we don't have to deal with the kind of corruption we face back home."

When I told friends in Brussels this story, they laughed out loud. They'd never imagined anyone would look at Italy as a paragon of upright living.

At the gurdwara that morning, the granthi was reciting prayers. "Pain is the remedy," he crooned. "The joy of Mammon is the disease." The irony of the sentiment was lost on the gathered congregation. They sat, men on one side, women on the other, heads covered, eyes closed in remembrance, or perhaps simply exhaustion, and rocked gently back and forth.

Outside the gurdwara, we were joined by Marco, the Italian sociologist. Gurtej and Harbhajan chatted with him easily, in heavily Punjabi-accented Italian. I asked them how they had learned the language. Had they taken classes? Harbhajan burst out laughing. After a whole day in the field or felling trees, who had the energy to attend classes? They'd learned it on the job.

"If we didn't know the language, who would hire us? We wouldn't be able to understand instructions," said Gurtej. Harbhajan added, "We've lived here ten years, madam. Even an animal would have learnt Italian in ten years."

I thought of all the unemployed Walloons in southern Belgium who hadn't learned Dutch in a lifetime, despite the availability of jobs in Flanders, which the language would have been the key to securing. And this was far from a uniquely Belgian problem. While in Italy, I came across an article in the *New York Times* about a French town, Sélestat, on the Franco-German border. Sélestat suffered from high unemployment, although there was plenty of work in the next-door German town of Emmendingen. But Sélestat's unemployed remained either unwilling or unable to learn German. The mayor of Emmendingen was quoted as saying, "There is a job here for anyone who can count to ten, but one needs to count in German."[15] The French couldn't.

Harbhajan was wrong. The reason the Indian immigrants had learned Italian was not because they had lived in Italy for ten years but because no one would pay them an unemployment benefit if they didn't work, and they needed to speak at least basic Italian to get a job. They had no choice. An accident of birth had meant they were shut out from the privileged world of the European work force.

But what of their children? That afternoon, Marco took me for a walk along Sabaudia's lake. Flanked by low-lying hills, the lake and the sea beyond it glowed palely in the weakening sun. I spotted three local teenagers sitting on an embankment, smoking cigarettes and guffawing at shared jokes. One of them was obviously of Indian parentage. What was his future going to be like?

Like other second-generation Indian immigrants who'd been born in places like Latina and gone to school with Italians, he looked like a Punjabi on the outside but dressed and spoke like an Italian. Since Indian immigration in the region was a relatively new phenomenon, the second generation was still mostly of school-going age. The few who were older had already begun to move up the economic value chain. In Rome, I noticed young Indian bus conductors and waiters in restaurants. Like their Italian contemporaries, they showed little appetite for the grueling farm work that had brought their parents to the country.

But given the economic stresses Europe, and Italy in particular, are facing, jobs as a whole are scarce. "Docile" Indians toiling deep in the countryside might have easily fitted into Italian society by virtue of being content with remaining hidden away from that society. Educated Italian-Indians competing for the limited number of jobs in the service sector, however, might not be accepted as easily.

These second-generation Indians are denied Italian citizenship and granted residence permits only if they can prove employment. The potential for friction is obvious, as expectations rub up against reality and pliant, "humble" first-wave immigrants give way to a disillusioned, "demanding" new generation of Italian-Indian residents.

WHAT WAS EVIDENT AS I TRAVELED around the continent was what a jumbled world immigration had created. In Spain, the Chinese are now the new Gypsies, having replaced the shawl-wrapped, gold-toothed, babe-clasping mamas as the chief street-corner flower sellers. In Rome, Bangladeshis have gradually taken over as the most ubiquitous corner store operators. In London, I found myself eating at a Michelin-starred Indian restaurant where all the waiters were immigrants from eastern Europe.

So, what does it mean to be a European in this world? There is no easy or immediate answer to this deceptively straightforward question. After all, even the single term "immigration" is formidably complex. It includes within its fold multiple and potentially contradictory identities, aspirations and behaviors. Immigrants could be economic or political, seasonal or permanent, of European or non-European origin, legal or illegal, highly educated or lacking in skills. Europe's immigrants include Indian diamond merchants in Antwerp and Punjabi agricultural labor in Latina; Polish plumbers in Munich and American multinational executives in Brussels; Jamaican taxi drivers in London and Bangladeshi geothermal engineers in Norway.

Cost-and-benefit analyses of immigration in the context of Europe are as varied as the kinds of immigrants themselves. There are studies to prove that they depress incomes lower down the social scale and studies to show they do no such thing. Critics rage that a third of professional jobs in cities like London are taken by foreign-born people. Immigration boosters counter that many of these jobs would not otherwise exist and that migrants create jobs for locals. And although immigration may benefit societies overall, it isn't clear whether those benefits accrue evenly across social strata.[16]

Are immigrants a drain on housing and welfare services? Or are their skills, energy, dynamism and willingness to work the salvation of entire economic sectors like Antwerp's diamond industry and Italy's dairy farming? The fact is that regardless of immigrants, the expansive welfare state that has become the norm in many European countries is going to have to slim down in the face of the economic realities of the new millennium.

At the time of my move to Europe, civil servants in Greece—the European country that would soon be at the vanguard of the region's fiscal crisis—were allowed by law to retire in their forties and collect a pension. They were awarded bonuses for the most absurd reasons, ranging from showing up to work on time to knowing how to use a computer.[17] Over the next few years, as Europe's sovereign debt and banking troubles spilt across borders into Portugal, Ireland, Spain, Italy and even into "core" eurozone countries like Belgium and France, the necessity of reforming labor and pension markets came to be accepted, albeit with varied enthusiasm, across the political spectrum.

The change was epochal although not apocalyptic. In Europe, the post-war social contract between the state and citizens was not being annulled as much as modified in light of global economic shifts. Given the rise of the rest, the West could not sit tight on its laurels and assume everything would get better and easier for the generations to come, as had been the assumption for large parts of the twentieth century. Just as Chinese and Indian immigrants put up with enormous hardships to ensure a better future for their children, the current generation of workers in Europe was being asked to tighten their belts to secure a decent future for their descendants.

In China, I had always been struck by the optimism of even hard-pressed migrant workers upon whose back-breaking labor the country's shiny new cities were constructed. They may have lived in dismal poverty, but they believed a different life was possible for their kids. The opposite was true for Europe, where people could no longer assume that upward mobility was going to be the norm for future generations.

Life for the child of a Spanish bus driver was probably going to remain superior in absolute material terms to that of the child of a Chinese bus worker for a long while to come, but relative decline was not an easy fact to come to terms with. And while immigration was not the root cause of Europe's economic insecurities, it was an easy target at a time when many felt the once-solid ground beneath their feet turn to shifting sands.

Unsurprisingly, despite having become an established fact in most European societies, immigration is not a popular phenomenon. As far back as 2007, a Pew Research Center Global Attitudes survey found that nine out of ten Italians saw immigration as a "problem" for their country. Germans are also largely unwelcoming of immigrants. Solid majorities in Germany (64 percent and 58 percent, respectively) said it was bad that people from the Middle East and North Africa and from Eastern Europe moved to their country.[18]

In a later 2009 Pew survey, 80 percent of Spaniards, 78 percent of Britons, 65 percent of Germans and 64 percent of French supported tougher restrictions on immigration.[19] An even later 2011 survey by Ipsos, a global research firm, had 72 percent of respondents in Belgium, 64 percent in Britain, 56 percent in Italy and 54 percent in Germany claim that immigration had a fairly or very negative impact on their country.[20]

Anti-immigration sentiment is often vague, conflating economic uncertainties linked to globalization, cultural anxiety related to visibly changing cityscapes, safety and security concerns in a post 9/11 world of cross-border terror organizations, and a general sense of pessimism and decline given the rise of emerging countries that has destabilized Europe's once securely dominant global position.

Immigrants who work are thus accused of taking away the "rightful" jobs of natives. And those who don't work are blamed for sponging off the welfare system. Whether they work "too hard" or not at all, complaints also focus on the dissonant culture and values of the new arrivals.

The combined result is a spate of policy efforts across many European countries to curb immigration from outside of the European Union and a simultaneous rise in the popularity of anti-immigration political parties.

For Indians, perhaps the policy reorientation that pinched the most was British Prime Minister David Cameron's imposition of a "migration cap" for those outside the European Union, intended to cut net migration from levels of more than 200,000 per year to less than 100,000 by 2015. Measures to discourage immigration being mulled include an increase in minimum skill levels for applicants, which could potentially bar entry to the United Kingdom for non-EU nurses, physiotherapists and financial technicians, among other categories of professionals. Another proposal that seeks to increase the minimum salary earned by potential immigrants to £35,000 would reduce the number of non-EU migrants and their dependents granted settlement by two-thirds.[21]

Other countries, including Spain and Denmark, are so desperate to get rid of immigrants that they have devised "pay as you go" schemes, under which immigrant workers get cash handouts to return to their countries of origin. During his re-election campaign in 2012, then French president Nicolas Sarkozy joined the immigrant-slimming club, pledging to reduce the number of immigrants to the country from 180,000 to 100,000 each year.

At the same time, political parties tough on immigration are showing strong performances. France's National Front (FN) was enjoying a resurgence under its new leader, Marine Le Pen, taking up to 15 percent of the vote in the local elections. Italy's Northern League took 8.3 percent of the national vote in 2008 and was an important coalition partner of the Silvio Berlusconi government until the financial crisis forced a change of leadership in late 2011.

The Dutch Freedom Party, led by Geert Wilders, won 15.5 percent of the vote in the general election in 2010, putting it in third place in the Netherlands. The anti-immigration True Finns took nearly 20 percent of votes in Finland's 2011 general election. In 2007, they had won only 4 percent of the vote. The Danish People's Party, which wanted to ban immigration from non-Western countries altogether, was the third largest party in Denmark's parliament.

BUT DESPITE ALL THE "IMMIGRANTS ARE TERRIBLE" noise, Europe's demographic makeup casts those same immigrants in a more desirable light. Rich, white, middle-class Europe is in demographic dire straits, particularly given the populous and dynamic composition of its new, emerging country challengers.

In 1900, Europeans accounted for 24 percent of the world's population; by 2000, that figure had more than halved and is expected to halve again by 2050. According to European Commission figures, from 2013 the working age population of the European Union will shrink by 50 million people over a period of 50 years, *despite* taking into account an influx of 58 million immigrants during that same period. And it's not as if Europe does not need these immigrants. Studies predict an estimated shortfall of 20 million skilled and unskilled workers by 2030.[22] Some of the figures are truly startling. For example, in 2008, there were 64,000 unfilled job vacancies for engineers in Germany alone, causing an estimated loss of 6.6 billion euros to the country's economy.[23]

Europe is thus all set to lurch from its ongoing credit crunch to the start of a long demographic crunch. With baby boomers set to hit retirement age within a few years, the impact of Europe's aging population on health and social services is likely to start kicking in by 2020. In the event of immigration being reined in, the inevitable result will be further cuts to the already shrinking welfare benefits. The former might be unpopular, but so are the latter.[24]

I found myself in a Brussels full of eurocrats feverishly working on a raft of directives aimed at balancing demographic imperatives with the popular suspicion of immigration. The focus, most agreed, had to be on culling the "right" kind of immigrants from the "wrong" sort, for whom the European Union was apparently a magnet.

The European Commission revealed that around 85 percent of global unskilled migrants headed to the European Union while only 5 percent went to the United States. At the same time, highly qualified foreign workers made up a mere 1.7 percent of the employed population in the European Union, but the equivalent figure for Australia was nearly 10 percent, over 7 percent in Canada and 3.2 percent in the United States.[25]

Even before the eurozone crisis hit, there had been much hand-wringing at the European Commission about Europe's inertia and inflexibility when compared, in particular, to America's youth, dynamism and creative energy. The differential ability of the two to attract skilled immigrants was zoomed in on. After all, studies had shown that the Chinese and Indian immigrants alone founded a quarter of Silicon Valley start-ups between 1980 and 1998. Moreover, immigrants were also behind a quarter of all American technology and engineering start-ups between 1995 and 2005.[26]

It didn't require an advanced degree in eurocratics to arrive at the conclusion that Europe needs to make itself more attractive to skilled foreigners. The Continent's byzantine visa rules are the stuff of legend in emigrant countries like India and China. A young Indian friend of mine, Rahul Venkit, who had worked in Beijing as a producer at a Chinese radio station, sent me an e-mail a month after I arrived in Brussels. He was bursting with cheer at the news that he'd been offered a great job as a multimedia producer for the International Diabetes Federation at its Brussels headquarters. "See you very soon," he had signed off.

These words proved less than prophetic, however, and it was several months before Rahul was actually able to move to Belgium, his once-youthful buoyancy rather dampened by the harrowing visa ordeal he'd been put through. At first, the Belgian consulate in Mumbai had refused to respond to his queries about what was beginning to seem like an inordinate delay in responding to his application. Ultimately, following many hours waiting on one end of a telephone, he was able to ascertain that his application was stuck on security grounds.

He was asked to produce police certificates for the last five years, clearing him of any criminal offences. But the youngster had lived in Pune, Singapore, London and Beijing during this time. He'd had bona fide jobs in all these cities, having worked as a newspaper reporter in

Pune and Singapore, in the Secretariat of the Commonwealth Games in London, and with China Radio International in Beijing.

With dogged persistence, he was eventually able to complete all the paperwork over a period of three months, and luckily for him, the Diabetes Federation held his job. "I used to think having international experience was an asset," Rahul told me later. "Little did I think it would actually be a hurdle to getting a visa."

Another friend, Mahesh, who'd initially been thrilled at having gotten a Brussels-based job with Hewlett Packard to help create a payroll engine for the Federal Police of Belgium, found his happiness short-lived. Despite kosher paperwork, he was unable to get a visa for his wife, whom he had married only a week before leaving for Europe. Nine months into trying, he finally gave up, quit his job and returned to India and his wife.

It is hardly puzzling that Europe finds it hard to attract skilled workers. After all, it seems to go almost out of its way to make it as difficult as possible to work in the region. There are considerable differences between European nations on immigration policy, with countries like Sweden rather more open than others like Belgium or Germany. But not a single one compares favorably with the United States, a fact that is all the more abysmal given that US immigration policy is itself hardly optimal.[27]

While Europe's inhospitable visa stand is mostly about protectionism, on occasion it elides into paternalism, making for a truly infuriating mixture. The unselfconsciousness of it all doesn't help to make it more palatable.

In September 2009, I joined a group of Indian journalists being trotted around the EU headquarters on a familiarization trip. One of the meetings was with an official from the Directorate for Education and Culture. He spent a while telling us about the wonders of the Erasmus Mundus program under which scholarship funds were made available for non-European students to pursue higher education in Europe. The journalists, aware of the keen interest this would elicit back home, began scribbling notes furiously.

"But don't worry," the official concluded reassuringly, "we make 100 percent sure that the students return home after finishing their degrees so that there is no brain drain." The journalists put down their pens.

Throwing out students immediately after they had finished university degrees, on the grounds of knowing what was good for them and their countries, regardless of their own feelings on the matter, ticked every wrong-headed box I could think of. It was pompous and self-defeating. It would act as a deterrent to attracting students in the first place. It would then get rid of precisely the kinds of people the Continent needed to meet its skills gap. And its paternalistic overtones were patronizing toward people already fed up with the European Union's constant moralizing.

But despite their muddled, and sometimes tone-deaf, approach, most people at the commission agreed that something had to be done to enhance the European Union's competitiveness. Enter Europe's blue card, the hoped-for retort to the United States' much-desired green equivalent.

The European Council adopted the Blue Card Directive a month after I arrived in Brussels. But three years down the line as I wrote this chapter, it remained largely unheralded, despite having been ratified by most EU member states.

To apply for a blue card, a professional needs either a university degree that had taken a minimum of three years to complete or five years of work experience in the relevant sector, a binding job offer from a European employer who has to certify that the post can't be filled from within the European Union, and a salary offer that is at least 1.5 times the average prevailing wage in the country concerned.

In return, a blue card holder is granted the same access to pensions, housing and health care as an EU citizen. Family reunification within six months is also guaranteed. The crucial clause is that, following an 18-month period, a blue card holder is allowed to move to any other participating EU member country if he or she is able to secure a job there.

The scheme's potential potency lay in the access it promised to not just a single European country but to the amalgamation of the 27 member states that comprised the European Union. However, following two years of controversy-bogged discussions, the eventual version of the directive that was adopted did not guarantee a card holder the right to move from one EU country to another and, in fact, made it almost as tough to move between member states as to reapply afresh from the country of origin.

Individual EU nations retained the right to reject any application by a blue card holder who consequently has no legal right guaranteed at the European level to move within the Union even after the initial 18-month period of residence has elapsed. The card holder merely has the right to apply for a transfer of job but without any certainty that the application will be accepted—an almost trivial improvement over the lot of non-card possessors.

Moreover, the United Kingdom, Ireland and Denmark opted out of the scheme altogether, a factor that further cripples its effectiveness, especially since it is English-speaking countries that have a natural advantage when it comes to attracting skilled workers. The upshot of all these caveats is that the queues at blue card counters in European embassies around the world remain rather short.

The architects of the directive at the European Commission were aware of its limitations, but immigration is one of the EU member states' most jealously guarded prerogatives. The ongoing process of the creation of the supranational European Union had itself provoked unresolved and conflicted issues related to immigration, identity, belonging and accountability.

Unbridled freedom of movement within Europe for member-state citizens, one of the European Union's crowning achievements toward European integration, remains deeply contested.[28] It continues to be resented by those who believe it to have been undemocratically imposed from atop by Brussels without sufficient regard for the sensitivities and wishes of national populations.

Non-European immigration is even more polarizing and emotive. Devolving national sovereignty to Brussels on the issue is unanimously seen as an unacceptable step too far. As it struggles to give form to its various directives aimed at addressing the demographic and skills lacunae, the European Commission is, as a result, simultaneously hampered by truculent member states and harangued by civil society groups.

In early 2011, I sat in on a hearing of the European Economic and Social Committee (EESC), a civil society consultative body featuring an assorted cast of trade unionists, representatives from national employment agencies and EU officials. The debate was heated, the warnings apocalyptic. The specters of rising xenophobia, "social dumping" and "fragmentation of local labor markets" were raised.

The issue at stake, although you wouldn't have known it given the panicked tenor of the statements, was another proposed European

Commission directive to attract skilled workers. This time around, the initiative was focused on a tiny group of managers, specialists and graduate trainees employed by multinational corporations (MNCs), dubbed intra-corporate transferees (ICTs).

The commission estimated that ICTs numbered a mere 16,000 in the entire European Union (although this figure excluded numbers from the United Kingdom, which would likely bump it up considerably). The directive provided for a combined visa and work permit, the application procedure for which would be standardized across the European Union's member states, guaranteeing a maximum 30-day processing time. Managers and specialists were to be allowed three years of employment within the European Union before having to return home, while trainees would be allowed to stay in Europe for a maximum of one year.

Once the ICT in question was in Europe, she would also be allowed to move freely within the EU member states, were the company that employed her to require it, on the basis of the first residence permit. Thus, an Indian working for a multinational corporation in Germany would be able to move to that company's Spanish branch office without having to apply for a fresh work permit or visa, as was currently the case.

At the EESC hearing, speaker after speaker brought up concerns about how the ICT directive could lead to a tsunami of low-paid IT workers from India crashing through Europe's doors and destabilizing the comfortable conditions enjoyed by their European counterparts today.

The case was repeatedly made that the entry of a few thousand of these workers would distort competition unacceptably. In essence, it was the same old fear of foreign workers agreeing to work harder for less money.

Other ingenious, or perhaps disingenuous, arguments against the proposal included concern for the human rights of the foreign workers; so a desire to protect them from exploitation by MNCs became the crux of one line of reasoning that sought to deny ICTs easier access to Europe. The paternalism was relentless.

A French member of the EESC study group on the ICT directive claimed to be worried about whether the workers in question would have access to social security in their home country once they had finished their stint in Europe and returned. Not a single one of the workers on whose behalf all these concerns were being expressed was actually invited to participate in the conversation.

Someone from the European Association for the Promotion of Human Rights stood up and announced that his organization promoted "equal rights to work without regard to nationality." But only a few sentences later, he made it clear that his real anxiety was about the directive promoting "inequality among workers *in the EU.*" Inequality between EU workers and those outside of Europe obviously did not exercise him overly. What he was supporting was an ever stronger wall to keep Europe's privileged labor market out of bounds for those who'd had the bad fortune to be born on the wrong side of that boundary.

The hypocrisy of the arguments made by some of the attendees was stunning. There is always a tension in the rhetoric of those who purport to speak for labor—that between the universal aspects of the labor movement and its stress on global solidarity among the working classes, and the particular, essentially selfish, protectionist concerns of the specific constituencies they, in fact, represent. From a global labor perspective, it is clear that unhindered migration is a moral and desirable outcome, despite any deleterious effects on Europe's disproportionately advantaged work force.

At the EESC hearing, a representative from business finally raised his voice, asking whether any of those in the room had actually met with an ICT. "These are usually an elite," he said, better paid than most Europeans.

An official from the European Commission's directorate in charge of home affairs chimed in. "Frankly speaking," she said, "the standard of life most of the ICTs would be used to in their home countries is actually better than in Europe." They had cars and drivers at their disposal back home; cooks and nannies; access to excellent schools and medical services; and the shops in their countries were usually open on Sunday. Worries that once in Europe they would proceed to live in sweatshop-like conditions, thereby forcing their European counterparts into a similarly demeaning existence, were preposterous. I had to contain myself from jumping up and down in vociferous agreement.

The tide began to turn toward sanity. An expert from the Swedish administration went on to share the experience of Sweden with labor migration. In 2008, the Swedish government undertook a radical reform of the immigration system, abolishing all quotas on migration.

Instead, they allowed employers to assess their own needs and freely recruit from outside Sweden, and outside the European Union if necessary, to meet their requirements.

The reasons for the move were primarily demographic. The country lacked not only sufficient numbers of doctors and engineers but also semi-skilled workers like welders, technicians and electricians.

Remarkably, despite the extreme—for Europe—liberalism of Sweden's immigration rules, only 30,000 work permits to migrants had in fact been issued in the two years between 2008 and 2010. Of these, only some 10,000 permit holders were actually working in Sweden at the time of the hearing. Given that the Swedish labor market had 4.9 million people, the impact of the opening had hardly been substantial, the expert concluded.

I was reminded of the German initiative in the late 1990s when, envious of the United States' thriving economy, Berlin had decided that it too needed to go high tech. In meeting their goals, the Germans had zeroed in on Indians, given that Indian entrepreneurs accounted for one of every three Silicon Valley start-ups. A German green card, especially for Indians, was thus created, 20,000 of which were issued in the first year. The program met with some resistance at home; nasty political slogans proclaiming *"Kinder statt Inder"* (Children not Indians) were raised. But fears of tens of thousands of Indians swamping the fatherland soon proved unfounded.

The program was a flop. A year after it was announced, barely half of the 20,000 cards had been issued, and after a few extensions, the program was abolished. Various reasons for the failure were mooted, including technical flaws in the design of the program and the fact that, unlike its US counterpart, the German green card was not a first step in the granting of citizenship. Indians also continued to prefer the United States for linguistic reasons.[29]

When I queried the Swedish expert at the EESC meeting about the tepid response from Indians (far fewer than expected had applied for work permits) to her country's attempts to lure them in, she shrugged. "Perhaps they find it too cold," she said.

Big emerging countries like India and China muddy the waters swirling around the fears and benefits imputed to immigration in Europe. Given their Dr. Jekyll and Mr. Hyde double lives as flashy, nascent superpowers-cum-Third World dystopias, they are unsurprisingly confusing.

These are countries where millions of middle-class citizens enjoy consumption levels and standards of living on a par with, or even exceeding, those of the West, but where at the same time millions more remain desperate to emigrate anywhere, as long as it is elsewhere. These are the countries of origin for Europe's diamond merchants as much as its illegal farm labor. These are countries that are home to both the "right" and "wrong" kinds of immigrants.

Moreover, these are also countries that have become magnets for foreign workers, so that immigration is no longer solely about one-way flows from the South to the North. A more multidimensional picture of migration is increasingly apparent.[30] As the *Economist* magazine put it: "Never before—or at least not in recent history—has the map of global migration been at the same time so varied and so changeable."[31]

In Chinese cities like Shanghai and Guangzhou, white-collar Westerners number in the tens of thousands. And substantial concentrations of immigrants have also set up in smaller cities in China like Shaoxing and Yiwu. Even more tellingly, certain categories of blue-collar workers from India[32] and Africa have begun looking to the Middle Kingdom for opportunities to better their lot.

At the EESC meeting, it took a representative from a Portuguese employers' association to make the point that rather than framing the ICT debate exclusively as one about whether and under what conditions non-European managers and specialists should be permitted to work in the European Union, Europe needed to begin looking at the issue in terms of reciprocity. There were more EU citizens working with multinational corporations in so-called Third World countries than the other way round. There were more Portuguese working in Angola than Angolans in Portugal, he claimed.

In fact, Brazil now admits more immigrants from Europe and the United States than from other Latin American countries. And World Bank figures show remittances from Brazil to Portugal being greater than those from Portugal to Brazil.[33]

Attempting to address immigration is akin to standing in a hall of mirrors, the issues seemingly endless, their often deceptive surfaces bouncing off each other, escaping easy solutions. But Indian, Chinese and other economic migrants are not the ones at the center of Europe's great immigrant-related moral panic. That position is the unhappy lot of western Europe's 20 million-odd Muslims.

THREE

The Veiled Threat

"SEE, IN ANY PLACE THE MAJORITY GROUP WILL WANT
to dominate. It's natural. And Europe is Christian territory. It's obvious they would not like Muslims to come here."

"But if that were the case, why did they let so many Muslims in?" I countered.

My interviewee spread his palms wide in a gesture somewhere between a shrug and an exclamation. "Europeans have become victims of their own laws. It's impossible for them to stop the Muslims now. They've cut off their own arms with all these rights. Human rights and women's rights and immigrants' rights."

I felt the irony of these sentiments keenly as I scribbled my notes. This was not some right-wing conservative from one of Europe's growing tribe of anti-immigration political parties that I was talking with, but rather the kind of person who was the standard object of their ire. Yet, Manzour Ahmad's views were of a piece with those who sought to cleanse Europe of his kind.

The 61-year-old Islamic scholar had grown up in India, where he studied at the conservative Darul Uloom Islamic school in Deoband. Following a stint in Saudi Arabia at the Madinah University of Islamic Studies, Manzour was sent to Brussels in 1982 to take up a teaching post at the Saudi-funded Islamic Cultural Centre, the oldest and largest mosque in Belgium.

After having taught Arabic and the Koran at the mosque for 17 years (during which time he also acquired Belgian nationality), Manzour switched jobs and began teaching Islamiat (Islamic religious studies) at two public schools, this time as an employee of the Belgian government. It is compulsory for children in Belgium under the age of 17 to either attend classes in non-denominational "ethics" or in any of the six religions officially recognized by the state.[1] While Islam had been nominally recognized as far back as 1975, it is only since 1998 that Islamiat has been widely made available as an option in Belgian schools.[2] There are currently around 800 Islamiat teachers on the government's payroll.

"What would you do if you were a European policymaker?" I asked Manzour. His reply came pat. "I would change their laws to stop all this immigration. It would be better for them to send all the Muslims back home. It's impossible for two cultures to live together. It's better for like to be amongst like."

I flushed despite knowing the need to keep a professional cool. But we were sitting in *my* drawing room, surrounded by pictures of my Spanish husband and "mixed" children, and Chinese cats! I reminded myself that Manzour's comments were not a personal attack. They were to him a banal statement of common sense. And these were far from the sentiments of fundamentalists.

From Harvard professors like Samuel Huntington of "the clash of civilizations" fame,[3] to kindly Indian aunties, the idea that there are clear lines between "us" and "them," to be crossed at one's own peril, is common enough. What lies on either side of the lines is mutable—class, ethnicity, religion, caste—but the lines themselves are deeply etched.

The *Financial Times* columnist Christopher Caldwell had just published a much-feted book, *Reflections on the Revolution in Europe,* which was in essence arguing the same thing.[4] Immigration (but in particular Muslim immigration) "erodes national cultures that have shaped and comforted people for centuries," he claimed. Of course, the invented nature of national cultures and the strife and exclusions such cultures glossed over remains unexamined in this line of reasoning. How "comforting" had these national cultures been to Jews in 1930s Austria, or indeed to the Roma (Gypsies) in present-day Romania?

Elaborating on the idea of the preference for cultural sameness, Caldwell referred to Swedish sociologist Ake Daun's work on how Swedes like being like each other. They apparently experience much distress when "foreigners" signal in traffic, which "normal" Swedes consider an undesirable expression of aggression, second only to the discomfiture caused by people who don't eat pea soup on Thursdays.

Cultural preferences do not in themselves have moral weight. There was a time when burning witches at the stake was a culturally preferred way of dealing with "difficult" women. Moreover, social preferences and notions of normality are fluid processes rather than rigid fatwas. I found it very hard to believe that most Swedes really found it so terrible to deal with people who chose not to eat pea soup on Thursday.

Caldwell and Manzour were both conservatives who, despite their seeming opposition to each other, actually shared the same world view. But all their hand-wringing was ex post facto. Numbering roughly 20 million, Muslims in the European Union comprise 4 percent of the region's total population. And in certain cities like Brussels, Amsterdam and Marseilles, they account for over a quarter of the citizenry.

For better or worse, Islam already lives in the heart of Europe. Literally. The Islamic Cultural Centre where Manzour worked when he first moved to Brussels is a corporeal symbol of the religion's presence at the center of European affairs. The mosque, where over 3,000 people congregate for Friday prayers, is located in a corner of a large public park, slap bang next to the buildings that house the European Union institutions.

Julio and I passed it every morning on our way to work. Ten minutes at the entrance to the mosque on any workday morning showed a window to postcolonial, post-national, twenty-first-century Europe. Eurocrats in fluttering ties walked hurriedly on their way to meetings, passing puffing women in sweatshirts and shorts, who only narrowly avoided bearded men in djellabas as they exited the mosque. A woman in tight jeans, knee-high boots and a headscarf smiled into a mobile phone, covering one ear with her palm to block out the noise of excited toddlers mucking about in the next-door sandpit. Elderly Bruxellois played a game of *petanque*[5] in the slender shadow of the mosque's crescent-topped minaret, while large dogs gamboled along happily sniffing for squirrels.

The mosque's circular building had originally been constructed as one of the pavilions for Belgium's 1880 National Exhibition, intended to showcase the might of the newly independent country on its fiftieth anniversary. Cinquantenaire Park, where the buildings were located, had been erected by King Leopold II, using the proceeds of the barbaric slave state he'd established in the Congo.

By the 1960s, the building had fallen into a state of genteel disrepair when it was offered as a gift by the reigning King Baudouin to the Saudi Arabian monarch Faisal bin Abdulaziz in 1967. The mosque, which was and continues to be fully funded by the Saudi, Mecca-based Muslim World League, was formally inaugurated in 1978. King Baudouin's gift of the building is widely interpreted as an attempted quid pro quo for securing infrastructure contracts in Saudi Arabia, motivated by economic opportunism rather than any religious demands that Belgian Muslims at the time might have had.

There is no clearer testament to the complexity of the contemporary social fabric in Europe than those ten minutes spent at the gates of Brussels's Islamic Cultural Centre. Caldwell and Manzour notwithstanding, there is no easy dichotomy between "us" and "them," "good" and "evil," "halal" and "haram," and certainly not between "Europe" and "Islam."

Multiculturalism is not an alien phenomenon to Europe. As the historian Tony Judt points out in his masterful work *Post War,* the continent was once a tapestry of intricately overlapping languages, religions and communities. Cities like Sarajevo, Trieste and Odessa were among the world's most syncretic and multi-textured. But that Europe was smashed between 1914 and 1945. The paroxysm of violence that rent the region during the Second World War formed the foundation for the post-war Europe of much tidier nation-states where "thanks to war, occupation, expulsions and genocide, almost everybody now lived in their own countries."[6]

But these "hermetic national enclaves" didn't last long. The governments of western Europe soon turned to former colonies and other large, poor countries to recruit the manpower for their booming post-war economies. In many cases the source countries for this labor were Muslim: Pakistan in the case of Britain; Morocco, Algeria and Tunisia in France; Turkey in Germany; and Indonesia, Suriname, Morocco and Turkey in the case of Holland.

The assertion that western Europe "became multicultural in a fit of absent-mindedness," as Caldwell claims, suffers from historical shallowness, given that it is the "pure" nation-state rather than multiculturalism that is the true novelty in the region. However, it is true that much of this immigration was initially believed to be temporary in nature. It was widely held by governments across Europe that "guest workers" from poor countries would sweat away in the continent's iron foundries, railroads, post offices and textile factories for a few years and then meekly return home. As a result, neither the political nor commercial elites who had devised these policies paid much heed to issues like devising plans for integration.[7] Nor was it thought necessary to consult with the general population before taking what transpired to be momentous decisions for their future.

The assumptions made about these foreign workers proved completely wrong. Far from returning home after a few years of hard work, the immigrants instead sent for their spouses and began to have children. Once the kids were in school, any plans of returning home were further delayed until they finally vanished altogether.

Meanwhile, the economy in Europe began to shift away from traditional industries. Increases in productivity led to a decrease in the need for labor at the same time as globalization was causing some of Europe's heavy industries to shut down forever. Since post-war European labor immigration actually met the needs of the old economy rather than the new, unemployment among migrants sharply spiked.

For example, Turks in Germany had a higher labor force participation than "native" Germans in the 1960s and 1970s. Today, there is 40 percent unemployment among Germany's Turkish community in some cities, including Berlin, and three times the national rate of welfare dependency. The number of foreign residents in Germany rose steadily between 1971 and 2000 from 3 million to 7.5 million, but the number of employed foreigners in the work force remained constant at 2 million.[8]

And so began a downward spiral of welfare dependency and economic exclusion, which in turn fed the social prejudice that further alienates many among the second and third generations of these immigrants. Since the 9/11 Al-Qaeda attacks on New York's World Trade Center, the conflation of Islam with terrorism and violence has intensified popular suspicion of Muslim immigrants. The train and metro bombings in Madrid and London in 2004 and 2005, both of which were carried out by Islamist terrorists, further entrenched anti-Muslim prejudice. But the roots of this bias stretch back beyond 2001.

AS IT BECAME CLEAR that the immigrants were not going "home" and that a new Europe with a new kind of citizen was being created, resentments against Muslims bubbled over. This was perhaps the natural outcome of what political philosopher Seyla Benhabib has called the "disaggregation of citizenship" whereby the political rights of citizenship are separated from national belonging.[9] If a nation is defined as a community where people are linked by shared languages, historical memories, common ancestry and attachment to a certain land, then Europe's new immigrants were not part of the nations of which they found themselves becoming citizens.

The new Muslim presence provoked among some Europeans feelings of alienation within their own countries. There were those who were embittered by having to share citizenship rights with people who they perceived as irredeemably different. Not only were Muslims "foreign," they were also seen as welfare spongers living off "real" European taxpayers' money. Their apparent refusal to integrate into "European" culture was offered as proof of the catastrophic consequences of having opened the Pandora's box of immigration.

Much antipathy stemmed from Muslim demands that European countries change some of their laws and customs to accommodate their religion. Over the years, Muslim groups had lobbied for and often succeeded in asking for provisions for halal meat in schools, prayer rooms in office buildings, exemption for girls from swimming classes and so on.

The idea that Muslims are all about insisting that Europe accommodate itself to them while steadfastly refusing to accommodate themselves to Europe meant that it had become quite respectable to voice concerns over Europe's Muslim "problem." Christopher Caldwell was described by a reviewer in the traditionally left-wing newspaper the *Observer* (the *Guardian's* Sunday edition) as a "bracing clear-eyed analyst of European pieties."[10] And Caldwell was merely following a path well trodden by a growing tribe of variably credible, but collectively significant, Eurabia exponents.[11]

The Eurabia thesis, in a nutshell, predicts the takeover of an "effeminate" and weak Europe plagued by wrong-headed notions of colonial guilt and misplaced liberalism by a resurgent and "masculine" Islam. Immigration in this interpretation is a Trojan Horse via which Muslims infiltrate Europe in order to prepare for an eventual conquest of the Continent. It predicts a Europe ruled by sharia law with a Muslim majority population within a few decades, unless exceptional steps—including a rediscovery of Christian belief—are taken to avert this outcome.

Much of the Eurabia line of reasoning is based on demographics. Never mind that Muslims are merely 4 percent of the European Union's population. For Eurabia proponents, the purported high birth rates among Muslim women combined with the low birth rate of "native" Europeans means that it's only a matter of time before Europe is overrun by the multitudinous progeny of Muslims.

There is, in fact, much data to prove such scaremongering wrong. Across Europe, the birth rates of Muslims are falling, to approach national averages. For example, at last count, Algerian women living in France averaged 2.57 children, higher than the "native" French rate of 1.9, but a significant decrease from the average of seven children they had in the 1970s.[12]

But I could also see why some in Europe might buy a version of the argument. In *Revolutions*, Caldwell provides lots of seemingly dramatic facts. Britain's far-right leader Enoch Powell (of "rivers of blood" notoriety), for instance, had predicted that the non-white population of Britain, barely over a million in the late 1960s, would be 4.5 million by 2002. This figure was dismissed at the time as laughably high. But, in fact, Britain's ethnic minority population numbered 4.6 million by 2001. The number of white British people in the capital of London fell by 620,000 over the first decade of the new millennium, equivalent to the entire population of Glasgow moving out. As a consequence, white Britons are now in a minority in London, making up just 45 percent of its residents.[13]

And in some European cities, the possibility of a Muslim-majority population is also no longer quite so ludicrous. One-third of newborns in Brussels, for example, are of Muslim origin, although currently Muslims make up only 25 percent of the city population.[14] A third of all children in Paris are born to foreign (although not necessarily Muslim) mothers.[15]

Islam is a very sensory presence in these cities. It's possible to walk through extensive neighborhoods where the scent emanating from *boulangeries* is the sticky-sweet *ittar* of baklava rather than the warm, flour-dusted aroma of freshly baked baguettes; the posters on the windows of travel agents scream discounts to Morocco and Tunisia rather than Venice or the Costa del Sol; and the snatches of chatter from TV sets permanently hooked up to satellite TV is guttural and unfamiliar.[16]

These are also usually the poorest, most marginalized quarters of a city. On the whole, Europe's Muslims are a dejected lot who must constantly fight unemployment and discrimination. Yet the idea that they are somehow politically potent, prospective conquerors of the Continent is fed by the comparatively greater religiosity of these immigrant communities in relation to the majority population of the host countries.

Islam mobilizes more people in Brussels than the church, labor movement or political parties, is what I read in newspapers that carried stories based on the Catholic University of Leuven's Professor Felice Dassetto's 2011 work, *The Iris and the Crescent*. This "mobilization" ostensibly happens via the city's 77 mosques and other cultural associations like bookshops.

I met with Dr. Dassetto one February morning in a French-language bookshop in central Brussels and found myself wondering whether all the people browsing the bookshelves that day could in any meaningful sense be considered to have been mobilized to a cause or an ideology by their presence in the shop.

Islam was apparently second only to football in its capacity to "mobilize" people in the city. These categories puzzled me: football, Islam, the labor movement, political parties. They hardly seemed equivalent or exclusive. Couldn't you be a Muslim trade unionist with a passion for football? Trying to classify humans on the basis of an isolated, singular identity rather than investigating the messy mesh of identities that constituted the lived reality of most people did not seem particularly helpful. And yet, it is the constant lot of immigrants from Islamic countries to be itemized as Muslims regardless of whether they are fanatics, devout, nominally observant or merely culturally affiliated to the religion.

As the *Financial Times'* Simon Kuper puts it, there is a danger of seeing "Islam as a bacillus that even secular former Muslims carry around, forever dangerous."[17]

Professor Dassetto was careful to stress his distance from Eurabia mongers. He did not approve of how some of his data had been used by the media. Of Brussels' 300,000 "Muslims," he said, only half were believers in the sense of attending mosques. Why then had they been categorized as Muslims by him, I wondered, but Dassetto was keen to make another point.

The neatly dressed, balding professor, himself a long-term Italian immigrant to Belgium, was keen that Europe did not "stick its head in the sand." In our postcolonial cities, he said, "religion was now a visible presence in public space." Given that "Catholicism" had become invisible over time, this reinsertion of religion into secular Europe was "traumatic."

But Europe is not as secular as it likes to claim. Religion is not so much absent from the public sphere as much as blended into the cultural background, and so rendered somewhat indiscernible. Virtually all the public holidays in Belgium are Christian ones. Not only Christmas and Easter but also a battery of others, including Ascension Day (when the resurrected Jesus is taken up to heaven), Whit Monday (the day of feasting following Pentecost—when the Holy Spirit descended on Jesus' disciples) and Assumption Day (when the Virgin Mary made it to heaven). Around half of all schools in Belgium are still denominated as "Catholic," as are a large number of hospitals.

Nonetheless, the kind of overt religiosity that had been a palpable part of the texture of European life only a few decades ago has indeed been extirpated. Consequently, the traditional Belgian mentalities described by Luc Sante in my dog-eared copy of *Factory of Facts* fitted immigrants from Morocco's Rif valley or Turkey's Anatolian interior far better than it did the contemporary "natives." If transported to modern-day Europe, Sante's grandmother would probably have a lot more in common with the waddling, headscarved matrons of Brussels's immigrant neighborhoods than with her grandson and his contemporaries.

"My grandmother was 'country' in the gravest sense," Sante writes, "absorbing all the moral certitude of life governed by God in the guise of the weather. The city must always have seemed remote and savage to her."[18] Indeed, much of the clash in the attitudes and values of some Muslim immigrants with the dominant culture of their host nations is attributable not to the religion of Islam per se as much as to the dislocation caused by the encounter of a traditional, rural sensibility with the social and economic individualism of modern, urban cultures.

Similar conflicts are in evidence not only in the Hindu or Sikh immigrant encounter with Europe but even within countries like India. As rural to urban migration accelerates in India, honor killings and other forms of violence against women have been on the rise over the last decade. The country has modernized rapidly following its fastest economic growth since Independence, but a simultaneous patriarchal backlash has resulted against the choices made by young people of a rural background emboldened by education and growing economic opportunities in urban centers.[19]

Sante goes on to describe how until the age of 13, even after his family's move to the United States, he was made to wear a cloth sack pinned to his undershirt with bits of linen and paper that had supposedly touched the bones of various Christian saints. "At the vital centre of Ardennais Catholicism," he says later on, "was a fear and hatred of sex . . . licentiousness and libertinism was the ultimate abomination, worse than murder."

The word denoting the attitude toward the physical in 1950s French-speaking Belgium was *"pudeur,"* and I must be forgiven for immediately picking up on its phonetic, if not etymological, similarity to "purdah," the custom shared by India and many Muslim countries whereby women are kept segregated from men by garments like the burka. *"Pudeur"* literally means "modesty" but with strong connotations of "shame."

"In the religion of the hills," says Sante, "good and evil were absolute, unshaded, jansenistically opposed forever and ever, per omnia saecula saeculorum."[20] The black-and-white dualities that characterize religions of the book like Christianity and Islam—good and evil; halal and haram; jannat, or heaven, and jahannum, or hell—give them the common flavor from whence sprang the affinities between some of Manzour's analysis of immigration and that of his Western right-wing detractors.

CLEARLY, SECULARISM IN EUROPE has been a long and difficult process rather than a fully formed "value" dating to Voltaire and the Enlightenment as is sometimes claimed. It was in fact only in the 1960s or thereabouts that most western European countries became secular in the contemporary sense. Anti-blasphemy laws were common in much of Europe until relatively recently.

By 2005, when a Dutch-Moroccan extremist assassinated the provocative Dutch filmmaker Theo van Gogh on a street in Amsterdam, it had become a badge of honor in the Netherlands to defend free speech (including van Gogh's common use of the term "goat fuckers" to describe Muslims).[21] But it wasn't that long before that novelists Gerard van het Reve and W. F. Hermans had fallen foul of Dutch "scornful blasphemy" laws in separate instances, the former as late as 1968.[22]

Theo van Gogh's assassination led to a proposal in the Netherlands to dust off its "scornful blasphemy" law. The argument is one that many Indians are more than familiar with. Unless deliberately incendiary statements aimed at religion, in this case Islam, are not checked, there can be no guarantee of avoiding future violence of the kind that van Gogh had fallen victim to.

The antecedents of threatened violence resulting from hurt sentiments of the Muslim community in Europe, or at least some purporting to speak for it, can most obviously be traced back to the 1989 publication of author Salman Rushdie's *The Satanic Verses*. The implications of the response to the book continue to reverberate not just in Europe but also across the world, including India.

India was the first country to ban *The Satanic Verses* on the grounds that it could offend Muslim feelings. India counted some 130 million Muslims among its citizens, more than the entire population of Pakistan at the time. Independent India was a country born out of the cataclysm of Partition in 1947 in which up to a million people had died in Hindu-Muslim fighting. When it came to religious sensitivities, the country had to tread uniquely cautiously, or so many argued.

In the years since the ban on the import of *The Satanic Verses*, the threat of violence by various aggrieved extremist groups had led to a spate of bans on artistic works in India.[23] And it's not only the works but the artists themselves who have on occasion found themselves "banned." Maqbool Fida Husain, one of modern India's greatest painters, was hounded out of the country because the government could not guarantee his safety from right-wing Hindu groups that criticized his depictions of Hindu goddesses.

And in 2012 the genie of the battle between religious belief and the secular right to free speech, let out of the bottle by *The Satanic*

Verses, was back in all its malignant complexity. In January of that year, Salman Rushdie was unable to participate in India's premier literary festival at Jaipur after unspecified threats of violence by various Muslim groups led the government to declare its inability to guarantee the safety of either the writer or his audience.

Freedom of speech has never been an absolute anywhere, but even less so in India than in most other democratic nations. The Indian Constitution guarantees free speech only within prescribed limits, and inciting hatred between communities is precluded. The penchant for censorship and bans in India of artistic works is often explained by the notion that India is a "special" case: a country whose ethos, mores and the resultant challenges of governance are too different from those of the West for "Western" liberal freedoms to be applied here.

Unlike Europe, India's is not a secular society in the sense of promoting public spaces blanched of religion, runs the argument. It is rather a deeply religious country where equal respect for different beliefs forms the bedrock of societal cohesion. Some people reason that the right to free speech, including the right to offend, cannot have primacy in a country like India where the vast majority of the population is poor and poorly educated; deeply devout, but with differing religious loyalties.

In the case of Rushdie and the literary festival, the government further defended its actions on the grounds that it did not prevent the author from traveling to the country, but that faced with the prospects of violent unrest by non-state actors, was unable to guarantee a peaceable outcome to his participation.

The choice, Indian policymakers claimed, was one between upholding a theoretical "principle" like artistic expression and the reality of potential riots that could lead to loss of life and fan the flames of already combustible relations between religious communities.

Rushdie-2012 provoked much soul-searching among India's intelligentsia with many aghast at the seemingly shrinking space for liberal, secular ideas.[24] An op-ed in *The Hindu* newspaper mourned the arrival of "India's new theocracy." In the meantime, Chetan Bhagat, the country's bestselling writer of lowbrow novels set in urban, middle-class India, piously declared that while he supported the right of people to offend, they should think about the consequences of their actions and self-censor to avoid causing offence. "This is India, you cannot hurt feelings here," he said.[25]

Sitting in Brussels, watching my friends post up a storm of related articles on Facebook, I was struck by how, despite all the claims of Indian exceptionalism, there were parallels to be drawn between some of the challenges facing it and those currently confronting Europe.

In Europe, too, the tensions generated by attempts to balance freedom of speech with freedom of belief are far from resolved. Out of the wreckage of the Second World War, the slow and difficult construction of new European identities and "values" has blended with new economic realities to create the individualist, consumer-oriented, secular societies associated today with Europe.

Shedding patriarchy and conservatism in favor of more permissive lifestyles oriented around personal choices has been only gradually achieved. Far from being some immutable Enlightenment value in Europe, gender equality, for instance, continues to be an arduous work in progress, trumped in certain aspects by some Muslim countries. Women were granted the right to vote in Pakistan at the time of its creation in 1947, a year earlier than Belgium, twenty years before Switzerland, and only three years after France.

But by the 1960s, the grip of the Church on morality was loosening in Europe. Tolerance toward individual choices of consumption, sexuality and belief was on the rise. Religiosity was on the wane.[26] And just at this point when a new consensus around societal values was emerging, in which religion's place was anemic at best, a more muscular, demanding shade of religiosity was back in the form of millions of devout immigrants.

There was thus a dissonance between the beliefs and practices of many of the region's new citizens and the constitutional laws that governed them, creating a curious parallel with India, which faced an inversion of this situation.

In both India and Europe, the power of governments to act flows from the democratic will of the people. But the "people" in both cases are not a homogenous, consonant entity. In postcolonial India, a liberal constitution was grafted onto a country where large parts of the social fabric remained dominated by conservative, traditional beliefs at variance with the values espoused by the newly independent state. In postcolonial Europe, immigration has created substantial pockets of traditionally minded, conservative citizenry at variance with the liberal constitutional values and social fabric that preceded their arrival.

Politicians in both India and Europe are attacked by "liberals" for pandering to "extremists" either for narrow political gain (as in India) or out of "foolish" colonial guilt and political correctness (as in Europe).

At the core of these debates is the collision between two competing sets of values, both of which are important to liberal, democratic societies. This is the clash between cultural relativism and the value placed on diversity, with the concept of universal human rights and the value placed on principles like free speech.

The idea of "tolerance" emerges as a vexed one. In liberal societies, one is expected to be tolerant of different ideas and cultures. But what if those cultures are intolerant of others? How much tolerance of intolerance is justified by liberal principles?

Neither India nor Europe has provided any definitive answers to these questions, as a consequence of which neither can serve as a straightforward model to the other. India is usually first aboard any censoring express. It bans books and movies with impunity. Similarly, many European countries ban the wearing of burkas in public or headscarves to school.

The last decade has been an inglorious one for Europe from the point of view of civil liberties. The Muslim "problem" has led to restrictions ranging from making it harder for citizens to marry foreigners to banning imams from abroad preaching in European mosques.[27] Headscarves, burkas, the Islamic call to prayer, and the building of minarets have all variously been banned in different European countries.

The laws passed across Europe aimed at restricting the public performance of Muslim belief are rarely in proportion to the reality of the Muslim presence. A 2009 Swiss ban on minarets was carried out despite the existence of a sum total of four minarets in the entire country, while the French interior ministry estimates that less than 1 percent of Muslim girls wore headscarves to schools before they were banned. The number of women who chose to wear burkas in the country before they were outlawed was around 350, a fourth of whom were converts.[28]

Even during the height of the 2010–11 Belgian government crisis, when the country lacked a federal government for more than 500 days, bitterly feuding Walloon and Flemish politicians were able to agree quickly on one matter: a nationwide ban prohibiting women from wearing the burka in public places.[29] Estimates put the number of women who actually wear the burka in Belgium at a few dozen.

Europeans are usually quick to censure authoritarian China for the restrictions on the practice of religion placed by Beijing on its western Muslim-majority region of Xinjiang. In Xinjiang, muezzins are banned from using loudspeakers during their call to prayer. Imams are not permitted to teach the Koran in private, and the study of Arabic is allowed only at designated government schools. But the difference between the constraints on Islam imposed by China and those by some European countries is arguably a matter of degree rather than substance.

BACK IN MY DRAWING ROOM in Brussels, Manzour leaned back into the sofa and slurped at his cup of coffee. My friend, whom I shall call Khan, an avuncular Brussels-based journalist for one of the Arab states' national news agencies, looked less relaxed. Khan is an Indian national who has lived in Europe since the 1970s. Originally from Calcutta, he'd studied in Germany before spending several years in Greece and eventually moving to Brussels.

It was Khan who'd introduced me to Manzour as someone who was well placed to tell me about the "true situation of Islam" in Brussels. Manzour's last comment about the inevitability of a majority community striving to dominate minorities seemed to have agitated Khan.

I knew Khan well and was familiar with the frustration he felt about his circumstances. Despite having spent the best part of his life in Europe, there was a stinging bitterness to his tone whenever he discussed his lot. "There is nothing for me here," he would often say. He spoke longingly of returning to India, to "home." He spoke of the country in idealized terms as one of boundless tolerance and harmony. "No one cares if you wear a burka or a lungi or whatever there," he would say.

I found his views astonishing. Yes, you could wear a burka in India, but it probably wouldn't have been a great idea to have been sporting one in Gujarat in 2002. But then, he hadn't lived in India through the rise of Hindutva and the BJP. His India was a thing of the imagination: a refuge to retreat to, that made the present more bearable. So, what was so terrible about genteel Brussels for Khan?

Khan was never very specific, but the sharp edge of resentment was clear under his generalizations. "Do you know what my son comes home and says about Arabs?" he would say darkly. "The kinds of prejudice he's picking up in school?"

On another occasion, we met directly after I'd attended a press conference at the EU headquarters where a spokesperson had been expounding on European "values" and their indispensability to securing human progress and happiness and peace. I had to suppress a giggle when Khan, unaware of where I was coming from, launched into a diatribe about the harm being caused to his son by his exposure to European "values." "They have no respect for the family, no respect for faith." He'd slumped into his chair and looked at me through eyes hooded in sadness. "What kind of a place is this?"

Whatever kind of a place it might be, Khan had chosen to live here for over three decades. It is a common schizophrenia among immigrants: the longing for a home that one had deliberately decided to leave. Khan always said the reason he stayed on in Europe was to see his son's schooling through. But this was the very school that he claimed fed the boy anti-Muslim prejudice. Ultimately, it seemed to me that Khan stayed on partly out of habit and also perhaps because of the barely acknowledged fear that life back in India would not in reality be the thing of glory that his imagination had shaped out of his childhood memories.

That day at my home with Manzour, I knew Khan wouldn't be able to resist jumping into the fray. Sure enough. "What about India?" he interjected, staring at his friend accusingly. "So many cultures live there together with no problem. No one cares if you are Hindu or Muslim or Christian. There is respect for each other. Europe should be learning from India."

Manzour looked shiftily at me as though assessing how much he should say. "There may have been respect when we were young, but not now. They [Hindus] deliberately provoke us." His voice rose in indignation and he set his coffee cup down.

"They take out [religious] processions with murtis [icons of Hindu gods] right in front of the masjid even when namaz is going on!" Islam is iconoclastic. "Where is the respect in that?"

Khan refused to back down. "No, no. It's much better now than before." He talked about traveling by train in India in the 1970s. "If people caught you doing the namaz in a train then, they would thrash you. But now, you go on a train and at least 15 percent of the people are Muslim with beards and everything."

I felt a stab of sadness. How terrible to be so vulnerable. To have to make quick calculations about how many others like you were there on a train, just in case.

Manzour was unconvinced. "My daughter and son-in-law were traveling from Lucknow to Agra just a few years back, in 2007. It was a late-night train," he said. "When they entered the compartment they saw that the others sitting there were wearing saffron clothes."[30] I felt a chill at the thought. Two young Muslims and a train compartment filled with saffron-robed thugs did not constitute the makings of a happy story.

"They wouldn't allow my kids to sit there with them." I actually found myself sighing with *relief*. Being bullied out of a public train compartment was not the worst that could have happened to the couple in that situation, by a long shot.

THIS EXCHANGE WAS ALL ABOUT the two ideas of India. There is the India of unique syncretism, of a civilization that lacks singularity save in being singularly diverse. This is the idea of an India with equal space and respect for every religion, ethnicity and language. Where a multiplicity of identities is celebrated and a propensity to spirited argument and debate is considered a cherished hallmark of the people. The India that is the only country in the world where Jews have never faced persecution and where Hindus and Muslims and Christians are known to worship at each other's holy places.[31]

And then there is the India of ground-level realities, where in practice the country's multicultural experiment with nationhood has given rise to a political culture where the threat of violence by extremist groups (both Hindu and Muslim) holds constitutional niceties to ransom. This is an India where mob action and intimidation trumps discussion. Where, as one leading columnist argued, the inability of the state to keep religion out of the public sphere has only led to "the perpetuation of caste and gender inequities, the stunting of reason and critical facilities needed for economic and social progress and the corrosive growth of religious nationalism."[32]

Both ideas of India are true, the truth rarely being singular. India's comfort level with religious and cultural diversity is often traced to the subcontinent's ancient popular religious practices, which eventually became described by the term "Hinduism." The habitual breaching of boundaries of gender, class, caste and sexuality were long an intrinsic part of the cultural fabric of the civilization.[33] Recently, an article used a contemporary metaphor to frame Hinduism as an "open source faith." Writing in the *Huffington Post,* Josh Schrei talks of how "Atheists and Goddess worshipers, heretics who've sought God through booze, sex, and meat, ash covered hermits, dualists and non-dualists, nihilists and hedonists, poets and singers, students and saints, children and outcasts have all contributed their lines of code to the Hindu string."[34]

The ascribing of India's uniquely diverse socio-religious fabric to Hinduism can be dangerous, in that right-wing Hindu extremists espouse a line of reasoning according to which, although the "Hindus" in their magnanimity may have "allowed" Muslims and other outsiders to live in India all these centuries, their generosity has been abused and is now finally wearing thin. It is therefore time, they claim, for all "foreigners" to shape up (i.e., declare their primary loyalty to a Hindu India) or ship out.

But of course the point is that "Hinduism" as a coherent set of identity and practices is itself arguably a modern construction. Historically, the Hindu tradition has embraced a vertiginously wide array of cultural practices, including atheism. For example, the Carvakas, Veda-rejecting materialists who lived as far back as 600 BC, are as much part of the Hindu tradition as the Vishnu- or Shiva-worshipping devout.[35]

A civilizational acceptance of pluralism, a high comfort level with contradictions and the absence of an insistence on singular truths, gods and loyalties has meant that even today India defies a linear, European-style narrative of modernity that would see it march forward from the feudal religious practices of the middle ages to the homogenizing secular modernity that is the assumed corollary of economic prosperity. In India, religious piety and modernity have not proved mutually exclusive. This is a country where nuclear scientists are known to keep shrines of gods in their homes and where Western-educated businessmen may well abandon lucrative negotiations to rush off on pilgrimage, should they feel the call of a Devi (Goddess).

And because of the enormous diversity of class, religion, language and customs that average Indians have to negotiate in their daily lives, they are used to adapting their behavior, dress and speech to suit different occasions. The middle class–urban and the traditional-rural live side by side and in different combinations in India's cities.

For most Indians, a certain amount of role-playing is an accepted part of life, and the contradictions between one's varied roles is not usually a matter of existential angst. An atheist bowing down before a shrine in a temple; a habitually miniskirted girl choosing to dress demurely to meet her more conservative relatives; an observant teetotaler Jain offering his dinner party guests a glass of beer: such common accommodations are not about lacking the guts to stand up for one's own beliefs as much as about expressing a respect for the beliefs of others. In Europe, this would probably have been frowned upon as hypocrisy. In India, it is considered tact. And tact has a definite advantage in a multicultural space.

The difference between India's cultural ethos and that of certain Protestant northern European countries like the Netherlands and its Scandinavian cousins was driven home when I read Ian Buruma's book on the murder of Theo van Gogh in which he talks about bluntness having been elevated to a virtue in the Dutch character. "The insistence on total frankness . . . that everything, no matter how sensitive should be stated openly, with no holds barred, the elevation of bluntness to a kind of moral ideal . . . is a common trait in Dutch behaviour," Buruma writes.[36]

It put me in mind of my Oxford days when I found myself seated to the right of Anders, a Danish physicist, at one of my college's weekly Formal Halls, a dinner at which students had to dress smartly and don academic gowns. The conversation at my table was focused on the upcoming elections to the social committee of the Middle Common Room, a very serious affair since it impacted the wine selection we would have access to for the rest of the year. Even as the chatter grew more animated, I noticed Anders's nose begin to twitch spasmodically. I turned to look at him sniff the air like a hound on the trail of a particularly plump bunny until he suddenly lifted his right arm and took a long inhalation at his armpit. "Yes!" he said with all the excitement of having a tricky hypothesis proved right. "I stink."

But for all of India's exceptional pluralism and ability to accommodate difference, the other India of grotesque communal riots and bloodshed is as much a reality. The country is stalked by the long shadow of the mass communal violence that its partition in 1947 had provoked. From the anti-Sikh massacres in 1984 following the assassination of Prime Minister Indira Gandhi by her Sikh bodyguard, to the riots that succeeded the destruction of the Babri Masjid in Ayodhya in

1992, and most recently the slaughter of Muslims in Gujarat in 2002, India's post-independence history is checkered with blood-baying mobs of Hindus and Muslims and Sikhs committing mind-boggling atrocities against each other.[37]

This makes it difficult to promote India as some kind of exemplar for Europe to follow, as my friend Khan would have it. India clearly does not have a tidy solution to the challenges of shaping a vast and diverse population with divergent beliefs into a harmonious ideal of civic-minded, public-spirited citizens who settle their disagreements with level-headed reasoning and vigorous debate.

Reading Ian Buruma's book about the murder of Theo Van Gogh in the Netherlands, what struck me most—as an Indian—was the muted reaction to the killing. Three mosques, in Huizen, Rotterdam and Groningen, were indeed targeted by arsonists bent on "revenge," causing minor damage to the buildings, but there was no pogrom against Muslims, no civil war, no counter-retaliations by jihadis.[38] The Netherlands did not burn, although an explosion of debate and "overheated commentary' in the media did produce a "feverish" atmosphere.

YET, EUROPE ITSELF ALSO FAILS as a paradigm of tolerance. As in the case of India, there are two ideas of Europe, which often do not fit easily together either.

There is the Europe of EU rhetoric: a touchy-feely yet high-minded post-national entity—what Parag Khanna calls a "metrosexual" superpower, focused on pooling sovereignty, cherishing diversity and soft peddling its "values" of human rights and democracy around the globe.[39] And then there is the ground-level reality of most European nations, where far-right parties are gaining ground, minorities are often vilified and intolerance is practiced in the guise of progressivism.

The ban on the burka and other kinds of "ethnic" or religious clothing like the headscarf is a case in point. Some supporters of these bans claim them as a victory for gender equality, a triumph of feminism. Politicians dress up the move on the burka as a security concern, since anyone with a covered face in public is apparently a security risk. I often wrapped up my face in a woolly scarf when venturing out in the winter wind of Brussels. But of course, no one seemed to find me a national security risk. There is much dissembling about the burka issue on all sides.

"I think the burka makes it easier for the police to catch criminals," Khalid Al-Ibri, the unctuous new head of Brussels's Islamic Cultural Centre, a recent arrival from Saudi Arabia, told me when I met him at the mosque one morning. "It's so much more difficult for a terrorist or criminal in a burka to make a getaway. Try running away from a crime scene in a burka. Not easy."

Neither the burka nor the headscarf is simply about an article of clothing. But a straightforward feminist reading of these bans as liberating for Muslim women can be crude as well. As the Indian writer and activist Arundhati Roy put it, coercing a woman out of the burka is not "about liberating her, but about unclothing her." Viewing gender "shorn of social, political and economic context, makes it an issue of identity, a battle of props and costumes."[40]

In *Another Cosmopolitanism*, political philosopher Seyla Benhabib describes how the wearing of the headscarf by a handful of French schoolgirls in defiance of the ban was far from a symbol of their oppression. It was rather a conscious political gesture, simultaneously an act of identification and defiance. By claiming to exercise their freedom of religion as French citizens, they both flagged their North African origins and forced their cultural and religious differences into the open, confounding any easy notion of school as a neutral space for unidirectional French acculturation.[41]

I met with Fatima Zibouh, PhD candidate, fashion lover, mother and headscarf wearer, on a weekday afternoon in Brussels to talk to her about the politics of the hijab. She strode into the coffee shop where I was waiting, dressed in jeans and a gauzy top. Drops of rain decorated her lilac flower-patterned headscarf, like jewels.

Fatima was a third-generation Belgian-Moroccan. "When people say 'your French is so good,' I get very annoyed," she said with a throaty, good-humored laugh. Fatima was the only one among the 50 grandchildren of her Moroccan-born grandparents to go to university. But her mother and electrician father had supported her decision to study. "Like most immigrants, my parents did not have much cultural capital, but they were progressive in their own way," she explained, sipping an espresso.

Growing up, Fatima's relationship with religion had been complex. Her parents were "culturally religious" in an unreflexive way, but her schooling had encouraged atheism. "My teachers in school always dismissed religion. They implied that believers were crazy. It hurt me because this was an insult to my parents, but for a long time I didn't believe in God."

In her late teens she found herself on an age-old quest for the meaning of life. And it was in Islam that she found answers. When she decided to begin wearing a headscarf at the age of 20, her father was concerned that it would hurt her job prospects. "'Don't do it. You will regret it,' he told me," Fatima grinned. But she was determined to go ahead.

"With a headscarf I finally found a way to express my identity. It made me so proud to be able to signal by my dress who I am." And who is that, I asked. "A European Muslim," pat came the reply. "There is no contradiction. You don't have to be either wholly Westernized or wholly Muslim, and through the hijab I was finally able to bring the two parts of who I am together. I felt complete."

At the time she began to wear the headscarf, Fatima was a student of political science at the Universite Libre de Brussels. She described her feelings on making the decision as "excited." "I wanted to open doors for Muslim women," she said. Fatima is currently the secretary general of an academic body called the Belgian Association of Political Science. "A headscarf-wearing woman becoming the secretary general of an association like that—it was something totally new in Belgium."

But it had been a bumpy ride professionally for the young Muslim woman. After graduating from university, she'd applied for a job at the Conseil d'Etat, Belgium's highest administrative court. She was one among 20-odd candidates selected for a final interview and was eventually offered the position.

"I was so excited, until they told me that while the job was mine, there was one small 'detail.' No headscarf. Because wearing a headscarf was against the idea of *laïcité*." Fatima turned down the offer. "For me that experience was violent. Like a slap. I was rejected simply because I had a different look."

Leaving clothing bans and restrictions aside, Europe has historically had a minority "problem." As Tony Judt makes clear, the modern idea of Europe as the embodiment of human rights and all things nice glosses over collective memories of brutal crimes in which almost all European states were complicit, including genocide, ethnic cleansing and colonialism. Europe's long-standing ethnic minority conundrum was only "solved" by "blasting flat the demographic heath upon which the foundations of a new and less complicated continent were then laid."[42]

It is bone-chilling to read about the massive scale of ethnic cleansing and population transfers that were carried out by so many European countries in the lead up to, and in the immediate aftermath of, the Second World War. Between 1939 and 1941, the Nazis expelled 750,000 Polish peasants eastward from western Europe—offering the vacated land to *volksdeutsche,* ethnic Germans from occupied eastern Europe. Slavs were removed and Jews were executed in the process. Hundreds of thousands of Germans from Romania, Soviet-occupied Poland and the Baltic states responded to Hitler's offer, all of whom were in turn expelled a few years later, once the war ended.[43]

Between Stalin and Hitler, "30 million people were uprooted, dispersed, expelled, deported and transplanted." The population transfers did not end with the war. Some of these movements were "voluntary," as in the case of Jews facing post-war pogroms in Poland who fled to Germany and elsewhere in large numbers. Over 63,300 Jews arrived in Germany from Poland between July and September 1946 alone. Similarly, up to 350,000 Italians left the Istrian peninsula rather than taking their chances under Yugoslav rule.[44]

But the bulk of the uprooting was the result of official policy during the course of the war. For example, 1 million Poles fled or were expelled from western Ukraine while half a million Ukrainians left Poland between October 1944 and June 1946 as a result of Soviet diktats. And thus, in the course of a few months, a centuries-old region of intermixed faiths and languages had been disaggregated into two separate, mono-ethnic territories.[45]

These population transfers were tantamount to ethnic cleansing. And although mostly confined to eastern and central Europe, they were agreed to by all the major western European powers as the safest solution to the continent's minority predicament.

Poland, whose population was only 68 percent Polish in 1938, became "Polish," just as Germany became "German." The ancient diasporas of Europe—Greeks and Turks in the south Balkans and Black Sea, Italians in Dalmatia, Hungarians in Transylvania, Poles in Ukraine, Jews across the continent—were greatly reduced.

And so was born the historically anomalous, ethnically homogenous Europe of nation-states that are currently being discomfited by the "new" presence of millions of Muslim immigrants. This discomfiture, says Judt, not only flags the region's current difficulties in dealing with variety but also "the ease with which the dead 'others' of Europe's past are cast out of mind."[46] Indeed, many right-wing parties active today, like the National Front in France and Austria's Freedom Party, have merely repackaged their foundational anti-Semitism into an anti-Muslim stance.[47]

"Europe" when used to refer to the European Union cannot rightfully be accused of this forgetfulness. Indeed, the European Union's existence is intended to serve as a reminder of the follies and atrocities of Europe's past, to ensure that these are "never again" repeated. Unfortunately, for most Europeans today, the European Union evokes either apathy or derision and is equated with bureaucracy and undemocratic diktats.[48] Identities remain strongly national, and despite the European Union's commitment to diversity, policies to address immigration are largely a national endeavor.

It's clear that neither European countries nor India have found easy answers to the thorny challenges of diversity. They haven't located the "correct" places to draw the lines between various kinds of freedoms and rights. But what is sometimes obscured is that the battle between individual and community rights, universalism and relativism, and the secular and religious also mask other divisions between the entitled and the excluded, the privileged and the marginalized. It is usually the more vulnerable in any society who cling to and need the protection of collective identity.

Buruma looks at the difference between immigrants with education and social connections and those without in the Netherlands. The former usually do well as individuals and assimilate, while it's the more vulnerable who hang on to their collective identities.[49]

In India, "liberals" (usually of the urban middle class) often ask why the offense taken by "illiberal" groups at, say, a book that insults their sensibilities, is prioritized by politicians over their own right to take offense at the illiberalism of those who would ban the said book. What is missed here is that the offense taken by a community over a book or a movie, the anxiety that is generated regarding the manner in which it is perceived and represented, is sometimes as much about exclusion as it is about the words or content of the work. And exclusion is not part of the lived experience of the country's liberal elite.

Europe's "others" are not rich foreigners. There is an unavoidable class element to the "Muslim" question. A Muslim middle class has not, so far, materialized here. Statistics to highlight the conflation of Muslim immigrants with pockets of poverty and deprivation abound. As one example, 50 percent of Muslims in Britain live in the most deprived housing conditions compared to 20 percent of the general population. Moreover, a huge 70 percent of Muslim children live in poverty and receive state support in Belgium.[50]

ONE LATE WINTER DAY I boarded a tram by my house to nearby Place Liedts to meet with the director of the European Network Against Racism (ENAR), a 600-odd-strong coalition of Europe-wide NGOs. Place Liedts is located in the commune of Schaerbeek, a "mixed" neighborhood with prosperous, cherry-blossom-lined neighborhoods, home to mostly white people, abruptly morphing into tree-less tenements with peeling paint and mainly Muslim inhabitants.

Place Liedts was buzzing with activity even though it was a weekday. People dawdled and gawped and clustered in groups, as they did in India, rather than striding along purposefully, in typical European fashion.

A statue of Nasreddin Hoca[51] riding a donkey backwards had been put up as a "tribute" to the area's Turkish community, just off the main square. A gaggle of rumpled, happy kids ran around the donkey, their headscarved mothers sitting on a nearby bench, occasionally calling out a warning to be careful. An elderly matron cloaked in an abaya came waddling out of the next-door Le Riad Hammam, her post-massage glow quite unmistakable. Shops displayed signs like Electro Ozcelik and Alimentation General Erdogan. The neighborhood boulangerie was called Kezban Firni. The travel agent had Turk Hava Yollari (Turkish Airlines) in large letters pasted onto its window.

Place Liedts was what one Belgian friend referred to as Anatolia Central. But its immigrant credentials were older than the Turks. I came across a fascinating article by Belgian historian Anne Morelli in an edition of the local Flemish magazine *KVS Express* that talked about the way immigrants in Brussels had been perceived over the decades, beginning with impoverished workers from the Flemish countryside itself.[52] The trams aboard which these country bumpkins from northern Belgium traveled were the only ones with stern signs that read, "No Spitting."

Later, Italian migrants replaced Flemish ones. By the 1930s, Place Liedts was a Polish-majority neighborhood. Morelli had dug up a telling passage from a 1933 edition of the *Bulletin de la Socieìteì Royal Belge de Geìographie*. Here's how it described the inhabitants of Place Liedts at the time:

> When they are sufficiently numerous in a neighbourhood, their fellow countrymen open hairdressing salons, grocery shops, bakeries . . . butcher's shops, where they sell meat from ritually-slaughtered animals. . . . Unfortunately, as a rule they pay little or no attention to their housing. One, two or three rooms, and sometimes simply cellars or small attic rooms suffice to house a family with the several children they usually have. . . . The way they live is also very different from ours . . . and disturbs the peace of the occupants of adjacent houses. . . . Do Belgian workers have any other complaints about the foreigners? In this period of very harsh economic crisis, and of astronomically high unemployment, work is also being taken away from the indigenous population. . . . And let us not forget that their religion and language do not ease any attempts at contact. . . . We can immediately say that there will never be full integration. . . . Their language is foreign to us, we know little about their religion, their customs are different from ours, and there is too great a social gap between the majority of these migrants and our population.

"They" in this piece referred to Jewish Polish immigrants but almost every sentence in the passage could have been written in the present day with Muslims as the subject. So much of the prejudice faced by Muslims in Europe today has to do with deprivation and poverty rather than the specificities of their religion. As Morelli puts it, the same causes—the grouping of a poor, foreign population in deprived neighborhoods—yield the same results.

Michael Privot, the director of ENAR, whom I had come to meet in Liedts, worked in a dilapidated building just across the road from the statue of Nasreddin Hoca. A 38-year-old Belgian convert to Islam, Michael had an infectious smile and round owlish glasses that bestowed on him a likeable earnestness. I went on to meet him several times over the course of a few months during which we talked about his worries and hopes for European Muslims. But it was only on the last occasion we met that he told me about his family.

He grew up, by coincidence, in the same Walloon city that my favorite Belgian memoirist Luc Sante belonged to, Verviers. His mother's side of the family, German Protestants fleeing religious persecution, had converted to Catholicism once in Wallonia and made it big in the region's wool industry before its collapse in the second half of the last century. His father's family were peasants from the Ardennes about whom not much was known.

Michael's father, a civil servant in the road administration in the nearby city of Liege, was an anti-clerical trade unionist. His mother's parents were very Catholic, but his mother, a bank clerk, was more agnostic than devout.

Theirs was an intellectually open family, which almost never went to church, although Michael and his brother had been baptized. By the time he was 15 or so, Michael became spiritually curious and began to read about various religions. He flirted with Buddhism, and at one point even met a rabbi to talk about possible conversion to Judaism.

At university in Liege, he chose to study Arabic in the Oriental languages department and from here on developed an interest in Islam. "I had never met any Muslims before I joined university, so I really had no preconceived notions of the religion," Michael told me. In the late 1980s, such ignorance was still possible.

He met a young woman, a fellow student, whose parents were Muslim immigrants from Dagestan in the Russian Caucasus. They fell in love and decided to marry. Michael converted to Islam at the age of 19, although he didn't start practicing seriously until he was 22. "Part of the reason for my conversion was because of my wife being Muslim. But it wasn't the whole story. I came to Islam from an academic perspective, and while it took me a few years, eventually I was sure this was the path for me," Michael said.

Unlike some converts, he insisted that his attraction to Islam had nothing to do with depression or feelings of anger against society. He was just strongly attracted to the simplicity of the religion's message. "Islam seemed to me a rational and clear path to get closer to God. Following it I could live a pious life but an active one. I didn't have to renounce anything and become a monk."

Michael's conversion and decision to get married did not go over well with his family. He recalled Amin Malouf's book *The Crusades through Arab Eyes* flying up and down his family dining table, literally. "It proved very difficult for my parents to look at the world from a non-Eurocentric perspective," he smiled.

Michael's in-laws so disapproved of his marriage to their daughter that the young couple was forced to seek police protection, fearing violence from his wife's family. Michael's own parents were "traumatized" by these happenings. Eventually, three years into the marriage, the wife's family re-established contact and polite, if not loving, relations have since been maintained.

The bizarre googly in this tale concerns Michael's own family. In 1998, four years after Michael's marriage, his brother too converted to Islam. Next, it was his mother's turn to convert, and she eventually cajoled her husband, Michael's father, to convert as well.

Michael did not dwell on the reasons behind these conversions, although he told me his mother later claimed to have discovered the "true Christian faith through Islam." The problem, Michael continued, was that the only mosque in Verviers at the time was a Salafi one that preached a strict version of the kind of Islam popular in Saudi Arabia.

Before long, Michael became branded as a semi-heretic by his own family. "My wife does not wear a headscarf, but my mother did. My father grew a full beard. They refused to sit at a dining table if there was wine on it. They claimed music was haram. My mother," sighed Michael, "was an extremist in everything, and Islam became no exception."

It was a strange story and an unexpected one. Michael had never referred to it during our previous meetings. I was left puzzled by a lot of what he told me. The motivations of his family members seemed hazy. But it did epitomize the polymorphic nature of Islam and Muslims in Europe, putting paid to any notions of homogeneity among these categories.

Fatima Zibouh, the political science researcher, had a similar story about her sister's husband, also a Belgian convert to Islam. "My brother-in-law took to wearing Pakistani clothes, like a long kurta and *shalwar*." Fatima thought the decision was strange. "I told him, you don't have to wear a *shalwar* just because you are now a Muslim. A *shalwar* is not an Islamic dress, it's an Asian dress. But you are European."

For Fatima, Islam had nothing to do with Saudi Arabian Wahabism. "I pay attention to fashion in the way I dress and put flowers on my headscarf. There is nothing in the Koran that says you have to wear a scarf in a particular way," she said with a flounce of her hijabed head.

Michael was a religious convert and Fatima a third-generation Moroccan-Belgian, and both insisted that in their cultural core, they were "European." "I cannot culturally become a Turk or Arab," Michael said, jabbing a clasped pen down hard on the table. "I am a Muslim, but that does not mean I have lost my cultural center. If Islam is universal, then it has to fit and adapt to my context, not the other way around."

Fatima echoed these sentiments. "I have only ever been to Morocco three times in my life. I don't speak Arabic, although I learnt to read it at university from a 'white' teacher. I prefer coffee to mint tea and *frite* to couscous. But at the same time, I don't drink, because I am a Muslim."

Michael and Fatima were essentially arguing for the existence and validity of European Islam, a controversial and confused creature-in-the-making, as distinct from Islam (rooted in other cultures) in Europe, which is a well-established fact. But it is still not clear what this European Islam will look like and what admixture will result from the intersection of the religious beliefs of second- and third-generation Muslim immigrants with their European identities.

Michael insisted that what was needed for Islam to grow and settle down in Europe was a negotiation of the manner in which the religion was represented in public. This was already happening via the hybrid norms of behavior that youngsters had begun to develop.

Manzour had referred to one of these with much disapproving head shaking. Talking about the teenagers he taught Islamiat to in Belgian schools, he spoke of their having developed a practice of "verbal nikahs." A nikah refers to the contractual marriage that Islam permits. Belgian Muslim youngsters, Manzour said, were increasingly desirous of dating, like their "native" counterparts. To assuage their guilt, they concluded some kind of personal nikah between themselves in the belief that this provided religious sanction to their relationship.

"Of course, it's complete nonsense," snorted Manzour. "There is no such thing in Islam." Strictly speaking, he was right. A verbal nikah between two consenting adults was merely an agreement to date, or at most, to consider oneself engaged. But in the absence of approval by a *Waki Amr,* or appropriate guardian, such a promise had no religious force.

However, it is probably more appropriate to say that there *was,* rather than *is,* no such thing in Islam. European Islam is very gradually developing its own cultural roots and adjusting the nature of religious practices accordingly. There are several examples of this.

The political theorist Bhikhu Parekh shows how young Muslim girls in the United Kingdom have begun to appropriate the Koran to defend their rights by invoking its authority to argue against sexist practices that are traditional but lacking a theological basis. By studying the Koran themselves, the girls are able to interpret it according to the feminist values embedded in their new cultural context.[53]

Fatima had talked to me about her own appropriation of Islamic texts in what she called her "feminist fight." For example, while studying for her undergraduate degree, Fatima found she needed to travel to Africa for a research project. Her mother was dead against it, claiming that women should not travel on their own. "I was able to advance Islamic arguments to convince her that they can and should travel by themselves, if necessary," Fatima recalled.

In France, leading scholar of Islam Olivier Roy points out that a hybrid form of French Muslim weddings has started to evolve. These weddings take place in mosques but with the couple hand in hand and the bride dressed in white and holding flowers.[54]

But for all the examples of the bricolage practiced by Muslim youngsters, it is also second- and third-generation immigrants who have proved most susceptible to radicalization. The supporters of an Al-Qaeda-style global jihad might be a small minority among European Muslims, but they are overwhelmingly young men who have been born and brought up in Europe.

The parents of these youngsters had seen themselves as temporary visitors to Europe. Michael recalled how his wife's parents kept a suitcase packed in readiness for departure back to Dagestan for close to 30 years. As a result, they had little anxiety about maintaining their homeland identity.

But their children faced a very different set of identity-related dilemmas. Unable to share fully in either their parents' or host nation's cultural milieu, many of these youth formed subcultures of their own, based on defiance and victimhood. Their interest in defining their identity increased with the experience of racism and exclusion that they suffered in school.

Michael pointed out that in the not-so-distant past Belgian schools sometimes divided classes up according to the color of the children attending. This was justified on the grounds of the children being differentially proficient in the language of instruction, but it had far-reaching repercussions on the way these kids felt alienated from the majority community. These feelings of exclusion only became more and more ingrained with the passage of time. "In Muslim areas, the police stop you if you are Arab-looking. I have never been stopped because I am white," said Michael grimly.

Moreover, many of these children were completely lacking in parental support and had in fact been forced by circumstances to act as the "adults" in the family, given their parents' inability to cope with practical and social life in Europe. Through interviews with Moroccan youngsters in the Netherlands, Buruma shows their resentment at having grown up helping their parents deal with all things quotidian, from filling out forms to talking with the postman. The result was mothers and fathers with little parental authority and kids who'd lost trust in their families.

Immigrant youth felt anger at their parents' helplessness and anger at the country that had allowed their parents to come and work but without any thought for how they would manage. "They let our parents clean the streets, work in factories, fix everything, but it's up to us, the children, to solve their problems," said Farhane, a young Moroccan actor whom Buruma interviewed.[55]

These young people lacked their parents' diffidence and inhibitions. They picked up on the condescension with which those around them treated their parents. Seeing their mothers and fathers diminished and humiliated in a hundred different covert and overt ways must have carried a lasting sting.

Fatima made the point about how despite being part of the modern history of European countries, Muslim immigrants were written out of the official histories taught in school. "My uncles helped build all the infrastructure here in Belgium after the Second World War. My father worked as an electrician in the buildings of the European Union. My family is part of this country. They were part of creating it. But does anyone acknowledge this?"

Many youngsters developed an increased interest in their identity as they tried to find a "home" that they could claim as their own and an authority to rely on that they found lacking in their parents. Religious identity was a less complicated focus for their search than national identity. And given that they had little connection to the national homelands of their parents, there was no modifying, secondary identity to temper their freshly discovered, and solace-providing, primary identity of Islam.

The ability to read Arabic is also something that distinguishes many of Europe's young Muslims from their parents. First-generation immigrants tended to speak the language of their home countries and were therefore unable to read the Koran directly, relying instead on traditionalist ulema for interpretations. But the younger generation often learn Arabic, which gives them direct access to the Koranic text. They can therefore interpret the Koran for themselves. While this can on occasionally lead to creatively syncretic beliefs, it can also lead to a purist, literal acceptance of the text. An Islam that is purged of local culture is not a taken-for-granted aspect of one's background, as had usually been the case with the first generation, but a self-consciously adopted insignia of commitment, and thus louder and more unbending.[56]

It is clear from the profiles of those who commit acts of violence in the name of Islam that those most prone to radicalization in Europe are youngsters who had found their attempts to fit into society thwarted in one way or another. Buruma describes how Theo van Gogh's assassin, Mohammed Bouyari, had been considered a "positivo" in school. The kind of kid who would do well, having embraced the idea that hard work would eventually lead to success.

Instead, a string of disappointments, from failed job applications to failed romances, gradually led an ever more embittered Mohammed to embrace the kind of radicalism he had shown scant appetite for while in school.[57] A former history teacher of Bouyeri told a newspaper reporter that the radical youths were generally the better educated ones. "I think they find ideals in fundamentalism that are impossible for them to reach in Dutch society when they leave school. Because employers won't take on Moroccans, for example."[58]

Several years later when 23-year-old Mohammad Merah, a Frenchman of Algerian descent, went on the rampage in Toulouse, gunning down French soldiers and Jewish civilians in March 2012, a similar profile emerged. As a youngster, Merah had loved fast cars and nightclubs, but when he landed in jail for having stolen a purse, he became despondent about his future. The Koran reading began.

Upon being released, he applied for jobs in the French Army and Foreign Legion but was rejected due to his criminal past. Attempts to find work as a mechanic, too, ended in failure. A brief marriage led to divorce.[59] And so on and so on until a crazed and vengeful Merah carried out the spate of attacks that left seven people dead and was eventually killed himself during a shootout with the police.

Only very few Muslim youth in Europe turn extremists in the Bouyari and Merah manner. But general disaffection is a more widespread malaise. I could only imagine how dispiriting it must be to have one's religion widely regarded as barbaric and somehow incompatible with (Western) "civilization." Since individuals develop a commitment to society and form a view of their place in it based on their experience of how it views, values and treats them, this widespread disillusionment was almost unavoidable.

There is such a triumphalist superiority about the constant touting of "European values" (in implicit opposition to Islamic and other non-Western values) as the panacea to the world's ills. And this opposition of Europe and Islam has a long pedigree. In a searing critique of Caldwell's book, Pankaj Mishra discusses research that connects the manner in which Muslims are perceived today to how they have been treated by European empires and their racial hierarchies in the past.[60] The veil, for example, the focus of much Islamic paranoia at present, was fixed in the nineteenth century by the French as a symbol of Islam's primitive backwardness and used to justify the pacification of North African Muslims and exclude them from full citizenship.[61]

In any event, what is clear is that no unambiguous trajectory of inevitable "assimilation'" has emerged among Europe's Muslim immigrants.

"But," Michael insisted, "it is early days yet." By the time we have sixth- and seventh-generation Muslims in Europe, would they really remain "foreign" in any plausible sense? India's Muslims had been a significant presence in the subcontinent for well over a thousand years, and the vast majority were converts. Western Europe's were barely a few decades old.

What has happened in Europe since the 1960s is a gradual unbundling of the nation, as a collectivity of shared cultural memories and morals, from its citizens. Moreover, the new, globalized technological environment, engendered by the Internet, satellite television and international air travel, has made it increasingly complicated to create an overlap between the two categories.

It is possible, as a result, for citizens of a country to remain isolated from any feelings of national belonging. You have youths who spend far more time surfing the Internet than talking to their neighbors. And one thing everyone from Michael to Manzour agreed on was the role played by Saudi Arabia in flooding the World Wide Web with Salafi literature and interpretations of Islam. The main formative influences on many youngsters thus often come from across national borders. Traditional means of constructing national identities via propaganda are disrupted by the ability of twenty-first-century citizens to choose to tune it out and participate instead in "imaginary communities"[62] that do not coincide with national constructs.

But I wondered whether national identity is as important as it had once been. The construction of the European Union, arguably the greatest achievement of post-war Europe, had undermined the primacy of the nation by disaggregating certain political and economic rights, like the freedom of movement and the right to work, from national belonging. While a concrete European identity still proved elusive for most "old" Europeans, the creation of the European Union allowed an alternative new identity for the region's new immigrants.

It is almost impossible for newcomers to insert themselves successfully into a community of belonging whose memory stretches back hundreds of years and is fed on songs and stories that have no place for them. The European Union, however, is an innovative, inclusive creature-in-the-making. If the development of nineteenth-century nation-states had the effect of simplifying society into the most homogenous common denominator, the European Union is a celebration of difference, of aggregation and multiplication.

Moreover, globalization has long smudged the national boundaries and certainties of the past. Companies and satellite signals and e-mails and tourists and supermarket produce criss-cross the world, puncturing national cocoons with such speed and in such quantities that almost everyone in Europe has dealings with and feelings about the wider world. Like it or not, aware of it or not, identities in the twenty-first century are more complicated, contradictory and cosmopolitan for the bulk of Europeans than ever before.

IN 2005, THE YEAR I MARRIED JULIO, my father wrote a column for the *Times of India* titled, "My Family and Other Globalisers." He began by talking about how his son, my brother, had married a German and now lived in the United States and how I had just got hitched to a Spaniard with whom I lived in China. He explained that while readers might assume our family to have been born on a jet plane, in reality, we were barely a generation or two out of an obscure village in south India called Kargudi.

My grandfather was one of six children, and so two generations later, the size of the Kargudi extended family is over 200. Of these, only three still live in the village, with the rest having moved across India and across the whole world, from China to Arabia to Europe to America. This single family accounts for 50 US citizens today.

"So," wrote my father, "dismiss the mutterings of those who claim that globalisation means westernisation. It looks more like Aiyarisation, viewed from Kargudi." But he clarified that "Aiyarisation" did not mean global domination by Aiyars, any more than he believed globalization meant global domination by Westerners or the Chinese or any other group. It meant, instead, the acquisition of multiple identities.

"I am a Kargudi villager, a Tamilian, a Delhi-wallah, an Indian, a Washington Redskins fan, and a citizen of the world, all at the same time," he said. "When I see the Brihadeeswara Temple in Tanjore, my heart swells and I say to myself, 'This is mine.' I feel exactly the same way when I see the Church of Bom Jesus in Goa, or the Jewish synagogue in Cochin, or the Siddi Sayed mosque in Ahmedabad: these too are mine. I have strolled so often through the Parks at Oxford University and along the canal in Washington, DC, that they feel part of me. As my family multiplies and intermarries, I hope one day to look at the Sagrada Familia cathedral in Barcelona and the Rhine river in Germany and think, 'These too are mine.'"[63]

My father's piece was hopelessly, or more accurately hopefully, Lennonesque in its imagined world. But was he only describing an elite class of cosmocrats who somehow float above the vast majority of "little" people whose mono-identities remain wholly shaped by the local and national? Of course not.

You just need to take a bus or metro ride in London or Paris or Brussels to understand what my father was getting at. Public transport is a ghetto-free, multicultural space where the natives are not distinguishable from the foreigners by the color of their skin, or their clothes, or their names, as much as by an expertise in negotiating the city and its codes. You can tell the locals by the assurance with which they ring the stop bell at the appropriate bus stop, by their brisk acceptance of the weather, by their knowledge of the quickest route home.

Regardless of whether you describe the cultural mélange evident in these superlatively cosmopolitan cities as soups, where the plural is blended into a shared consistency, or tossed salads, where different textures are maintained, there is no escaping their eclectic energy. They are powerful magnets for the world's peoples, which have made them powerful, full stop.

These are cities that have experienced the enormous cruelty and moral debilitation of ruinous wars. And yet, they have not only survived but flourished and allowed newcomers to try and flourish along with them. The results have been variable. As is evident from the deep veins of anxiety created by the presence of immigrants, Muslim and others, multiculturalism remains a fraught progression rather than a happy accomplishment.

But it is also clear to me that these cities have proved wrong the inevitability of a clash of civilizations: the idea that different kinds of people simply cannot live together.

My Bruxellois friends talk about how their children's conception of what it means to be from Brussels is already wholly different from the one they themselves had grown up with. How could it be otherwise, given that more than 30 percent of the city's population is of foreign origin? Youngsters from every kind of cultural background mix in school, check each other out on the bus, and hang out on sunny days in the city's public parks and squares.

On any evening, the streets that knit together Matonge, a largely African neighborhood that claims to be home to 100 nationalities, are like the proverbial global village. Rotund Africans and lean Swedish *stagiaires* from the European Commission rub shoulders with harried Vietnamese waiters and garrulous Congolese vegetable sellers. The shocking pink of a Roma's skirt cuts a flash of color. There are many headdresses adorning bobbing heads, from scarves to patterned turbans. A few dozen meters away, a massive bronze statue of the infamous Belgian colonizer Leopold II, mounted atop a horse, gazes sourly over the scene, like some Berber grandmother from the Rif, tut-tutting at what a strange pass the world has come to.

FOUR

Tilting at Windmills

WEEKENDS IN BRUSSELS WERE NOT A PERIOD OF RELAX- ation and repose. They were, instead, an alternatively exhausting and dull two days, which made Monday feel as alluring as chocolate cake for dessert after a main course of pig's innards.

Every Saturday, Julio and I hauled the kids (we had a second son, Nicolas, in 2011) to the supermarket for our weekly grocery shopping. The store would be more crowded than Mumbai's Victoria Terminal at rush hour, since this was the lone day Brussels residents with jobs could make it to the supermarket at a time when it was open. In Belgium, shops not only closed on the Sabbath with a religious fervor, they also pulled down their shutters on weekdays at 6 p.m. with a 9 a.m. start.

More than once, I found myself in a sepia-tinted reverie involving our local corner store in the hutong where we had lived in Beijing. The owner had slept in the back room and was always willing to wake up to sell a pack of biscuits with a smile, regardless of the time. As for department stores, they were usually open for business until 10 p.m. on weeknights. But it was Sundays that were true commercial manna, the Chinese retail industry operating on the sensible principle that it was best to sell to consumers when they had the time to buy.

In Brussels, Saturday mornings at the supermarket involved me lugging around a yowling Nicolas strapped to my chest in a Baby

Björn, while pushing a shopping cart with an invariably squirmy Ishaan sitting in it, while snapping at Julio in misplaced irritation as the last unbruised avocado in the pile was whisked away by someone else, while cursing the self-scanning machine (with which we had to total up our own grocery bill, supposedly for our own convenience) for failing to scan the items I was trying to purchase.

We would usually make it out of the store with our sanity well on its way to some faraway place that was not Brussels on a Saturday, when it would begin to rain and our umbrella would break in the headwind and the car alarm would go off for no visible reason.

The only thing worse than a Saturday in the city was a Sunday. Sundays were death by boredom. Everything was closed. The streets were deserted. And, since this was Brussels, it was a fair bet that it was raining. Again.

Did I mention there were times I missed Beijing? And Delhi? Life for the elite in these places, the lower rungs of which class were occupied by people such as myself, could be so much easier. Most especially for parents of young children.

Affordable labor in all places "emerging" considerably lightened the burden for women looking after kids and working outside the home. Before moving to Brussels, I had written an e-mail to a long-time friend from China who now lived in Belgium with her husband and two young children. While still in Beijing, she had introduced us to Peng Shifu, a marvelous handyman who'd over the years painted our walls, helped put up pictures, built us a table and become a much-loved part of our household. In my e-mail, I'd asked my friend, Tuva, if she could recommend anyone like Peng Shifu to help us to settle into our new home in Belgium. "No, I can't," she'd replied dryly, "but I do know a very good hardware store called Brico. It sells excellent drills."

Moreover, the comparative comfort of life in emerging countries was not only about abundant and affordable labor, a.k.a. people-a-lot-poorer-than-you. Nor was it only about consumerism and all those Sunday-opening malls oozing global brand names.

In late 2007, I'd spent several months at Oxford University on a Reuters journalism fellowship and often found myself huddled with a gaggle of complaining Chinese students. It wasn't just the food, weather and service that we'd moaned about, but tellingly, the infrastructure. Large bits of London's metro always seemed to be closing down for repairs even as Beijing was opening extensive new lines in the run-up to the Olympic Games. While I was at Oxford, Beijing had actually lowered its metro fare by 1 RMB to make it a total of 2 RMB (which in those days was equivalent to 15 pence) for the majority of metro rides across the city. In London, the cost of a one-way metro journey had simultaneously reached 5 pounds.

It all got me wondering. Certainly, some of the received wisdom's "labeling" was in need of an update, the example of "communist" China's "capitalism" being a case in point. Could an argument be made for the former Third World having emerged as the contemporary First World?

I might have been tempted to agree on particularly bleak weekends, but my body, quite physically, rejected the proposition. In the years I lived in China, despite some pollution-hardened lungs from my childhood in India, I'd developed a persistent low-level cough. But it took only a couple of weeks in Brussels for it to disappear, pretty much for the next three years.

A Swedish friend in Beijing used to joke that one year of living in China felt like a dog year, in that it aged you by seven years. But in Brussels, despite the lack of domestic help and available plumbers, I felt healthier and less anxious about what my family and I were eating and drinking than ever before.

What really differentiates the developed and developing world, at least from an elites-in-emerging countries perspective, is not the availability of consumer products or efficient service, but clean air, safe water and equitable access to quality health care.

Calling countries like China a "hardship" posting for European diplomats, as is still the norm, may partly be symptomatic of a kind of conceited insularity. But the cold fact is that the average Chinese lives a full decade less than her European counterpart, and the average Indian two decades less. According to the Global Alliance Against Chronic Respiratory Diseases, these diseases account for 17 percent of all deaths in China, compared to less than 4 percent of deaths in Europe. Around 90 percent of deaths worldwide due to pulmonary illnesses like bronchitis and emphysema occur in the developing world. While hundreds of thousands of children in India and China die of diarrhea every year, such deaths are almost non-existent in Europe.[1]

In the months leading up to the Olympic Games in August 2008, I had watched Beijing, a city where cars spewed 3,600 tons of pollutants into the air every day, struggle to clean up its foul air.² Extraordinary measures were put into place, including the banning of millions of polluting vehicles from the roads, in addition to the closing down of several factories in the city's outlying areas. And *still* the air failed to meet China's own national air quality standards for several days heading into the Olympics.³

My friend, Tuva, who'd had to embrace hardware stores and transform herself into a dab hand with the drill in the absence of willing handymen in Brussels, did not regret her move to Europe. With two boys under the age of three, she hadn't wanted them to grow up breathing Beijing's dirty air.

And it isn't only the air that is fetid. The Chinese government itself estimates that 70 percent of the country's rivers and lakes are polluted to some degree, while the water of 28 percent is unsuitable even for irrigation. Ninety percent of the groundwater in China's cities is too polluted to drink.⁴

Things are barely better in India, where waterways are gagging with waste and excreta, and air pollution takes an enormous toll on health.⁵ According to the World Health Organization, India had 168,601 deaths in 2008, directly attributable to outdoor pollution, less than the 470,649 deaths in China, but hardly a number to sneeze at.⁶

A journalist friend with the BBC who moved from New Delhi to Brussels said that although he missed reporting the "India story," his health couldn't have taken much more of Delhi. While researching the spike in dengue fever cases in the run-up to the Commonwealth Games in October 2010, he had not only contracted a case of dengue himself but topped it off with typhoid.

In China, stories of contaminated food, medicines and baby milk were rife. In 2008, the year Ishaan was born, upward of 300,000 people were confirmed by the state authorities to have been poisoned by milk and baby formula adulterated with the chemical melamine. Julio and I were sick with worry when difficulties with breastfeeding meant Ishaan needed to be topped off with formula. We bought imported milk powder at inflated prices, and he remained healthy. But at four months of age, he was wheezing like an elephant with apnea and was diagnosed with bronchiolitis, a respiratory tract infection. Doctors warned us that this would likely be a recurrent problem for him through childhood and possibly beyond. But three months later, we moved to Brussels, and voila, his lungs magically cleared. In the coming years, he rarely suffered even a cold.

Luckily for him, our second son, Nicolas, had a truly First World infanthood. We never had to worry about formula for him because well-trained lactation consultants had helped ease the breastfeeding challenges we'd encountered with Ishaan. Nicolas's body was unblemished by the tuberculosis vaccination scar that punctured Ishaan's arm. We could brush his teeth with water that flowed straight from the tap, unlike the expensive mineral water that we'd had to use to clean Ishaan's first few incisors.

Viruses, water and air are far more democratic indicators of the level of well-being in a society than rude waiters or seasonal slippers. They are undeterred by the watchmen that guard the gated communities of the rich. They are unimpressed by the number of credit cards in a wallet or Jimmy Choo shoes in a closet. And on these indicators the "First World" remained firmly in the West, a fact that had not gone unnoticed by European authorities.

Nevertheless, in many ways, the glory days of the undisputed supremacy of the West were already waning by 2009, the year we arrived in Europe. In Brussels, there was a striking pessimism in the tenor of policy discourse, especially for someone used to China. In Beijing, everything was on the up: the economy, the sky-scraping new buildings, nationalism, sporting prowess, even the art market.

But here in Brussels, there were furrowed brows aplenty, worrying about gloomy predictions of uncertainty, irrelevance and decline. This was an insecurity rooted in the fact of China's rise and amplified by the chatter of analysts and think tanks, all driving home the point that Europe's clout was weakening.

Perhaps the rhetoric was louder in Brussels than elsewhere in Europe (this was before the Greek bankruptcy sparked the euro crisis in 2010), because it was in the European Union's interest to convince its member states of their supposedly inevitable declining importance. In a world of Asian mammoths like China and India, only the European Union, united and speaking with one voice, could hope to compete, the argument ran.

Having momentously admitted a number of former eastern bloc communist countries into the Union in 2004,[7] the European Project, as the process of creating an ever more closely bound Europe was called, had run out of steam. The 2005 attempt to bring a new European constitution into force was stopped in its tracks when French and Dutch citizens voted "no" to it in referenda. The result was a generalized glumness about the prospects of a "grand European project."

The original, overarching goals that underlay the creation of the European Union—the bringing of peace, stability and prosperity to a warring continent—had become normalized by the twenty-first century. Youngsters in France did not spend their days gasping in wonderment at the fact that they didn't live in fear of going to war against Germany.

The creation of the European Union was a truly radical event in the history of Europe, but this epochal change was just so much water under the bridge for most. It was normal to be rich in Europe today, just as it was normal to be secure (random acts of terrorism notwithstanding). The European Union got scant thanks and was thus left scrabbling to devise reasons that could persuade its audience about its continued importance. One that fortuitously happened to be up for grabs was climate change.

Taking up the self-proclaimed leadership of delivering the world from the perils of global warming ticked several boxes for the European Union. It exploited an area where Europe was demonstrably superior to rising Asia: the environment. It was, moreover, a sufficiently grandiose and worthy goal, in keeping with the weighty objectives of the European Union's past, like peace and solidarity. It provided a narrative that people could identify with and invest in, unlike the minutiae of the important but unsexy work that the European Union did around customs and internal markets. It was easier to rally support for saving the world for future generations than for instituting measures for improving the functioning of the VAT system.

Moreover, given its cross-border nature, climate change was uniquely suited to an EU-wide response, since no country could hope to address it adequately on its own. Common EU targets for greenhouse gas emissions reductions also allowed for richer member states like the United Kingdom or Germany to subsidize the emissions of poorer, more coal-dependent eastern European countries like Poland.

Climate change shifted the focus away from a Europe of exhausted possibilities and failed referenda, struggling to claim popular legitimacy, outward to a Europe supposedly leading the world along the path of moral righteousness.

EU leaders could indignantly point to the "irresponsible" behavior of the new powers of the world, China and India, with their massively increasing emissions. They could wag the occasional finger at the status quo power, the United States, as well, which defiantly refused to face up to the great damage being done to the world's environment.

I moved to Brussels in the months leading up to the fifteenth meeting of the United Nations Framework Convention on Climate Change (COP 15) that was to be held in Copenhagen in December of that year. It was a time when every EU leader and official was on-message, driving home the belief that the European Union stood heroically alone in the attempt to save the planet. Only the European Union cared. Only the European Union was ready to act now.

Not only did the cause of climate change allow the European Union to feed its own ego, it provided the region with a foreign policy role at a time when the geo-political world was increasingly dominated by the United States and the emerging powers. And best of all, it allowed the European Union to do all this with little or no pain.

The European Union's leadership position was attributed to the fact that it was the only group of countries to have taken on legally binding emissions reductions target under the Kyoto Protocol of 1997, the UN treaty that aimed to combat climate change. The European Union had agreed to reduce its emissions between 2008 and 2012 (the first commitment period under the protocol) by 8 percent compared with 1990 levels. Going into the Copenhagen meeting, the European Union was promising a further 20 percent reduction in emissions by 2020 over 1990 levels, with a "generous" offer to up this to a 30 percent cut in the event of other big emitters agreeing to similar reductions.

But it was not as straightforward as may have appeared at first sight. For example, mitigation targets were defined in terms of carbon production rather than consumption, which allowed the European Union to meet them by merely exporting emissions to other parts of the world like China. With European companies in the process of shifting manufacturing en masse to the cost-competitive East, this was in fact what was happening. The European Union's target of 20 percent reduction by 2020 could therefore easily be achieved without reducing any carbon emissions globally at all.[8]

There was no scientific basis for the European Union's targets of either 8 percent under the original Kyoto Protocol (KP) or 20 percent by the 2020 pledge. The European Commission itself admitted that the 20 percent target was inadequate to meet the goal of an increase of no more than 2 degrees Celsius in temperature above pre-industrial levels by 2050: the level most climate scientists agree on as the limit over which catastrophic consequences would probably occur.[9]

But leaving aside the studies and the statistics, it was difficult for me to take a ten-minute walk around Brussels with my eyes open and remain unaware of the acts of self-delusion that underlay claims to the "moral" leadership of Europe when it came to climate change.

The inequality that was embedded in Europe's climate change discourse was a physical presence as I made my way to the regular press conferences the European Union held, trumpeting its "leading" efforts to vanquish emissions in the run-up to the Copenhagen meeting.

On the way to the Schuman area, where most EU institution buildings were located, I walked past tall *maisons de maitre* town houses with four-meter-high ceilings, the preferred residences of many European officials. The houses were centrally heated for the long winter. They looked cozy and inviting when one peeked in, revealing rooms strewn with laptops and televisions and electrical plug points in abundant use. The cars that sat parked outside these homes were huge family cars; many were seven-seaters. The same EU officials who casually lectured me on India's "lack of vision" on climate change drove these cars and recommended them to me as "convenient."

Life had indeed long been convenient in Europe and continued to be so, largely untouched by the European Union's vaunted emissions targets. A few minor changes in lifestyles had been enforced. A graduated ban on the traditional incandescent light bulb, beginning in 2009, had some artists, who felt their work would look aesthetically unacceptable in the cold white light emitted by the replacement compact fluorescent lamps, all riled up. EU policymakers were also accused of robbing children of the magical experience of traditional fairground lights. Recycling of paper, plastic and glass into differently colored disposal bags was enforced in some neighborhoods. People were made to pay a small amount to buy plastic bags in supermarkets, and so on.

But these amounted to a relaxing massage of the conscience. They allowed people to have their cake, by feeling environmentally enlightened, and eat it too, by making easy, cosmetic changes to their lives.

And implicit in the European Union's policy position going into the Copenhagen meeting was a denial of an equal-sized piece of cake to others who wanted their share.

Of course, I wasn't the only one walking around Brussels with my eyes open. Yet, most Europeans did not seem to see what I did. Perhaps it was because I had double vision. When I looked at the heated *maisons de maitre* and convenient family cars, they were superimposed by other images: of the rotating blades of the single fan that was all the defense houses in Delhi had against temperatures of 45 degrees Celsius, shuddering to a deafening halt, signaling another power cut to be patiently borne; of the veins of sweat slicing into every crevice of the multitudes cycling to work or standing in buses stuck to the bodies of stinking, sticky others.

This double sight would have been terrifying to Europeans, offering as it did the glimpse of an alternative life of great hardship that could have been theirs but for a different roll of fortune's dice. For most Indians and many Chinese, however, such a life was not only normal, but even clasped with a steely embrace, given their knowledge of how lucky they were to have fans and jobs to take dangerously overcrowded buses to. They suffered power cuts stoically because at least they had access to electricity.

Four hundred million people in India did not. Debates about the aesthetic effects of a particular kind of light bulb felt almost grotesque in this context. And 668 million Indians depend on traditional biomass—wood and cow dung—for cooking, even though the consequent pollution they live with often blinds them or kills them with tuberculosis.[10] As many as 500,000 women and children die in India every year as a result of using biomass as cooking fuel.

There are no official figures for the numbers who die from diseases contracted while going over the maggot-infested garbage dumps that line the outskirts of every Indian city. But of the estimated 300,000 ragpickers active in Delhi alone, a substantial number are children, often as young as five, picking over rotting refuse for anything salvageable to sell at prices of 15 cents a kilo. This is the kind of recycling that fills distended bellies with a few grains of rice at the end of an eight-hour day—a far cry from the blue-and-white-and-yellow bags I had to purchase from the supermarket in Brussels to divvy up my plastics, paper and food waste. This is the difference between subsistence recycling and luxury recycling, mirroring the moral distinction between the subsistence emissions of poor countries and the luxury emissions of the rich.

And so I spent those months ahead of the Copenhagen meeting sitting in seminar rooms flooded with lights so bright I could have worn sunglasses indoors and scarcely noticed. People made Power-Point presentations. They held forth on the European Union's great achievements in leading the climate change fight. And they fretted about how these progressive moves were canceled out by the growing emissions of emerging countries like China and India.

As for me, my double vision grew more acute. Every time a speaker paused to take a casual sip of the bottled water inevitably placed in front of her, I would see a toddler thirstily drinking from a communal tap in a slum and dying of diarrhea a few days later. Over 200,000 children die of diarrhea in India every year from the bugs they pick up from their drinking water.[11] And here in Europe, where tap water is as safe as mother's milk, people *choose* to drink bottled water while waxing eloquent about climate change.[12]

The cold fact was that putting carbon into the atmosphere, given the way our societies function, is still a fundamental part of securing food, shelter, warmth and other necessities. The standard of life enjoyed in the European Union and other wealthy countries today has been secured not by virtue of innately superior abilities but by the burning of fossil fuels on an enormous scale and the subsequent plundering of the world's limited carbon commons.

To root any global climate change policy in just foundations, one needs to be able to locate the responsibility for who should take action and on what scale. An answer to this requires an investigation into three temporal directions: the past, on the basis of past behavior; the present, taking into account the current distribution of resources and capacities; and the future or obligations to future generations.[13]

Since the start of the Industrial Revolution and leading up to the Copenhagen meeting, human beings had put over 600 billion tons of carbon into the atmosphere. The United States had been responsible for almost 30 percent of these cumulative emissions, the European Union for 26.5 percent and Germany on its own for 7.6 percent. China was responsible for 7.6 percent of cumulative global emissions and India 2.2 percent.[14]

But the waters were clouded by the changes between the historic share in global emissions and their current equivalents. While the rich world had certainly got the warming ball rolling, its share of global emissions was declining just as those of the large developing countries were taking off.

Going into Copenhagen, the European Union, for example, had only accounted for around 15 percent of global emissions, while the current share of emissions of many developing countries like China and India was more than double their cumulative shares. By 2009, China's emissions of carbon dioxide had reached 7.5 billion tons, and thus Beijing added one more record to its list of global titles, overtaking the United States to become the world's largest emitter of greenhouse gases.[15]

But even setting aside historical emissions and focusing on the present, the chasm between the per capita emissions of rich countries and those of the emerging countries remained wide. For the 20 tons emitted by the average American, the average Chinese emitted just under 5 tons and the Indian only 1.2 tons.[16] The average for the 27 members of the European Union in 2009 was just over 10 tons.[17]

A few months before the UN meeting at Copenhagen, I attended a climate change seminar held in the Danish capital where the Princeton-University-based moral philosopher Peter Singer claimed that the failure of the major industrialized nations to reduce their emissions to a level that would not cause serious adverse effects to others was a moral wrongdoing on a scale that exceeded the wrongs of colonialism. The only really fair basis on which to formulate a global climate change policy, he said, was one where every person on the planet was accorded an equal per capita allocation for carbon emissions.

This would allow countries in the developing world room to grow and increase their emissions but require rich countries to make large cuts. It was the most intuitively fair solution to the problem, where one human life was considered on par with another, but not a single leader from the rich world was in favor of it. Given that oratorical dressing aside, climate change policy was all about interests rather than morality; this was scarcely surprising.

Various developing country leaders had, however, made use of the per capita measure as a basis for articulating ideas and positions. At a UN meeting in September 2009, President Paul Kagame of Rwanda suggested giving every country an annual per capita quota for CO2 emissions and allowing developing countries below the quota to trade their excess quota with countries that were above theirs. Indian Prime

Minister Manmohan Singh had also drawn attention to the fairness of the "per capita emissions" argument by pledging that Indian per capita emissions would never exceed the average per capita emissions levels of the rich countries at the time.

A promise like this wiped the past slate clean by "forgiving" historical wrongs and focused instead on the present. It was therefore a concession to rich countries in order to get them on board a global deal. There were, however, some obvious flaws with the per capita approach.

It could be argued, for example, that someone living in Norway, where it is extremely cold for large parts of the year, needed a larger allocation of emissions than someone who lived by the Mediterranean. It also drew attention to the politically difficult but crucial issue of population control. A per capita approach would reward those countries that had "failed" to control their populations.

These complications aside, any per-capita-based policy would result in massive financial transfers from the North to the South and was therefore unacceptable to the rich world, regardless of its ethical validity. Nobel laureate Michael Spence points out that Kagame's solution would, for example, lead to enormous windfalls in developing countries in the short term.

Take India as an example. It had 18.5 percent of the world's population but accounted only for 5 percent of total emissions. On a per capita basis, India would receive 13.5 percent of total credits that it currently didn't need. With total emissions of about 31 billion tons, India could thus sell in excess of a billion tons of credit that the advanced countries would have to buy. And moreover, such a system did not even guarantee significant carbon emissions mitigation.[18]

But the rejection of per-capita-based arguments is not only about rational economic calculations related to windfalls. A more fundamental problem lies with its fundamental fairness. It assumes an equality between all people that does not exist in fact and is not truthfully desired even in societies where egalitarianism is an acknowledged and purposefully inculcated ideal.

Put baldly, people everywhere have sharply circumscribed moral constituencies of concern. We are usually willing to do the right thing by our friends and family. We are able, if pushed, to stretch our moral constituencies further, to include villages, castes, religions and nations. But climate change requires us to extend our sense of moral obligation spatially to a global community of people we have no contact with and have in fact been conditioned to think of as outside our realm of concern.

Were the effects of climate change localized to, say, the inhabitants of Papua New Guinea, it is doubtful there would be much concern in the rich world, even if the historical and present greenhouse gas emissions of these countries were known to be a substantial part of the cause. Any political leader trying to persuade people to curtail their carbon footprint in the absence of direct consequences for themselves, purely on the grounds of global responsibility, would have a tough time garnering votes.

What gave the European Union's climate change charge resonance among its constituents were the new (for Europe) circumstances of the twenty-first century whereby the choices made by people in countries outside their borders, and hence outside of their control, had a potentially large impact on their own future. But while Europeans wanted others to exercise their choices in a way that would be beneficial for Europe's future, they had patently not exercised their own choices, either in the past or the present, with the benefit of others in mind.

The whole climate change policy game was a show of smoke and mirrors, where high-minded talk of global concerns and scientific imperatives masked selfish, interest-based goals.

Emerging countries were no exception to this rule. The schizophrenic duality of nations like China and India, with their expanding First World oases set amid a Third World desert, complicated their role and responsibilities in the climate change discourse. Not only had these countries emerged among the world's top emitters, their emissions were likely to continue to grow exponentially so that their share of future emissions would eclipse those of many rich countries today. On the issue of the future sustainability of the planet's environment, China and India have a major role, indeed an ethical obligation, to ensure that their economic growth inflicts the minimum possible damage.

Given their large populations, their per capita emissions remain modest, but what of the considerable number of Chinese and Indians whose emissions are on par with or exceed those of the First World emitters? What standards should they be held to? With the benefit of hindsight, did "modernity" necessarily mean glass-fronted constructions that hemorrhaged energy? Did the historical inequities that have led to the present asymmetries in the allocation of global carbon space demand that the emerging countries repeat the mistakes of the past?

AT GLOBAL CLIMATE NEGOTIATIONS, the world's large emerging countries continued to beat the drum of historical responsibility, but it was in neither China's nor India's interest to cut off their nose to spite their face. And so action was being taken to ensure a less carbon-intensive growth trajectory. India had been able to cut its carbon emission intensity (the amount of carbon dioxide emitted for each unit of GDP) by 17.6 percent between 1990 and 2005. New fuel-efficiency standards for cars and trucks, a green building code, and a mandate that 20 percent of India's energy come from renewable sources by 2020 were all in place.

China was implementing its National Climate Change Program, which included mandatory targets for reducing energy intensity and major pollutants, while increasing forest cover and the share of renewable energy. Beijing had promised a cut of 40 to 45 percent below the 2005 levels by 2020.

But for the emerging world, the overwhelming priority remained in creating and sustaining the economic growth that would continue to lift the hundreds of millions of people that remained mired in debilitating poverty. And while there was a consciousness of the need to try and ensure that this growth was as carbon neutral as possible, the emergence of a real alternative to the carbon-dependent model of growth still at the heart of rich-country economies had not yet been demonstrated.

What had been demonstrated by the rich world's growth trajectory was that copious pollution was the route to the comfortable lives enjoyed there today.

It was the attitude among European officials that irked me: their smugness at being environmentally conscious rather than the fact of this consciousness. Far be it for me to criticize someone spending a few minutes a day recycling their glass and plastic. What got my goat was the righteousness that often underlay this act and the absence of a sense of humility. The environmental ethics of people in the West was born of privilege and prosperity and the environmental destruction in which these were rooted.

And the evangelistic fervor of it all compounded my irritation. Climate change, I was endlessly and solemnly told, was the greatest problem facing the world today. Really? What about diarrhea and malaria and famine and female feticide? These might not have been Europe's problems, but in India and other parts of the developing world, problems were as numerous as sand in a dune. I found convincing arguments lacking for prioritizing the limited resources at their disposal to address climate change over the sea of other immediate, and more long-term, challenges.

The Danish writer Bjørn Lomborg's arguments about the disturbing disconnect between the rich world's environmental concerns and those of the majority of the world's inhabitants reverberated with me. He pointed to the 900 million people who remain malnourished globally, the billion lacking clean drinking water, the 2.6 billion without adequate sanitation and the 1.6 billion without electricity. Roughly 15 million deaths every year—a quarter of the world's total—are caused by diseases that are easily and cheaply curable. The key environmental concerns for most people, he said, are indoor air pollution, the lack of clean drinking water, poor sanitation and poverty itself.

Lomborg argued that poverty is an environmental problem because environmental consciousness is a distant luxury for those subsisting on less than $1.25 a day. "If your family is freezing, you will cut down the last tree for fuel; if they are starving, you will strip the land bare to feed them. And if you have no certainty about the future, you will provide for it in the only way possible: by having more children to care for you in your old age, regardless of how much they will add to humanity's demands on the planet."[19]

At multiple dinner parties with EU officials, I was indignantly told how "unfair" the Kyoto Protocol was for having tied the region to legally binding targets that the rest of the world was free of. "It's not fair," they would whine even as their transatlantic allies in the United States claimed much the same thing: it wasn't fair for the United States to take on commitments while other big emitters like China went scot-free.

This was a strangely blinkered conception of fairness. These were the countries that had caused the problem to begin with and continued to contribute to it disproportionately in the present, despite having the knowledge of the consequences of their actions. These were, moreover, the countries that had the financial and technical capabilities to do something to fix the problem.

They were the countries best placed in terms of present capacities to take on the challenge of mitigation. Their room for emissions reductions, a large proportion of which were luxury emissions, was patently larger than the room for reduction in countries where the majority of emissions were of the subsistence variety. They led the world in terms of both cumulative and per capita emissions and were likely to do so for a while to come.

Finally, from a philosophical point of view, a morally demanded action was not contingent on the action of others. If doing something is the right thing to do, it remains right whether or not others are doing it. Refusing to act unless others did, as was the case with the United States, and increasingly with Europe, is tantamount to ignoring the moral demands on oneself while placing moral standards on others.

I had grown up in a Westernized household, speaking English as a first language. I had studied Wordsworth and Dickens in school and Descartes and Kant at university in Delhi. At 20, I had gone off to Oxford and thereafter spent time in London and Los Angeles. I married a Spaniard. I was, in short, the kind of person many Europeans "forgot" was Indian, automatically assuming I shared their assumptions and cultural background. And this was true, to a degree.

But my immersion into the world of climate change policy debate in Brussels sharpened my Indian identity. Following stormy debates over breakfast at home, my husband began to call me an "unreconstructed Third World-ist," to which I would toss my head and declare that in this case I was proud to be one. But banter aside, I was gnawingly aware of how, while I might well point an indignant finger at rich-country behavior, at an individual level, the finger pointed straight back at me.

Everything that could be said about the double standards of Europeans was equally true about rich Indians or Chinese. These people had their own brand of hypocrisy, using the cover of their country's poverty to avoid facing up to their own actions. As did I.

Even as I wrote incensed op-eds critiquing Europe's climate change position, I spent my afternoons sipping bottled water over lunch, jetting around the continent on cheap flights for research, and often forgetting to switch off my laptop at night as I tumbled into bed.

I would have occasional frissons of guilt brought on by reading up on global warming science, but when life with its deadlines and more immediate problems overcame me, these would fade away quickly enough. It was a bit like smoking. We are all addicted to these lifestyles, and the immediate gratification they provide proves a mighty match for potential long-term, diffused harm in the future.

Unlike smoking, this harm would not necessarily be borne by oneself but by generations to come. And the precise nature of the harm was fuzzy too. The moral equations engendered by climate change, given their spatially and temporally extended nature, are convoluted. The individual responsibility for something as cumulative as global warming is hard to pin down and easy to evade. The causes, effects and agents of climate change are globally dispersed and go back and forth in time between the actions of our ancestors and the future of our descendants.

Such complexity did not bode well for a global UN-led deal to tackle the problem. Regardless, as December 2009 rolled around, I was off to Copenhagen to report on the scrimmage in full gory detail.

The fifteenth conference of the parties to the 1992 United Nations Framework Convention on Climate Change (UNFCCC), known as COP 15, had attracted unprecedented global interest. The European Union was upping the pressure for global leaders to "seal the deal," and environmentalists billed the meeting as a make-or-break event that would decide the future course of mankind.

Some 115 heads of state and government were expected to attend the final couple of days of the two-week-long conference, marking one of the largest gatherings of world leaders. One thousand two hundred limousines and 400 helicopters were pressed into service to accommodate the VIPs. Around 40,000 people had registered for the meeting, including shoals of enthusiastic journalists and civil society activists.[20]

Copenhagen had been rechristened Hopenhagen, as a wave of optimism crested upon the announcements made by several countries of voluntary emissions mitigation targets. The European Union had long been tom-tomming its pledge to cut emissions by 20 percent below 1990 levels by the year 2020, with a 30 percent cut as a bait to persuade other significant players to follow suit.

The United States, the most recalcitrant of climate offenders, had promised change under President Obama and had declared an emissions cut "in the range of" 17 percent below 2005 levels by 2020. Its main aim at COP 15 was to ensure a scrapping of the Kyoto Protocol, a treaty Washington had refused to sign. Instead, it was angling for a new treaty that would see legally binding targets set for large developing countries, which were exempt from Kyoto Protocol commitments.

China, the United States' emerging world double at the talks, had pledged a carbon intensity cut of 40 to 45 percent below 2005 levels by 2020. New Delhi, for long viewed with exasperation in the West for its "unhelpful" focus on historical responsibilities to the exclusion of all other discussions at UNFCCC meets, had also promised a carbon intensity cut of 20 to 25 percent from 2005 levels by 2020. Both India and China were dead against the scrapping and replacement of the Kyoto Protocol, which had clearly placed the onus of mitigation on the developed countries.

Various other countries from Japan to Russia had come forth with pledges and objectives, setting up COP 15 at "Hopenhagen" as the best chance to date for securing a substantial outcome.

I CAUGHT A FLIGHT TO COPENHAGEN on the Sunday before the second week of the negotiations. Environment ministers from around the world had already been battling it out for a few days, attempting to set the stage for a deal that world leaders could sign onto.

The main protagonist from an Indian journalist's point of view was Jairam Ramesh, India's mercurial environment minister, who was quickly acquiring rock star status in the climate negotiations world.

At the pre-COP 15 seminar in Copenhagen I attended, Ramesh's intervention had received a standing ovation. India will go to the UN negotiations as a "deal maker *not* a deal breaker," he'd announced to an applauding audience consisting of 300-plus editors from countries around the world.

Since taking over as environment minister, Ramesh, an engineer and economist by training, had made it his objective to change India's positioning from a victim to that of a responsible world player. Foreign journalists lavished praise on his commitment to voluntary mitigation efforts undertaken by India, as they did on his wavy, pepper pot coiffure.[21]

Ramesh had been stressing flexibility, pragmatism and a constructive approach to the talks and seemed to have Indian Prime Minister Manmohan Singh's ear. He'd been making the case that it was in India's own interest to tackle climate change, irrespective of Copenhagen, because of the country's primary economic dependence on monsoons and the large-scale potential damage from shrinking Himalayan glaciers, among other factors.

As my plane swooped down toward the Copenhagen airport, a forest of rotor-headed offshore windmills reared into sight, their slender necks glinting in the mid-morning sun (which was pretty much the only kind of sun that Denmark knew in December). These were the new temples for the twenty-first-century environmentalism in which Denmark was the world leader.

The country was home to more than 4,000 onshore turbines, making it the global Number One in terms of turbines per capita. The Danes had reduced their greenhouse gas emissions by 14 percent since 1990, even though Danish energy consumption had stayed constant and Denmark's GDP had grown by more than 40 percent over that time. It was also the most energy efficient country in the European Union. Renewables supplied almost 30 percent of Denmark's electricity.[22]

The country was supposed to house the world's happiest people and often topped the kinds of charts that tried to quantify such things.[23] The de facto minimum wage was around $20 an hour. The government paid for college education. Free health care and outstanding child-care support no doubt contributed to the general well-being of the citizens. It felt most implausible that countries like India and China, with their smog, stench and sores, even shared the same planet with this utopia.

On the way to the hotel, I looked out of the taxicab at all the intimidatingly trendy people in rimless glasses walking about. I felt a stab of envy every time I spotted an inevitably slim young mother pushing her designer-looking baby about in the lofty heights of a Stokke stroller. Ever since having a baby, I noticed things like strollers, objects that had once upon a time been invisible to me. But post-baby, nothing stung with greater burning jealousy than the sight of a Scandinavian-made Stokke stroller, the Rolls Royce of strollers—so stylish, it provoked every mother unable to afford its 1,000 euro price tag into contemplating a fire sale of the family silver.

I imagined myself sashaying down the streets of Copenhagen in stilettos with an equally well-groomed Ishaan ensconced in a Stokke, ne'er a smear of banana puree in sight, but was rudely jolted out of this reverie by the angry tinkling of a passing bicyclist, who barely avoided mowing me down. The taxi had spilled me out right into the bicycle lane that ran along the pavement by the hotel and this was obviously somewhere one did not dawdle in Denmark, if one valued one's life. Like all other aspects of Danish society, bike etiquette was designed to operate like a well-oiled machine—disrupt the order by oafishly standing around for a moment too long in the bicycle lane and the machine is instantly thrown out of gear.

That night I had dinner with a friend of a cousin whom I'd met in India a few years earlier at a wedding. She was possibly the most miserable person ever, putting paid to the orthodoxy of happy, content Danes. She spent all evening moaning about how expensive everything was in Denmark and how she'd kill to be able to afford servants like the middle classes in India. Don't get taken in by appearances, she warned. All those slick-looking moms wheeling Stokke strollers around were crying on the inside, exhausted by the daily drudgery of shopping and cleaning and cooking and working. When I made noises about getting a taxi to return to the hotel, she turned solemn. Be careful with the taxi drivers, she said, her pale blue eyes darkening. Particularly avoid the ones that look like Pakistanis.

The next morning I rose bright and early, except it wasn't bright at all, but pitch dark outside. It was seven in the morning by the time I reached the Bella Centre, a sprawling complex of buildings on the outskirts of Copenhagen where the COP 15 was taking place. My heart sank the moment I emerged from the metro. Through the winter gloom I could make out a great mass of humanity already queuing outside the gates. I reckoned it would take an hour or two to make it inside and begin the accreditation formalities, which would then finally allow me access to the conference.

I walked toward the back of the line and found myself still walking ten minutes later. It was freezing and little whorls of snow were drifting down on the huddled, gathered crowds. The minutes and then hours passed, and we had only shuffled a few feet forward. At around 9 a.m., a grey dawn began to break. Beefy cops patrolled the length of the line but offered no information when we begged for some.

Rumors circulated. The accreditation machine had broken down. There was a terrorist threat and no one was being allowed in. The Bella Centre was simply too full to have any more people enter. It later transpired that the center's capacity was 15,000 people, but the United Nations had accredited close to 40,000. And the accreditation machine had indeed broken down.

The result was a surreally cold, eight-hour wait in the line to enter a meeting about global warming. A few bleak jokes about this irony passed up and down the queue.

"We are coming from India," groaned a middle-aged climatologist from the northern state of Uttarakhand, through layers of mufflers. "We are feeling very cold."

"If this kind of organization had happened in India, people would say it was typical Third World organization, but I have never in my life seen anything as bad in India as this COP 15 organization in Denmark," her colleague chipped in.

By this time I had banded together with a group of Indian journalists who were accompanying Sunita Narain, the feisty head of one of India's leading environmental NGOs, the Centre for Science and Environment. "If only these Danes had outsourced the damn logistics to an Indian IT firm," quipped someone.

I was panicking at the thought of wasting an entire day without being able to file a story. But Sunita had several colleagues on the inside who intermittently called her with news. It sounded like business as usual.

The island of Tuvalu had staged a walkout. The Association of Small Island States (AOSIS) was up in arms. The Europeans were up to their usual tricks, trying to spring a last-minute "Danish draft" to supplant the texts being worked out by the UN's ad hoc committees. Indian newspapers had taken to dubbing any draft emerging from the developed country camp as the "Danish draft," and one of our main jobs was to sniff out and expose the details of this nefarious being.

By the time it was lunchtime, the gates of the Bella Centre remained a distant fantasy. I was so dizzy with fatigue that I assumed I was hallucinating when I saw several large chickens walking toward me bearing sandwiches. It turned out these were in fact (human) vegans, dressed up in chicken outfits. It mattered not. They were bearing (vegetarian) sandwiches and distributing them for free. "Less meat means less heat," they chanted as they passed out the food to frozen hands.

This was true enough. The methane released when ruminants like cows and sheep pass gas (which they do copiously), combined with the indirect emissions associated with their life cycles, contributes 18 percent of greenhouse gas emissions worldwide, according to a United Nation's Food and Agriculture Organization study.[24] Small wonder then that Australia's Cooperative Research Centre for Sheep Industry Innovation was busy identifying sheep that were genetically predisposed to less flatulence.[25] The lack of any toilet facilities for those lining up did not help take one's mind off enteric emissions either.

By three in the afternoon, the twilight that was Copenhagen's daytime had once again begun to fade to black, and the barricaded gates of the Bella Centre remained as out of reach as ever. The stony-faced cops had, however, begun to speak. Go home, they told us. Try again tomorrow. But I found myself pathologically unable to leave, or perhaps my legs had become welded to the ground by the cold.

I kept thinking about how if the United Nations couldn't even manage the logistics of a conference, there really couldn't be much hope for it to organize a global deal. It was five in the evening when I finally gave up and took a taxi back to my hotel, disheartened and exhausted. The driver looked Pakistani but the journey was unadventurous.

The next morning I was outside the Bella Centre at half past six. The accreditation machine had been fixed and the queue was actually shuffling forward. By 9 a.m. I was accredited. Badge flapping around my neck, I took a deep breath and walked into the maelstrom.

Everywhere arrows pointed to signs that read PARTIES. The headlines of Indian papers that morning had quotes from Jairam Ramesh insisting that he would only stand for texts that were "party driven" so that he came across to the uninitiated like a teenager headed to the disco. But the "Parties" in question of course referred to country delegations to the UNFCCC rather than any Scandinavian bacchanalia. It had, however, certainly been harder getting into the Bella Centre than any nightclub I'd known.

As I, hitherto a UN virgin, looked around at the hectic scurrying of humanity from virtually every country on the globe, I was afflicted by a moment of moist-eyed idealism. How wonderful that despite all the deep-seated historical enmities and injustices, human beings managed to gather together to talk and negotiate, rather than fight and kill.

It reminded me of a grand Tolkienesque alliance of dwarves and elves and hobbits and men, when menaced by an overarching enemy like Sauron—or climate change in this case. If there was any redemption for humanity, it had to be through a process like this, where talk trumped arms; where common adversity forced the peoples of the world to reach deep, beyond their mutual suspicions, in defense of the values they shared.

The moment lasted the few minutes it took me to find the India office amid the mass of country delegation spaces at the far end of the Bella Centre. From then on, an intensive submersion into the realpolitik of the workings of the United Nations meant that every shred of idealism I had briefly felt was pretty much vacuumed up and tossed, replaced by the cynicism spawned by the virtuoso performances of back-stabbing and finger-pointing I encountered over the next few days.

It fast became clear that this whole process was not about sealing a deal as much as about ensuring that one was not blamed for the failure to seal one. Moreover, my misty vision about all the world's peoples sitting around a table to thrash out a compromise was pretty much poppycock too. The United Nations did not work like that.

Although everyone spent a lot of time complaining about the informal (i.e., "non-Party" driven) drafts that were doing the rounds, there was tacit acceptance of the fact that deals were never going to be made by 195 countries in reasoned discussion. Agreements at the United Nations were always struck behind closed doors by the big guns, with the majority of smaller countries persuaded to sign on, ex post facto.

Countries like India and China might have been shrill in their condemnation of the European Union's "coalition of the willing"— the countries seeking to replace the KP with a new protocol—but they were busy cooking up their own drafts that were equally divorced from the formal work of the formal UN working groups.

India and China were part of the BASIC faction, which comprised in addition the emerging economies of Brazil and South Africa. BASIC's primary agenda was to resist supplanting the KP with any protocol that would force legally binding emissions cuts on them.

I found myself quite literally bumping into BASIC that very first morning at the Bella Centre. I located the India office just as Jairam Ramesh was exiting, coiffure undulating in the wake of a gaggle of excitable reporters who trailed him. I inveigled my way through to the minister and managed to deposit a name card into his hands.

He took a brusque look. "You're the one who used to write from China," he said, without breaking his stride. I scurried along beside him, elbowing away my fellow journalists. "Yes," I said, "I've just flown in and missed your briefing. Can you fill me in?"

Ramesh paused for a brief moment, a glimmer of indecision in his eyes changing into what can only be described as a naughty smile. "Well, you speak Chinese. Come along with me."

Before I could catch my breath, I'd been swept along with him and an aide into a boxlike room off one of the criss-crossing corridors that threaded the country delegations' space. Seated in front of us, along a narrow table, were several Chinese people in dark suits who looked almost as startled to see me as I was to behold them.

"Please take a seat," a youngster stood and indicated a chair to Ramesh, who took up the offer. I was left standing without any introduction. It had dawned on me that the jowly, bespectacled gentleman at the center of the row of Chinese was Xie Zhenhua, China's climate change chief and vice chairman of the all-powerful National Development and Reform Commission.

I looked at Ramesh desperately, but he wouldn't meet my eye. The silence grew pregnant with expectation as everyone on the Chinese side of the table continued to stare at me. I finally broke the ice with a limp, "Ni hao," and mumbled that my name was Pallavi Aiyar.

"Oh!" said Xie, losing interest and looking away, "a translator." I smiled noncommittally and sat down uninvited, in a chair next to Ramesh. And thus began the most harrowing 15 minutes of my professional life, in which I oscillated like a shuttlecock between unbelievable excitement at the journalistic scoop and the ignominy of going down in Chinese history as the worst translator ever produced at a high-level meeting.

When it became apparent, startlingly soon, that I had no idea how to say, "monitoring, reporting and verification," or "carbon intensity cuts" in Mandarin, Xie's interpreter shot me a contemptuous look and took control, allowing me to shrink into the role of note-scribbling lackey.

The meeting, it transpired, was a bilateral called by the Chinese side to discuss how India and China could counter the infamous "Danish draft." Xie (through his very capable interpreter) told Ramesh that the Chinese side had reliable information that Australia and the European Union were planning to launch a surprise "attack" later in the evening.

"The Danish text does exist and we have information that the rich countries are going to go public with it," said Xie gravely. Ramesh looked suitably agitated. How much of this was theatrics, I wondered.

Xie continued, "When they present it, we must respond to it in a united way. And we must get all the G77 to stand united in opposition. Because, if the developing world shows cracks, then it will allow the developed countries to shift the responsibility onto the developing nations, which is what they are planning." Ramesh nodded in solemn acquiescence.

Xie went on to express concern that AOSIS (the Alliance of Small Island States) was already leaning toward the Danish text. A small ministerial meeting was to be held that evening by the European Union and Australia where heads of state who had already arrived in Copenhagen, such as Australian Prime Minster Kevin Rudd, would be asked to lobby other countries to sign on to the idea of a single treaty to replace, rather than extend, the Kyoto Protocol, he concluded.

Ramesh cleared his throat. It was now his turn to speak. "We are with you and with BASIC in every way, Minister," he intoned. He suggested that the BASIC countries make a public announcement to the effect that they would "not accept any text that is not UN Party driven."

Ramesh had, in fact, already made this same statement almost every day over the last week. But as I was soon to learn, repetitions uttered with indignation, determination or weary resignation, as the situation demanded, were the bedrock of global climate negotiations. Xie and Ramesh ended the meeting with the rather convenient agreement that in the event of a breakdown in talks, the BASIC countries were not to be blamed.

I staggered out of the room ashen-faced, and Ramesh looked at me disapprovingly. "Uff, your Chinese is pretty bad," he said. "I'd have done a better job if I'd had some advance warning," I replied reproachfully. Ramesh grinned. "We're working very closely with these guys [the Chinese]," he said. "Did you see? They had called this meeting just now. We're meeting six times a day." But before I could splutter out a follow-up, he was whisked away by a BBC crew to his next media interview.

"Yes, we are closely coordinating with the Danish chair," I heard him tell the British reporter as he disappeared into the Bella Centre's bowels. "I talk to Connie [Hedegaard, Denmark's chief climate envoy and chair of COP 15] six times a day."

I was left bemused about what had just happened. Ramesh was famously a maverick, but what on earth had propelled him to sneak me into a closed-door bilateral? There had been no mention of anything being off the record. He obviously wanted me to write about the meeting. But why?

It almost felt like he did it because he could, or because he was bored and wanted to stir things up a bit. It had been such a snap decision. But of course, there had to be more to the minister's move than impish impulse.

Given the flak he was getting in India for his purported deal-making on behalf of the United States, it wouldn't hurt Ramesh to highlight how close he was to the Chinese. Ramesh was, after all, the coiner of that over-used and under-realized portmanteau, "Chindia." In his 2005 collection of essays, *Making Sense of Chindia*, he'd argued with passion for a mature and engaged economic diplomacy between New Delhi and Beijing.

By 2009, the high noon of Chindia—a period in the early 2000s when diplomatic relations between the neighbors had been thawing following a decades-long freeze—was decisively over.[26] Tough talk on the disputed border had once again come to dominate the India-China dynamic, putting paid to the kind of fantasies about hardware-software collaboration that Chindia boosters had once prophesied would be the hallmark of an Asian-dominated twenty-first century.

Cooperation via BASIC at the climate negotiations was thus a significant silver lining around a darkish India-China cloud—a development for which Ramesh was understandably keen to take credit.

But while the minister was eager to publicize his efforts at promoting a cross-Himalayan climate change partnership, I couldn't help wonder how wise this was. It suited China to have the backing of other emerging economies like India and Brazil in the context of the negotiations. Without this support, Beijing would have been isolated and found it considerably harder to position itself as the spokesperson for the developing world.

But by allying itself so closely with China, India was punching above its weight, and with consequences that were not necessarily beneficial in the long term. Despite their frequent hyphenation, India and

China remained as far apart on the parameters of carbon emissions as they did on most other fronts, from infrastructure and global trade to literacy and maternal mortality. Beijing was, as usual, far ahead.

China had actually overtaken the United States as the largest emitter of greenhouse gases, and India's total emissions were barely one-fourth that of its northern neighbor. On a per capita basis, India emitted about 1.5 tons compared to China's 5 tons. India, moreover, lacked China's technological and financial heft and was in far greater need of transfers and assistance from the West, if it were to attempt a low-carbon developmental path.

To complicate matters further, not only was China a more significant emitter than India, it was conversely doing much more to reduce its carbon footprint. Already by 2009, it was clear that Beijing was not going to lose out on the business opportunity presented by green tech, and China was well on the way to becoming the global leader in solar and wind production. The price of "Made in China" solar panels were to drive down the cost of solar energy by two-thirds between 2009 and 2012. By 2011, American imports of Chinese-made panels had soared to $2.65 billion from $21.3 million in 2005.[27]

When I met him in Brussels in early 2012, Tom Brookes, the communications head of the European Climate Foundation, was categorical in stating that China's twelfth five-year plan (for 2011–15) was "the most progressive piece of climate legislation in the world."

Back at Copenhagen, China was also making much of the green credentials of its three-decades-old experiment with demographic engineering: the one-child policy. Population tends to be the elephant in the room of climate policy debate, but at COP 15, China was determined to shine a spotlight on it, indicating another potential fault line in its climate alliance with India.

Several members of China's National Population and Family Planning Commission (NPFPC) were part of Beijing's official delegation to the UN meeting. I attended a press conference where Zhao Baige, NPFPC vice minister, had a simple message: China's one-child policy had been a boon to the earth's environment.

Ms. Zhao said that China's birth rate was down from over 1.8 percent in 1978 to around 1.2 percent by 2007, resulting in an estimated 400 million fewer births in total. "Such a decline in population growth converts into a reduction of 1.83 billion tons of carbon dioxide emissions in China every year," Zhao claimed with a flourish.

Given its enormous and growing population, and heavy reliance on the per capita argument, India was implicitly cast in an unfavorable light by China's stance on population control. It had become fashionable in recent years to frame what was once referred to as the "population problem" in the positive terms of a "demographic dividend."[28] But in a world of limited carbon space, uncontrolled population growth was not going to be a straightforward asset.

In light of these divergences of interests in their climate change objectives and positions, I was skeptical of the sustainability of the India-China or BASIC partnership over the long term. Were Beijing to remain the chief fall guy for the failure of global negotiations and continue its trajectory into uber-emitter status, being bracketed with China could hardly be to India's advantage.

Conversely, were China to pull off its transformation into green-hero, with its cheap solar panels and strict controls on population growth, India would be left wearing the badge of villain-in-chief. Moreover, siding with China did not help India achieve what should have been one of its leading objectives at the talks: securing the technological and financial assistance necessary to undertake a greener road to development.

It could have made strategic sense for India and the European Union to cozy up, thus putting pressure on the real heavyweights: the United States and China. But this was not an approach that either side seemed interested in following. The Indians remained convinced of the two-faced nature of the European game. There was a sense in New Delhi that with the Americans, the cards were on the table—what you saw was what you got. The European Union's high-minded rhetoric, by contrast, came across as exasperatingly disingenuous.

And breaking ranks with the United States in any serious way remained out of the question for the Europeans (opening them up to further charges of hypocrisy). Ultimately, a lot of history sat fatly between India and Europe. The two had been on opposite sides of so many geostrategic fences for so long that a lack of trust was endemic to relations. And so both the European Union and India remained in sidekick position, playing second fiddle to the United States and China, as was their wont.

Over the next couple of days, I settled into a predictable rhythm of briefings, press conferences and filing copy, just as COP 15 proceeded

with its predictable rhythm of leaked drafts, walkouts, finger-wag-
gling and the dogged defense of entrenched positions. Outside the
Bella Centre, environmental activists flooded the streets of Copenhagen in colorful protests. Inside the venue, the world's leaders began to
trickle in, ahead of the meeting's final Friday.

Negotiations remained stalled on almost every major issue, from
emissions cuts to their verification and financing. Ramesh continued
to bounce around, dispensing quotable quotes. "The Kyoto Protocol is
not dead yet, but it's in the ICU [intensive care unit]," he said, rushing
off to yet another BASIC bilateral. "It desperately needs a cylinder of
oxygen in the form of some US flexibility."

Beyond the slog of deadlocked working groups, the broader significance of the meeting lay in the manner in which it exemplified
how the geostrategic contours of the twenty-first century were shifting. These were contours in flux, not wholly settled, but increasingly
discernible. The shaping and breaking of old and new alliances, and
the multiple centers of power that the COP 15 talks wound around,
heralded the emergence of the kind of multipolar world that could
scarcely have been imagined even a decade ago.

Robert Zoellick, the president of the World Bank, walked through
the conference site almost unnoticed because reporters were busy
rushing behind Lumumba Di-Aping, the Sudanese spokesperson for
the G77 plus China group. This was not an isolated incident. Day after day, the headlines tapped out on keyboards from the Bella Centre's
cavernous media center were dominated by Meles Zenawi and Wen
Jiabao as much as by Angela Merkel and Gordon Brown.

But although the "new" world as revealed by COP 15 was clearly
multipolar, the climate summit also showed that while all poles are
equal, two are more equal than others. In the end, as expected, it all
came down to the United States and China.

The so-called "Copenhagen Accord" that was the summit's main,
rather tepid, outcome, was not the dreaded Danish draft by another
name, but a US-China accord that surgically cut the Danish hosts of
the conference right out of the final deal.

The final day of the conference was febrile with anticipation and
disappointments. The United States and China circled each other
like wary pugilists. When Obama had arrived in Copenhagen that
morning, he had immediately gone into a huddle with 18 other world

leaders. But Chinese Premier Wen had been conspicuously absent, sending junior vice minister for foreign affairs, He Yafei, to attend in his place. The entire meeting appeared to be on the verge of implosion.

In the end, Obama maneuvered two unscheduled meetings with Wen Jiabao, the second of which was also attended by China's BASIC partners, during which he brokered what came to be known as the Copenhagen Accord: a non-legally binding, three-page-long political statement. The US president went on to present the accord at a midnight press conference as a fait accompli that other countries could sign on to, or not, before rushing back home, ahead of an expected snowstorm.

The accord amounted to signatories (of both the developed and developing varieties) agreeing to list their domestic climate change mitigation actions. Steps taken by developing countries that entailed some international support were to require "international consultations and analysis," but precisely what this would entail was left unspecified.

The accord caused a furor, with a battalion of developing-world nations complaining at the manner in which a closed-door US-BASIC meeting had hijacked the whole UN process. Although the European Union reluctantly endorsed the agreement, the Conference of Parties ended on Saturday morning without adopting it. Instead, the accord was merely "noted."[29]

COP 15 closed with a whimper. And as a test of the European Union's global leadership, it had only served to underscore Europe's declining heft. For two weeks, European leaders had embraced the role of mediators, attempting to bring the United States on board, while persuading the major developing economies to make stronger commitments. They failed. Their "Danish draft" became the main whipping boy of the BASIC countries, while the United States brokered a deal without any representation from the European Union in the room.

The Copenhagen Accord was the worst possible outcome for the European Union, leaving Europe still tied to legally binding emissions cuts under the Kyoto Protocol, while Washington and Beijing got their desired non-binding pledge and review systems in place.

Ignored and a tad bewildered, EU climate change officials retired to Brussels to lick their wounds. In early February 2010, I met with Connie Hedegaard, the erstwhile COP 15 chair, who had been newly anointed as the first EU Commissioner for Climate Action. She remained uncowed and insisted that despite appearances, Europe had been central to the final Copenhagen Accord.

And she countered the suggestion that when it came to climate change, the European Union was a leader without followers. "Europe *is* the leader," she declared with a toss of the head. "We have delivered the most so far and we are also the leader in committing to a unilateral 20 percent emissions reduction target."

She tempered her optimism with a call for the need for Europe to "act with a uniform voice" and secure a "flexible mandate" from the European Union's 27 member states to avoid any deadlock between them. But even as Hedegaard spoke, a fiscal storm was brewing on Europe's periphery, with the news of an imminent Greek bankruptcy beginning to displace climate change from European headlines.

THE CLIMATE COMMISSIONER WAS TO BEGIN her tenure at the start of a years-long banking and sovereign debt crisis that would strip global warming of its mantle as European priority Number One. Resource prioritization had always been the key issue when it came to environmental politics in countries like India. When faced with innumerable immediate and intractable problems that ranged from malnutrition to sanitation, it had been impossible for climate change to gain the kind of precedence it had in rich, healthy, educated Europe.

And the moment global warming found a competitor for the attention of European leaders in the form of the structural flaws in the workings of the eurozone, it began to struggle to remain as the issue du jour in Europe as well.

Hedegaard spent the next couple of years striving to claw climate back to the forefront of the European policy agenda, but in vain. Her office repeatedly made the point that the economic slowdown in Europe had, in fact, slashed the cost of cutting greenhouse gas emissions by as much as a third.[30] But it failed to inspire enthusiasm among member states focused on spiraling borrowing costs and spiking unemployment.

In the meantime, coal-dependent Eastern European states like Poland found their voice and began openly to block every proposal to move the European Union's climate agenda forward.[31] Once-generous subsidies to renewable technologies that had underlain Europe's claims to climate leadership were also increasingly getting the axe by cash-strapped governments from France and Greece, to Spain and even Germany.[32] And as the euro crisis forced the European Union to marshal all its resources toward battling the financial crisis, talk of Europe's global leadership in climate change was increasingly looking like a case of tilting at windmills rather than steering their spread.

FIVE

The Austere New Boss

TEN MONTHS AFTER I RETURNED FROM COPENHAGEN, we learned that we'd soon be doing our bit to help ease Europe's demographic deficit, with a baby brother for Ishaan due in mid-2011. Pregnancy in Europe brought culture shocks of its own to someone whose previous experience as a mother-to-be had been in China. In Beijing, a pregnant woman was pretty much treated as an invalid. As my belly had begun to grow with Ishaan, it had been quite common for complete strangers to leap up unsolicited and literally offer their shoulders in support, as I waddled about shopping and the like. There were times when this over-solicitousness had been quite infuriating, but it had its advantages: throughout the 2008 Olympic Games in Beijing, as we approached the security queues at the match venues, dozens of eager volunteers were invariably galvanized into herding us into a "special lane" billed as catering to "The elder, the little, the sick, the disabled and the pregnant."

In a Europe of evolved feminists, however, the aim of the pregnant mother was to carry on as close to "normal" as possible. I was quite in awe of some of Julio's female colleagues who thought nothing of driving themselves to the hospital for checkups, days before being due to give birth. My Belgian gynecologist advised me to swim, walk and indulge in the occasional massage through the major part of the pregnancy, all activities that are anathema to pregnant women in

China. I was even advised not to eat too much, an instruction which would have been enough to make most Chinese people pass out. In any event, I didn't have either the time or the appetite to eat much, not only because for much of the time I felt more nauseated than Silvio Berlusconi after a particularly wild *bunga bunga* party, but also because Europe was suddenly big news.

In the history of random coincidences, an honorable mention must be made of the convergence between my pregnancies and the Western world teetering on the verge of economic implosion. The collapse of the investment bank Lehman Brothers, in the same month that Ishaan was born, had sparked off a global financial crisis, destabilizing long-held beliefs about the self-correcting nature of free markets. And when, almost three years later, Nicolas emerged in a hospital in Brussels, it was the eurozone about which plangent obituaries were being written. Greece's sovereign debt crisis was spreading unrelentingly across the 17-country eurozone and, having already taken down Ireland and Portugal, was now knocking on the doors of Italy and Spain.[1] There were fears of a double-dip recession and talk of Europe's "Lehman moment."[2]

Unsurprisingly, climate change had faded as the primary focus for the energies of the European Union, the lamenting over Chinese and Indian carbon recalcitrance being replaced by hand-wringing over Athens's fiscal shenanigans and the European response, or lack thereof, to these.

So what exactly had happened? On the surface, it was a case of naughty Greeks and thin-lipped Germans. The Greeks, despite their status as the antique font of all European civilization, had an embarrassing penchant for corruption. They had cheated and lied for years about their finances, which it was fast becoming clear, were rotten to the core. With massive levels of sovereign debt acquired at a time when membership of the euro club had offered them undeserved, but seemingly bottomless, liquidity, the Greek government could no longer find creditors willing to lend to it.

Having given up the right to devalue its currency upon adopting the euro in 2001, the most obvious path for staving off imminent insolvency was closed to Athens. Nor could it turn to the European Central Bank (ECB) for help, because under existing eurozone rules it was bound by a no-bailout clause. Greece found itself stuck between a rock and a very hard place, or to put it another way, between bank-ruptcy and Germany.

It was Berlin that controlled the purse strings of Europe. And Germany was the only country in the region with pockets deep enough to convince markets not to totally forsake Greece. Any eurozone under-writing of Greek debt would of necessity be German-led, with German taxpayers bearing a substantial burden.

But the Germans were not rushing to write the check that many believed was needed to save the euro from collapse. They were instead circumspect and suspicious and seemingly more interested in tut-tut-ting than action. When confronted with the Greek begging bowl, they pursed their lips and talked disapprovingly of moral hazard, or the idea that people who don't have to bear the consequences of their actions are unlikely to mend their ways.

In other words, it was the (very plausible) German belief that were Athens just handed the money with an eye to calming the markets, but with scant conditionality attached, it would only serve as encouragement for the Greeks to continue with their profligate ways.

Berlin had thus made it clear that in return for any cash, the Greeks, and anybody else who was asking, needed to offer up a suitable pound of flesh. "Austerity," the Germans repeatedly intoned even as Greek trade unionists took to the streets in unprecedented numbers. Cuts in public salaries and welfare benefits were met in Berlin with unempathetic demands for even deeper budgetary lacerations.

Some framed the German response as part and parcel of the country's austere Lutheran heritage, and the ideas of sin and suffering that north European Protestantism stressed, as distinct from the ostensibly more forgiving, wink-and-a-nod-and-a-few-Hail-Marys culture of southern Europe's Catholic nations like Spain and Italy.

But of course, the euro crisis in all its laborious, long-winded unfurling over the months and years was about much more than bad Greeks and unforgiving Germans. It was the almost inevitable result of blatant structural flaws in the design of the common currency, where monetary union between eurozone countries was not accompanied by an equivalent fiscal conjoining. So although the ECB set interest rates for the eurozone as a whole, it did so in a vacuum, with constituent governments retaining control over fiscal and economic policy.

The crisis threw into relief the difficulties—many would claim folly—of yoking together countries with such disparate levels of economic development, and perhaps even more importantly, economic culture. Did fiscally conservative, export-driven, inflation-despising Germany, and big-spending, import-dependent, inflation-accommodating Greece really belong together? Before the euro was introduced, exchange rate adjustments served to dispel tensions that resulted from these divergences in developmental levels between Europe's constituent states. But now the individual members of the common currency zone lacked the option of adapting to a crisis with currency devaluation.

And it was not only bonds and debt and balance of payment issues that were exposed by the crisis, but existential dilemmas of identity and culture that the development of the European Union had helped sublimate but not solve. The reason for the structural flaws of the euro was the reluctance of member countries to cede national sovereignty beyond sharply circumscribed limits. After all, if the countries were to enter a true union, say, along the lines of the United States, who would set the rules for the new entity? What kind of political culture would prevail? Whose values?

The crisis was making it increasingly clear that the answer, however unpalatable for some, was Germany.

GERMANY HAS ALWAYS BEEN at the heart of the European Project. The European Union and its precursors (the European Economic Community and the European Coal and Steel Community) were entities implicitly conceived of as vehicles by which Germany was to be both contained and rehabilitated, following the carnage of the Second World War.

As a nation, Germany represents the Continent's deepest psychological scars, but it has also come to embody the best of "European" values: diligence, resilience and solidarity. Herein lie the seeds of Europe's German schizophrenia, apparent with Technicolor clarity in the commentaries and debates that swooshed around as the eurozone crisis deepened.

It was Germany, above any other country, that was looked up to enough to provide leadership for the region. But as soon as Berlin showed any signs of gathering up the reins, the country was condemned for imposing German interests on Europe.

With fiscal contagion blowing across the region, it was embarrassingly apparent that Europe's major nations were in a state of disarray. Enraged mobs baying for the blood of politicians, burning buildings, the elderly reduced to destitution: these were not scenes from some faraway Third World hell but from the countries that formed the beating heart of rich Europe.

France was ruled by an increasingly unpopular president, Nicolas Sarkozy, whose hyperactive posturing had done little for the country's fortunes domestically or internationally. Spanish youth unemployment was nearing 50 percent, a number higher than in Egypt or Tunisia, where unemployed youth had played a key role in the overthrow of governments. Belgium was breaking world records for the longest period a country had gone without a government, taking over the title from war-torn Iraq. And Italy's prime minister, Silvio Berlusconi, was in and out of court on sex-related and corruption charges.

At the center of these choppy waters, Germany was an island of calm and confidence. More than 20 years after reunification, the country had healed its historic scars and emerged as successful, democratic and rich. A manufacturing powerhouse, Germany had turned its economy around over the last decade to become the moneymaking dynamo of the European Union. It had crested the financial turmoil of 2008 to grow at over 3.5 percent in 2010 and 2011, even as its fellow eurozone members grappled with recession or stagnation.

Despite being at the heart of sclerotic Europe, German GDP per capita had risen more than in any other G7 country over the past decade. Unemployment was at a record low, as were bond yields. Manufacturing was booming, leading to hefty trade surpluses. With only about 1 percent of the world's labor force, Germany accounted for approximately 10 percent of global exports. On almost every economic parameter, Germany was at odds with the general trend in Europe.[3]

Gone were the days when France set the European agenda and Germany automatically acquiesced, unquestioningly conflating its own national interest with that of Europe. A new generation of Germans, the 89ers, whose identities were shaped by the tearing down of the Berlin Wall rather than the atrocities of the Nazis, had reached adulthood and the "normalization" of Germany was perhaps no longer a goal as much as a fact.[4]

The idea of Germany having metamorphosed from cautionary tale to exemplary model was one that most Germans had only just begun to grapple with, when it was lit up in neon and thrust upon them by the eurozone crisis. Poland's foreign minister Radoslaw Sikorski reflected the wider European mood in a speech made in the shadow of Berlin's Brandenburg Gate in November 2011.

"I will probably be the first Polish foreign minister in history to say so but here it is: I fear German power less than I am beginning to fear German inactivity," he said, alluding to Germany's 1939 invasion of Poland that sparked World War II.[5]

That it was a Polish representative turning openly to Germany for leadership was quite extraordinary, given Poland's uniquely fraught relationship with Berlin. Over the course of its occupation by Hitler's troops, the country had lost a fifth of its population. Between 1939 and 1940, in a prelude to the Holocaust, the Nazis had practiced mass killings and ethnic cleansing in Poland, with plans to deport 31 million Poles to Siberia to make way for German settlers in Poland.[6]

But while all of Europe was now looking to Germany for a cure, when Berlin offered up some medicine, it was condemned by many as too bitter. Ms. Merkel steadfastly refused to hand out sugar-coated pills in the form of Eurobonds or other instruments of debt collectivization, which would have meant a German guarantee for the rest of the eurozone's borrowings. Instead, she insisted on austerity for debtor countries in return for limited bailouts and the slow slog toward developing the institutional rules for closer fiscal and political union between euro-using states.

In Brussels, the acronyms multiplied as fast as the worry wrinkles on the faces of Messrs. Barroso and Van Rompuy (the presidents of the European Commission and Council, respectively). The hard-fought-for EFSM (European Financial Stabilization Mechanism) and EFSF (European Financial Stability Facility), temporary bailout funds established in the aftermath of the Greek crisis, were eventually followed up by the ESM (European Stability Mechanism), a permanent eurozone rescue fund. As push came to shove toward the end of 2011, LTROs (long-term refinancing operations) and OMTs (outright monetary transactions) were added to the alphabet soup, as the ECB (European Central Bank) finally overcame German reluctance and swung into action, pumping in hundreds of billions of euros into roiled financial markets. One of my favorite headlines from this time is the *Economist* magazine's story titled "The ECB and OMT: OTT, OMG or WTF?"[7]

Through the entire drama, it was Germany that had to be convinced and reasoned with, listened to and accommodated. At eurozone fire-fighting summits, which began to ping around with alarming frequency, it was Merkel who dominated like a leviathan. French presidents Sarkozy and, later, Hollande, once the stalwarts of such meetings, played at best a supporting role. The fig leaf that France had once provided to German power was slowly but steadily being dispensed with.

In calibrated fashion, and too sluggishly for the tastes of some, Germany agreed to put money on the table. The EFSF had not inconsiderable firepower at its disposal, with a lending capacity of 440 billion euros and a maximum guarantee facility of around 780 billion euros. And by the end of 2012, Berlin had agreed for the fund to lend Greece a whopping 144 billion euros.[8] Germany shouldered the largest burden of all the bailout programs. Its share of the EFSF's 440 billion, for example, was a meaty 211 billion euro, calculated on the basis of its capital share in the ECB.[9]

Merkel also worked to develop the skeleton of closer fiscal coordination, supporting new eurozone legislation referred to as the "six pack" that set rules for member-country budget deficits and debt levels. Similar rules had already existed since the inception of the euro. Termed the Stability and Growth Pact (SGP), these regulations ostensibly limited member countries to budget deficits of no more than 3 percent of GDP and government debt to less than 60 percent of GDP. In reality, several countries had flouted the SGP regularly.

Germany, which was ironically the nation that had insisted on instituting these rules in the first place, was as guilty a party as any other. Berlin, in fact, flouted the SGP for four straight years from 2003, without suffering any punitive consequences. There were grumblings, therefore, that the "new" Germany was increasingly resembling the United States, in that while it sought to corral others into toeing a certain line, it chafed against being bound by the same tenets.

Berlin claimed that it would be as bound by these new rules as any other country. But Chancellor Angela Merkel's efforts to make bailouts palatable to a skeptical domestic audience, while simultaneously attempting to forge a longer-term solution to the eurozone's structural flaws, were not proving easy. The country's Nazi past was inevitably raked up and mumblings about the dangers to Europe of a Germany that was once again becoming too powerful were not uncommon.

In Greece, a variety of newspapers ran commentaries and images to suggest parallels between the Third Reich and the current German leadership. A daily newspaper, *Eleftheros Typos,* for example, carried a doctored photograph depicting the golden statue atop Berlin's Column of Victory holding up a swastika. Others ran pictures of Ms. Merkel in Nazi uniform. Greek politicians, from Athens's mayor, Nikitas Kaklamanis, to socialist stalwart Theodoros Pangalos, made public statements to the effect that Germany still owed Greece billions of euros in war reparations and should therefore just pay up the bailout money with no strings attached.[10]

Germany stood accused of conspiring to recast all of Europe in its own image, and Merkel's conception of fiscal union was disparaged as a plan to subjugate member countries to German hegemony. Some went as far as to suggest that Germany was the greatest threat to Europe today. One article by a leading news agency claimed this should scarcely come as a surprise since "this [the German threat] has happened twice before since 1914."[11]

To me, these criticisms appeared either overblown or unwarranted. But it was clear that even as eastward shifts in the geopolitical balance of power had left Europe with less influence than it once boasted, there had also been internal power shifts within Europe, away from those who had emerged strongest at the end of the Second World War (most notably France) and toward the country that had been defeated and humiliated, Germany. And just as a re-orientalizing world had added fuel to China-bashing, raising anew the specter of the Yellow Peril, a powerful and increasingly vocal Germany was discomfiting for some within Europe.

After a wrenching period of adjustment, the reunification of West and East Germany in 1990 had eventually led to the emergence of a united, dominant economic giant. This was a power that no longer mechanically bowed to the diktats of the European Union. In 2009, the German constitutional court ruled that the European Union lacked the democratic legitimacy to push European integration any further, a volte face from the country's earlier lubricating role in EU expansion.[12] More and more German institutions, from the Bundestag (Parliament), to the Bundesbank (central bank), to the constitutional court, were openly seeking to curtail Brussels's influence over their decision-making prerogatives.

Germany's twenty-first century voice, increasingly untinged by war guilt, no longer shied away from expressing dissenting opinions. For example, prior to the 1990s, policymakers in Germany used to press for a European seat at the United Nations Security Council. Now they called for a German seat.

The idea that the German national interest and the wishes of its domestic constituency could and would take primacy over European interests and agreements was of a piece with Berlin's refusal to be bullied into coughing up bailout cash quicker. It was also evident in Germany's 2011 surprise abstention from the United Nations vote on the imposition of a no-fly zone in Libya, despite the move having received strong backing from its EU and NATO allies, Britain and France.[13]

In the past, Germany only tended to say "no" to European matters via a carefully constructed coalition. But over the last decade, the "no" was more often than not an independent, and even solitary, one. German analysts I met with stressed the role that reunification had played in enabling the German national interest to emerge as an unapologetic force. Josef Janning, the director of studies at the European Policy Centre, a Brussels think tank, explained this to me further.

"A divided country in a cold war is bound to be more outward-oriented, paying careful attention to the needs and trajectories of its neighbors and other important powers." But following unification, Germany, for the first time in a long time, found itself surrounded by friends. The ensuing decrease in threat perception allowed it to become more inward-focused. "It was like going from a situation where you feel like North Korea to one where you are as comfortable as Ohio," Janning said. The manner in which other countries perceived Germany simply became less relevant to it, compounding the confidence that its increased size and economic heft had created.

"Germans still overall have a positive view of Europe. But many no longer see it primarily in terms of the peace, stability and economic prosperity of the continent, but about wasteful bureaucracy, over-regulation, wasteful spending, and lack of transparency," Janning claimed. It sounded almost like a classically British take on Europe, a momentous change, given Germany's history as the European Project's most ardent supporter and Britain's as its most vocal skeptic.

Another analyst, Olaf Boehnke, the head of the Berlin office of the European Council on Foreign Relations, agreed that the role

Germany played within Europe was in flux and its new contours still unclear.

"As a child, I could never imagine being patriotic," Olaf reminisced. "I even felt embarrassed to say I was German and used to stress that I was from Berlin instead." He talked about being shocked during his first visit abroad to Switzerland as a 15-year-old in 1986. "They [the Swiss] had national flags in their gardens. It was astonishing for me. In Germany, a national flag equaled fascism. Patriotism was very difficult for us."

Olaf recalled how German football fans never waved national flags at matches, unlike supporters of other teams. But he noticed this had begun to change by the turn of the century. It had certainly transformed by 2012 when Germany took on Greece in the Euro Cup quarterfinal. The match had been dubbed by the media as the "Battle of the Bailout," and flags aplenty were in evidence, as close-ups of German Chancellor Angela Merkel showed her chortling and cavorting in delight every time her team scored. The Germans won the game 4–2, and for Greece it was yet another blow to national self-esteem, deepening their already bitter resentment of their northern creditors.

The Germans, however, appeared oblivious to the finer feelings of the Greeks, with fans bellowing, "Without Angie, you wouldn't be here," referring to the majority German-funded bailouts that Athens had received from the European Union. "We'll never pay you back," countered the Greeks.[14]

As the euro crisis deepened, I became convinced that the manner in which Europe adjusted to a fresh role for a newly empowered Germany, and conversely, the manner in which Germany adjusted to the kind of leadership role in Europe it was evidently not well prepared for, would be crucial to the future of the continent.

And so I set off to visit this country, which was alternately vilified and deified. I wanted to try to understand this anomaly—in particular, what made it so strong when others in the region were so weak. Why had the German economy been able to buck both European and global trends? How had this high-wage country become, and remained, so successful as a top-end manufacturer and exporter?

The answers to these questions appeared inexorably to lead down one path, to the humble, yet mighty, German mittelstand. Mittelstand is a German term that refers to small and medium enterprises, which are usually family-owned. These are omnipresent but obscure, modest but far from puny. They are Germany's "hidden champions," companies you've never heard of, in places that even many Germans would be hard-pressed to locate on a map.[15] And yet, they form the backbone of the German economy, driving the country's impressive exports and employing upward of 60 percent of the work force.

The Bonn-based Institut für Mittelstandforschung (Institute for Mittelstand Research) estimates that in 2010 over 99.5 percent of all companies in Germany qualified as mittelstand, defined as having up to 500 employees with less than 50 million euros in annual turnover.[16] There are 3.5 million such firms thought to operate in the country. And the resilience of the German economy in the 2008 crisis and beyond has largely been attributed to their flexibility in responding to changing circumstances.

While large German firms cut jobs between 2008 and 2011 by 2.4 percent, the mittelstand actually increased employment by 1.6 percent.[17] The confidence of these firms, even in the face of a world dogged by crises and shifting power relations, was reflected in a poll conducted by the Federation of German Industry in 2012, where more than half of the mittelstand rated their own business situation as "good' or "very good," and only 8 percent felt that it was "bad."[18]

A defining characteristic of the mittelstand is an aversion to the Anglo-Saxon model of deregulation with its stress on maximizing shareholder value and using debt as a strategy of growth. Mittelstand firms frown upon bank debt, and many choose not to go public, their traditional prejudices confirmed to them by the financial chicanery that underlay the 2008 crisis.[19]

The mittelstand are conservative and paternalistic. They are determined, if slightly dour, hedgehogs, who preferred to perfect their art in a chosen niche, rather than run off in myriad directions, like flashy but fickle foxes. This strategy has enabled them to charge premium prices, allowing for continued production in Germany despite the country's high labor costs. China's rise as a manufacturing powerhouse has neither put these German firms out of business nor seen them scrambling to relocate wholescale to the lower-wage countries of Asia.[20] Instead, many mittelstand have been able to increase the sale of their "Made in Germany" products to China, turning the erstwhile Middle Kingdom's rise into an opportunity to be exploited rather than resented.[21]

READING ABOUT THE MITTELSTAND reminded me of the kind of firms that operated in the southern Chinese city of Wenzhou, one of the most enterprising places in all China. At the time of my visit to Wenzhou in 2007, 80 percent of the world's metallic shell lighters had been produced there and another 80 percent of its zippers. The tens of thousands of workers in the city's factory assembly lines also manufactured 25 percent of China's shoes, 80 percent of the country's spectacles, 60 percent of its razors and 65 percent of its electricity transformers. Ninety-five percent of Wenzhou's produce was exported.[22]

Like the mittelstand, Wenzhou firms were world-beaters in their chosen niches. They also tended to be family-owned and-run. Because banks in China had in the past been forbidden to lend to private enterprises and continued to discriminate against them even in the present day, Wenzhou firms had also relied upon financial assistance from family and friends rather than depending on the formal banking network.

But while Wenzhou's companies largely made low-value-added products like buttons and lighters, the mittelstand were strong in high-end engineering products. Ranging from pistons and pumps to faucets and valves, their wares were produced to last. These tools, parts and components might have been hidden to the average consumer's eye, but the mittelstand's offerings were the haute couture of the world of industrial components.

COLOGNE'S DOM IS A HIGH-GOTHIC cathedral that soars, its ceilings so high that you can't look up without feeling you are going to fall off something, even though you are standing on flat ground. As I stepped out of the train station, and the Dom hit me full in the face, I reeled and felt alternately inspired and cut down to insignificant size. Nothing could have better encapsulated Germany's engineering might than this cathedral that took over six centuries to complete. And it was thus apposite that it so thoroughly dominated the skyline of Cologne, the largest city in the western German state of North Rhine-Westphalia (NRW).

I had decided to visit NRW because it was the beating industrial heart of Germany and densely clustered with mittelstand. This was the Rhine-Ruhr region, *das land von kohle und stahl* (the land of coal and steel), which had long been Germany's principal mining and energy-producing area. It was the birthplace of the German industrial revolution, and for decades its landscape had been overrun with blast furnaces and rolling mills.

Industry in this region had played an important role in the production of military ammunition during the Second World War and had consequently been a prime target for Allied bombing. It was here that post-war attempts to dismantle, and later to channel, German economic strength were focused. The setting up of the international authority for the Ruhr in 1949 gave control of the region's coal and steel industries to a coalition of Allied powers.

The international authority was replaced a few years later by the European Coal and Steel Community (ECSC), the body that eventually grew into the European Union of today. And it is here that we clearly see how the roots of the European Union lay in efforts by western Europe, in particular France, to both contain and mobilize German industrial might, in a non-threatening, advantageous way. Much of pre-war Europe had been interlinked with and dependent on the German economy.[23] And so, even as the Allies distrusted the country, they understood that substantial benefits would accrue to them from a revived German economy.

And on West Germany's part, it was through its participation in the ECSC, by sublimating itself into a larger European whole, that the *Wirtschaftswunder* (the economic miracle that refers to the rapid reconstruction of the post-war West German economy) in all its transformatory marvelousness was able to get under way, without setting off alarm bells. The ECSC allowed Germany to enter an international organization on equal terms with other independent states, something that would have been hard to conceive of at the end of the war.

Pooling coal and steel allowed the country to regain control over these resources, shaping a German mindset where pooling sovereignty was seen as a way of regaining it. Recalling this history helps to clarify why contemporary Europe is finding it so agonizing to adjust to Berlin's new leadership and also how a Germany decoupled from the European Union is so shocking for many.

As I sat on the steps leading up from the railway station to the cathedral in Cologne, I smiled at the ghost of my younger self. This city had been the first stop on my euro-railing adventure as a teenager, some 20 years earlier. I had fallen in love with Germany on that brief, youth hostel-filled romp across Europe. It was everything that was not India: Peruvian buskers in patchwork ponchos, efficient public transportation, attractive museums, well-tended parks, well-mannered dogs.

And here I was, a long time later, back at the spot where Europe and I had first become acquainted. Peruvian buskers (a new bunch, I assumed) were still whistling away with gusto at the base of the cathedral. But I had little time to enjoy a prolonged wallow in nostalgia, my agenda being packed with appointments to do with all things mittelstand.

NRW was the right place for this. In 2009, the state's exports were worth 138.6 billion euros, ahead of its main economic competitor Baden-Württemberg. Nineteen percent of the German population lived in this territory and 17 percent of the country's exports originated here. A brochure I'd been handed by the office of the German Chamber of Commerce in Brussels informed me that were NRW a nation in its own right, it would be the world's eighteenth largest exporter.

My first stop was at the regional business archive of the Rhineland, apparently the oldest such archive in the world, dating back to 1906, where I met with archivist Christian Hillen in his office. "The mittelstand," he began musingly, "yes, they are very special. It is really their family structure, which they still retain, that is interesting. In most other parts of Europe, family firms grew and eventually went public. But here, they have preferred to stay a modest size and remain in family hands."

This is why talk of a German model that the rest of Europe should emulate should be treated with caution, he said. German success rested on the shoulders of the mittelstand, and further, on a unique societal attitude to economic relationships that stressed cooperation over confrontation.

"We are," said Hillen very seriously, "not French." I must have sniggered, because he hastened to clarify. "Culturally, we are not like the French or Italians who are more volatile and temperamental. But Germans don't like confrontation, we are conservative, we prefer compromise."

Sure, I found myself thinking, like that nifty bit of confrontation-avoidance with the Jews. But I immediately felt guilty for such an uncharitable thought. It was cheap and easy and unfair. Like Greek papers displaying images of Ms. Merkel in Nazi uniform. I felt a quick surge of sympathy. How difficult it must be for ordinary Germans. Even today. Despite coming from a decent, hard-working, law-abiding, wealthy country. It must be virtually impossible for them to totally escape that uncomfortable feeling in the pit of the stomach where shame and embarrassment lived.

Or perhaps I only imagined this to be the case. Hillen certainly betrayed none of these emotions as he continued to explain why the mittelstand were the product of a unique German spirit. He was not alone in his belief. It was widely held in Germany that the mittelstand was not a term that just referred to numbers like the size of a company or its turnover. Instead, as Ludwig Erhard, the minister for economics, who was the architect of West Germany's post-war renewal, wrote in 1956, "It [mittelstand] is more an expression of a state of mind and a specific attitude."[24] More recently, Ralph Wiechers, chief economist of the German machine makers' association, called the mittelstand "a philosophy rather than an order of magnitude."[25]

Hillen was meanwhile fleshing out his point about the German penchant for compromise, referring to the country's system of collective bargaining. This is an arrangement that works against the kind of frenetic street protests that French trade unionists seem to be perpetually enacting. Pay and work conditions in Germany are usually determined at the industry level between individual trade unions and employers' organizations.

The way Hillen described the process, it sounded almost unbearably civilized. Representatives of workers and employees sit around a table and weigh up the conditions of the local and global economy, and eventually everyone agrees on what would be best for the long-term good of the whole. The system works because the employers are conscientious and the employees diligent, and each side trusts the other to keep their word.

It sounded precisely the opposite of how these things functioned in many other parts of Europe (and indeed, most of the world), where the selfish, short-term benefits of vested interests tend to shape outcomes. Hillen picked up a newspaper and pointed to a headline.

Discussions on pay raises had just been concluded in the state of Baden-Württemberg. It had taken three days of amiable chatting, and the steel industry bosses had apparently come around to the workers' point of view that business was good enough to allow a (Germanically precise) 4.3 percent pay rise over the next two years. OK, in the interests of full disclosure, the steel workers' union had threatened a full-blown strike and even carried out a few partial "warning strikes" to get the employers to up their initial offer of a 2.6 percent hike.

"But it's all theatre. Ultimately, the bosses here see their companies like their families. While they might on occasion be strict with their children, they want the best for the family," said Hillen, using an analogy I was to become nauseatingly familiar with in the following days. The paternalism of the family-owned businesses in Germany was overt, with the boss openly referring to himself (mittelstand are overwhelmingly headed by men) as the father of the company, working for the benefit of the entire family, including the employees.

But despite the penchant for treating workers like children, employees in Germany do have a say in management, through their participation in workers' councils. This corporatist *Mitbestimmung* model with its emphasis on consensus has withstood wars and globalization and bouts of reform to remain strong today.[26] In fact, it is one of the reasons Germany had been able to push through difficult structural reforms in the early part of this century, in tandem with holding down wages.

Currently, Germany was economically in the ascendant, but just two decades ago, the country had been condemned as the "sick man" of Europe. The unification of West and East Germany in 1990 was followed by the sharpest recession since the Second World War. Some 500,000 manufacturing jobs were lost as the country's economy reeled from the effects of competition from nimble Asian challengers, coupled with the huge costs that unification had entailed.

It was difficult to believe now, given how confident and healthy the German economy had become, that as recently as 1997, then president Roman Herzog spoke of "the loss of economic dynamism, the torpor of society, an unbelievable mental depression."[27]

In response to the crisis, German policymakers decided to retain the core of their system but make it more flexible, a move that German workers eventually accepted as necessary. Rather than lose their jobs to eastern Europe or Asia, workers made a bargain with their employers. "They [the workers] got job security in exchange for flexibility on wages and work hours," said Hillen.

In the early 2000s, Gerhard Schröder undertook a series of labor-market reforms that reduced unemployment benefits and liberalized temporary work. His successor as chancellor, Angela Merkel, raised the pension age from 65 to 67 and amended the Constitution to require state and federal governments to cut their structural budget deficits to more or less zero (these were the kind of reforms that Berlin was now seeking to have the rest of the eurozone sign on to as well).

Benefits that were once considered sacrosanct were cut. As a result, income inequality rose. But so did employment and exports. Germany had pulled off quite a coup, altering the fine print of the social contract that held its society together while preserving the form.

It was a most amazing story, especially given the sorry state of much of the rest of Europe, where ossified entitlements were defended to the death as fundamental rights. In France, for example, it had taken a superhuman effort by then president Nicolas Sarkozy to raise the country's retirement age from 60 to 62 in 2010. The measure was pushed through in the face of repeated street action by upward of a million people. But less than two years later, the socialist government of Francoise Hollande rolled back the move for workers who had entered the work force at the age of 18. The French were clearly not German, as Hillen had so pithily indicated at the outset.

The archivist suddenly jumped up and started rummaging through a phalanx of files stacked along the length of a bookshelf. "Look at this," he said waving one at me. "It's the archive of Deutz AG. You have heard of Nikolaus August Otto?" I had to admit my ignorance.

"He is proof of how we Germans are mechanically minded by nature. We are tinkerers. We like to experiment and invent and make things go," gushed Hillen. Otto, it transpired, was the inventor of the four-stroke internal combustible engine, widely used in motorcycles and cars. A one-time traveling salesman and the son of a farmer, Otto had culled much of his engineering knowledge from reading the newspapers, having lacked formal training.

NA OTTO & CIE, the business he set up on the outskirts of Cologne in 1864, was still going strong, now named Deutz AG. Later in the day, I passed a sign for it on my way to visit a rather unusual mittelstand firm: SQS (Software Quality Systems). This company was atypical in that it did not manufacture anything, being a service provider, and was publically listed, rather than in private hands. Yet it shared many features in common with other mittelstand firms, including being headed by a founder-manager father figure, with a distrust of banks and a strong belief in niche development. It was, in addition, surprisingly global, demonstrating an ability to withstand the competition from the East, in this case India.

SQS is a company that specializes in testing software, the kind of tech firm one might imagine flourishing in Bangalore rather than the Rhineland. It is housed in a modest building on the outskirts of Cologne, a far cry from the flashy campuses of Indian IT companies. But then SQS is not about size as much as specialization, as is the case with so many of the mittelstand.

I was welcomed by Rudolf Van Megen, who had co-founded the company in 1982 and still ran it with a firm hand. A bit too firm for my liking—my own paw felt quite shattered after being crushed in his uber-manly handshake. Van Megen was asparagus-tall and neatly dressed. Two tufts of silvery hair flanked his otherwise bald pate. A short, bristly moustache adorned his upper lip.

His booming voice thundered with enthusiasm as he described his business: SQS operated in the narrow segment of software testing. Van Megen recalled that at the time he'd decided to set up the company, the general consensus in the tech world was that it would soon be possible to develop perfect code from specifications, allowing no room for error, hence making software testing redundant.

Undeterred, Van Megen and his partner pushed ahead with their idea. Back then, it was almost always the software developer who also tested the product. "But it was so obvious to us that a good developer is a bad tester and vice versa. A good tester is analytical and not creative. And a developer testing their own software is a conflict of interest." His mouth relaxed into a smile. "You should not be allowed to test your own homework, should you?"

Like many other mittelstand, SQS had met the challenge of globalization by embracing it. "By the mid-1990s, we realized that to remain market leaders in Germany we would also have to become world leaders." And so, the company began to spread its tentacles further and further afield, starting with a joint venture in Spain, continuing on to Austria, the United Kingdom, the Netherlands and eventually to non-European countries. By 2012, SQS had 500 people working in a test center in India and 120 employees in Egypt.

Along the way, the company had learned the one lesson that all mittelstand seemed to carry around like a badge of honor: a distrust of bank credit. Van Megen was emphatic when telling his story. SQS had financed an acquisition in the United Kingdom with a bank loan in 2000, which turned out to "be a disaster" when the dot-com bubble of the 1990s burst. "Let me tell you one thing we now know. Never get dependent on banks. You can grow without loans."

SQS was what was called a "pure play tester," in that it only operated in the field of testing, unlike the "system integrators" that combined a range of services from development and IT processes management to testing.

Van Megen revealed that there were 160 other pure play testers globally but that most were small, with a handful of employees and low turnover. By contrast, SQS employed 2,200 staff in 15 countries and boasted revenues of 200 million euros. The pure play tester that ranked immediately below SQS had revenues of 28 million euros. SQS's "real competitors" were the systems integrators like Indian heavyweight Wipro, whose software-testing arm generated revenues upward of 420 million euros.

But how could SQS hope to take on low-cost IT services giant India? Van Megen became heated in response. "India cannot and will not prove competitive in Europe," he said, slapping the table in front of him with a copy of SQS's financial report for 2011. The company was currently number five in Europe in its field despite its relatively small size precisely because it was a European company.

"We speak German. Language matters. Why would a German company work through translation with an Indian firm when it could have us? This is why we win deals over Accenture, IBM, Infosys. If you had a chance to work with a European company or an Indian one, of course you would prefer a European one." He paused, the spittle glinting on the edge of his mouth, before adding slowly, "For cultural reasons."

SQS had the right number of people on site in Europe, he claimed—58 percent of its work force, to be precise. For Indian companies to build up their centers in Europe to SQS levels would be "very difficult." Besides, SQS was not just a tester but also a "thought leader and standard setter," providing the most cutting-edge methodologies in testing, which the Indian systems integrators themselves used.

I was slightly uncomfortable with all this self-aggrandizement and had to fight the feeling that there was an underlying sneer to Van

Megen's tone every time he mentioned the word "Indian." He didn't notice and continued irrepressibly, "We are not cost leaders, like the Indians, but we are efficiency leaders."

I decided to try and encourage him to stretch this line of thinking to see how far down it would go. "Yes," I murmured admiringly. "It's so amazing how efficient the Germans are in whatever they do."

Van Megen's muscles uncoiled. It was like watching a flowering tea unfurl in a cup of hot water. "It's because of German culture," he beamed expansively. "A culture of innovation. Indians only do what they are told, but in Germany people dare to think. Our employees are trained to come back with a good idea and try and do things better than before. The workers have a high sense of self-responsibility. And they understand the concept of short-term loss for long-term gain. We can withstand crises because immediate profit is never our bottom line."

This was an explanation I was to hear repeatedly during my visits to several mittelstand: that Germans were more efficient, more rational and more responsible than others. In their self-perception and self-promotion, the Germans I met were confident, bordering on the arrogant. There was scant evidence of any discomfort with exhibiting pride in their German-ness. Instead, the idea of German exceptionalism was unselfconsciously common. The once-bulky shadow of the Second World War was fading away into irrelevance.

THIS FEELING WAS REINFORCED the following evening as I drove around the city of Dortmund with 29-year-old Tim Dolezych, the scion of an eponymous, archetypical mittelstand firm. With his gelled blonde hair and easy laugh, Tim had the air of a bit of a lad about him. His English was tinged with an American twang. He was a huge fan of the local football team, Borussia Dortmund. He radiated confidence and youth and good health.

As we chit-chatted, I mentioned how I'd been to university in England. I liked the English, I said, because they had this ability to poke fun at themselves. They kind of got how others might perceive them less than favorably. To this, Tim responded that Germans were the same too. They understood what foreigners thought of them.

Poor chap, I thought. Still haunted by Germany's Nazi past. But just as I was about to reassure him that there were foreigners who realized that young Germans today bore no responsibility for the sins of their forefathers, he giggled. "Foreigners tend to think of us as perfectionist, but actually we slack off sometimes, just like everyone else."

His answer reminded me of those job interviews where people get asked to list their most negative personality trait and they answer with straight faces that they are perfectionists. Except that Tim wasn't being insincere. He really meant it.

Dolezych had been founded by Tim's grandfather in 1935. Like the majority of mittelstand, the company had played a supporting role in the region's economic mainstay: the mining and steel industries. It manufactured the wires, ropes and slings that were used in these sectors. Then the war broke out and the company was bombed into rubble. But it was rebuilt in 1948 with the kind of "get on with it" determination that played such an important role in West Germany's wider *Wirtschaftswunder*.

"We could recover because we are like a centipede," Dr. Karl Peter Ellerbrock, head archivist at the Dortmund Business Archives, had told me earlier in the day. "Our body is the big companies like the steelmakers. But we have a hundred legs, the mittelstand, that carry us forward."

Ellerbrock's face was weathered, furrowed with lines. But his eyes were bright when he talked of the local businesses. "These companies have known how to withstand crises for 150 years. In the Ruhr, crisis is the norm, not the exception. It's made them very quick to adapt to changes."

In the nineteenth century, the region had to make the dramatic adaptation from a subsistence, rural economy to an industrialized one centered on the mining and steel industry, he explained. The mechanical age spawned the mittelstand, transforming artisans into entrepreneurs.[28] Then, even as Otto Von Bismarck successfully united disparate German states into one powerful Prussian-led empire, a huge stock market crash kicked off a 23-year-long recession. This *Gründerkrise* (as the two-decade period of economic stagnation was referred to) forged new ideas about how capital, labor and the state should relate to one another, laying the foundations of the German "coordinated market economy," with its particular blend of capitalism and state control.

Workers' representations on company boards and other elements of the welfare state like health insurance have their roots in this period, as does the vocational system of education that continues to stand the German economy in such good stead today.

Warming to the subject of the crises from whence the mittelstand were wrought, Ellerbrock reeled off the series of twentieth-century catastrophes that the businesses in the region had to cope with: the French occupation after the First World War, followed by a period of hyperinflation, the Great Depression, the rise of national socialism and yet another devastating all-out war.

"These companies know to always be prepared for the worst. It's because of their history of adjustment to these successive crises that they have such, such . . . what do you call it in English?" Ellerbrock stopped to think long and hard, literally scratching his head, but finally gave up. "You understand *Existenzgrundung?*" he asked hopefully.

I did not. But I wrote it down and looked it up later. The term refers to the spirit of entrepreneurialism, to the starting up of a business. To that seemingly unquenchable German spirit that had allowed companies like Dolezych to dust off the devastation of the Second World War and start up, yet again.

That afternoon I spent several hours at the Dolezych headquarters, talking with Tim and the company CEO Karl-Heinz Keisewitt. Tim's father, Udo Dolezych, had been the firm's president since the late 1980s, but the youngster was now poised to inherit the role.

Dolezych was currently the market leader in Europe in its business of lifting and load-fastening equipment. It employed 600 people around the world, including in China, Chile, Poland, Ukraine, Russia and Switzerland. But the largest part of the work force, 180 people, remained on German soil, in Dortmund.

"This is our secret," said Keisewitt, the bespectacled manager who played the role of faithful family retainer. "Our commitment to our employees over the long term, and in return, their loyalty to us." Tim jumped in with a story about a worker who had just celebrated his fiftieth year of employment at Dolezych. He'd joined the company at the tender age of 15. "The identification of the workers with the firm is excellent," said Tim. Keisewitt added, "Our people know whom they are working for. There are no anonymous shareholders but a person they can trust. Mr. Udo is like a father to them."

There we go again, I thought.

"We are what we call a dicmocracy, a mixture of democracy and dictatorship," Keisewitt continued. "The workers are encouraged to give their input, but ultimately it is the boss who decides, without the interference from banks or shareholders. He can take quick decisions and even unpopular ones." How very Chinese Communist Party the mittelstand were.

I was then treated to the standard mittelstand anti-bank invective as Keisewitt joked that all Dolezych was interested in seeing of banks was the back of their managers. "We are self-financed 100 percent," he growled proudly, "so we can retain 100 percent independent decision making. We might not make as much money, but money is not our final value."

So what is this value, I asked. "Pride," Tim answered. "Pride in the quality of the product. And pride in the family. The pride in having something to pass down to your sons and daughters. In our kind of company, you can cut the leaves but not the roots," he summed up. "The family structure means that from generation to generation the rules and ethics are passed down."

'Yes,' agreed Keisewitt, "the values of the company don't change simply because a new CEO is around." I felt a tad embarrassed for the chap as he eviscerated his own position as CEO of the company. "Stability is very important. To the workers and the company."

Gosh, the Chinese communists would love these guys. I had to resist a smirk. Tim was looking earnest. "I think our secret is that we mittelstand are innovative and conservative at the same time. We like to stick to our core business, what we can really do well, but innovate within it."

He gave the example of how his father had innovated the manufacture of textile slings using nylon and polyester rather than the steel slings of yore. His grandfather had initially been skeptical but had eventually given his permission for experimentation. Today two-thirds of Dolezych products were textile-based rather than steel-based.

"But we still make slings," Keisewitt interjected. "We make 20,000 different articles, but all in the same sector. *Schuster bleib bei deinen leisten*." "Schuster what?" I said, pausing in my note-taking.

"It's a German proverb," explained Tim. "It means like, 'Shoeman, stick to your trade.' Like you should stick to the things you understand." With this resounding endorsement of the caste system, I could imagine the mittelstand going down quite well in India too.

But sarcasm was easy. The fact was that Dolezych, like the German mittelstand more broadly, had been hugely successful, resiliently rising to challenges ranging from war to financial crises. In fact, the German economy as a whole resembles one large mittelstand firm, given how it prioritizes stability over growth and prudence over profit. These were values that had served the country, and its businesses, well.

Dolezych's strategy for dealing with the 2008 crisis, for example, was a case study in the German way of meeting business adversity. In 2009, the firm's turnover fell by 22 percent. "This was something new for us. It had never happened in the 30 years before," said Keisewitt somberly. But the company did not lay off or lose a single employee. Instead, it introduced part-time work. The deal was that employees would keep their jobs but temporarily accept fewer working hours and lower wages. "Within one minute of offering the deal, everyone accepted it," smiled Tim. And by 2010, business was back to normal.

In fact, 2011 had been Dolezych's best year ever, despite the eurozone crisis. The growth was coming from Germany's steel and pipe companies, which were flourishing. It was hardly surprising that Tim expressed such complete confidence in the future.

Later, when I asked him over a drink whether he worried about a potential collapse of the eurozone, he was nonchalant. "I think we'll be OK," he smiled, sipping his beer. "Whether there is a euro or no euro, everyone who produces something anywhere in the world has to move it, to lift it, lash it, secure it. They are all our potential clients. If demand slumps in Europe, we'll find it elsewhere."

TIM'S CONFIDENCE NEEDS TO BE SET in context. At the time of our meeting the bestselling book in Germany was titled *Europe Doesn't Need the Euro,* written by Thilo Sarrazin, a former member of the Bundesbank's executive board, also known for his anti-immigration views.[29] Newspapers were regularly running debates and publishing poll results on the question of whether Germany ought to leave the eurozone, often with answers in the affirmative winning out. Popular and business sentiment was surging with pride and assurance in Germany's muscle.

But impressive as the mittelstand are, I believed such brazen confidence to be foolhardy. The German economy is hardly invincible, nor is German exceptionalism all that exceptional. The idea that Germans are "thought innovators" while the Chinese and Indians just do as they are told, essentially providing the hands and feet to the great German brain, smacks of hubris. The impact that rapidly growing China and India are having on Europe in economic terms will be examined in detail in the next two chapters. It is certainly not a foregone conclusion that Germany will remain on top.

Moreover, the notion that Germany can breezily decouple itself from the rest of Europe, the ensuing slack getting picked up by rising demand from Asia, does not hold water either. Germany is deeply entwined with the European Union, not just politically, but economically, and any slowdown in the eurozone is bound to have consequential implications for it.

In 2011, 71 percent of German exports were to European countries, and almost 40 percent to eurozone countries alone. It is estimated that three-quarters of the total German trade surplus that year was due to its surplus with the other 26 countries of the European Union.[30]

In 2012, the country experienced a paltry 0.7 percent growth, sharply down from the brisk (by European standards) 3 percent of 2011. The slowdown was thought to be the result of a decline by companies in plant and machinery investment, given the overall recessionary environment of the eurozone.[31]

That the euro had allowed Germany to export at a cheaper rate than its currency-sharing partners is a fact often pointed to by countries like Spain and Italy. There is a line of reasoning that claims Berlin had benefited from the euro at the "expense" of southern European countries whose own economies had suffered from an overvalued currency. This is not the whole truth. Several analyses show that it is precisely the countries in most trouble now—Greece, Portugal and Spain—that had benefited most from the euro, a currency that had brought rising standards of living, stability and international acceptance to them.[32] Yet, the sentiment that Berlin was asking for too much pain in return for too little support, and without adequate understanding of the cost of what it was asking of others, had some merit.

Berlin itself had certainly carried out some of the tough reform measures, like the opening up of labor markets, that it was asking of others. But this didn't exactly amount to walking the talk, since Germany had carried out its reforms at a time when economic buoyancy in the rest of Europe had created a strong demand for German products. In contrast, Italy, Spain and other struggling "peripheral" countries were being asked to do the same at a time of economic stagnation, even contraction, which made it much harder and, arguably, counterproductive.

Now, clearly, shoring up the eurozone is not about asking Germany to undertake some wholly altruistic piece of charity. There are sound political and economic benefits that would accrue to Germany from doing so. In the event of a euro collapse and forced readoption of the deutsche mark, Germany's exchange rate would surge, potentially crippling the exports that have been so fundamental to the country's economic growth. Moreover, the direct costs of a eurozone breakup to the German economy would be substantial, estimated at a minimum of 10 percent of the nation's GDP.

One report by the Swiss financial services firm, UBS, quantified the cost of a German exit of the eurozone to be between 6,000 and 8,000 euros for every German citizen in the first year and in the range of 3,500 to 4,500 euros per capita in the following years. That is the equivalent of 20–25 percent of GDP in the first year. In comparison, it was estimated that the cost of bailing out Greece, Ireland and Portugal entirely in the wake of the default of those countries would be a little over 1,000 euros a person, in a single hit.[33]

However, Germany's pockets are not bottomless. And for all its dynamism, the kind of bailouts that would be required by large countries like Spain and Italy in the event of their financial collapse would be a difficult task, even for Berlin. Some analysts concluded that Berlin could potentially end up with debts equal to more than 40 percent of its annual GDP.[34]

Ms. Merkel wasn't being disingenuous when she claimed in a speech to the Bundestag in mid-2012 that "Germany's strength is not infinite." Her call for a "realistic sizing up of our [German] powers, so we can use them for Germany and Europe with full force" made sense.[35] The worry, however, was not her lack of logic, as much as the mismatch between the speed of the cautious, piecemeal solutions that Germany was putting forward to the crisis and that of the urgent, full-throated solutions that the markets seemed to be demanding.

Through much of the crisis, the main criticism of Germany's handling of the situation was its reluctance to pull out a "big bazooka," the kind of shock-and-awe weapon that would allow the policy leadership to get ahead of the markets and ostensibly help stabilize investor confidence and stem contagion. Suggestions for this bazooka ranged from tripling the firepower of the EFSF bailout fund up from its original 440-billion-euro kitty to unequivocal debt pooling within the eurozone—in effect, an unconditional guarantee by Germany of the weaker countries' debts.

The "big bazooka" approach was originally advocated by former US Treasury secretary Hank Paulson during the 2008 financial crisis. But in my thinking, to promote the idea of a big bazooka solution to the euro crisis was either to totally misunderstand the nature of the beast that is the European Union or to deliberately root for its failure.

Acting quickly and decisively might work for actors like the United States and China. But for an entity like the European Union, it can be perilous. Perhaps it takes an Indian to understand this, for we resemble the European Union in our cumbersome, coalition-constrained, procedure-oriented decision-making process.

LIKE EUROPE, INDIA IS OFTEN ACCUSED of doing too little, too late. As much as China's economic reforms have been spectacular and strategic, attracting all manner of superlatives, India's have been tepid and muddled, in constant danger of being subverted by a surfeit of debate. And just as the United States, with its armory of capital injections and big bailouts, has demonstrated its willingness and ability to do whatever is needed to tame the markets, Europe is stuck playing catch up with the markets, one step behind, rather than ahead, of them.

But to deride either India or the European Union for their shuffling and equivocation, while understandable when the need for results is pressing, misses the point that both entities owe their existence and continued survival to these very phenomena. Protracted debate and sluggish consensus building are existential demands for India and Europe, not just some annoying character flaws.

Calibrating the kind of diversity of interests and identities that New Delhi and Brussels have to contend with on a daily basis necessitates the type of measured response that is the unexciting, and often ambiguous, opposite of a big bazooka. Quick, unilateral or forceful reactions to complex matters of import hold the potential to unravel the delicate knit that allows these two unions, of India and Europe, to cohere and persist against the strong centrifugal forces of narrowly defined nationalisms.

India and the European Union are not just cumbersome polities; they are huge political achievements that allow the world to imagine alternative, inclusive configurations to the exclusions and bigotry of national tribalisms. This is not to claim that either lives up perfectly to its own underlying idea. Both remain messy and contradictory and half-baked. But in their idealized potential there resides considerable hope for humanity.

And so it is imperative to resist impatience when willing Europe to solve its problems. Wrong-headed haste could derail, rather than strengthen, the fine balancing act that is the European Union.

Were Merkel to have listened to her many international would-be advisors and agreed to an unconditional bailout for Greece right off the bat, giving the markets their wish, would she have solved the problem? Perhaps for a brief moment, but such a bailout would merely have kicked the substantive ball further down the line. It is ironic given how Germany's critics accused Merkel's tendency to agree to just enough at every eurozone summit to avert complete disaster as short-termist behavior, when in fact handing the markets and their boosters a blank check is what would have really qualified for that label.

Rescuing Greece without a fuss would have left the underlying flaws of the eurozone as unaddressed as they were at the inception of the common currency, inevitably setting up another future crisis along the same lines. It would have sent out the message that rash and deceitful fiscal decisions would be rewarded with cash. It would have done little to stem the tide of countries with access to cheap credit that they did not deserve spending beyond their means. It would have allowed populist politicians to continue to skate around the difficult but necessary reforms needed to remold their economies into competitive shape. It would, in other words, have allowed the great lie, that things could remain the same in Europe, to persist.

And it would have been dangerously undemocratic, quite probably undermining crucial support in Germany for the European Project. A majority of Germans had opposed the introduction of the euro in the first place but had taken some solace in the fact that bailouts between European countries were prohibited. Understandably, many felt betrayed at this basic rule of the common currency being twisted out of existence by the crisis summitry of the last few years.

How much worse would this sense of duplicity have been, had an unconditional bailout been agreed to at the outset? The drawn-out process via which the German public was nudged and pushed along in the direction of accepting greater fiscal responsibility for its struggling eurozone partners did considerable service to the cause of preserving the common currency.

Furthermore, Germany was also aware that abandoning Greece to its own fate, however well deserved, was not an option. An unmanaged bankruptcy within the eurozone would have exacted a heavy price from every member country, with the contagion quite possibly arriving to knock at Germany's own door. The consequences of an economically weak country leaving or being expelled from the euro would need to include the costs of sovereign default, corporate default, collapse of the banking system and even the potential collapse of international trade. And this was excluding harder to quantify, but arguably even more destabilizing, political costs.

It was therefore incumbent on Germany, and indeed the eurozone as a whole, to stop, look and weigh up options before leaping. Finding the right balance between the inconsistent demands of national democratic responsibilities and unpopular supranational needs, and the short term and the long term, were not the kinds of tasks that could be carried out with ease, speed or efficiency. They required a fair degree of "crossing the river by feeling the stones," a Chinese proverb that effectively translates into English as "muddling through."

Within months of the Greek crisis going public in early 2010, pundits of all stripes were busy opining that the time for "muddling through" was over, that the eurozone had arrived at a crossroads where only two possible outcomes awaited: full fiscal and increased political union, or disintegration into some version of the pre-1999 euro regime. In fact, the much-derided third option of muddling through is the one I understood as necessary.

Dissolution of the euro would have been expensive and politically dangerous. A strong push toward federalism, a "United States of Europe," would have been undemocratic and lacking in popular support. Consequently, the halfway house between these two extremes that Europe attempted to construct in the ensuing years was the only choice. The muddling through from 2010 to 2012 was a legitimate— possibly the only legitimate—tactic for handling the crisis.

BY THE END OF 2012, it was beginning to appear that this approach had gone some way in accomplishing the very difficult task of prodding Europe toward the second scenario of closer union. The creation of eurozone bailout funds, the ratcheting up of their firepower, the introduction of the "six-pack" legislation that set out new fiscal and budgetary rules for euro-using countries may not in isolation have been a single big bazooka. But collectively, they were beginning to form the outlines of a longer-term answer to the needs of the eurozone without precipitating a politically unpalatable shock to the system.

After months of striving to ensure that Europe's response was shaped by three of Germany's priorities—to prevent moral hazard, to avoid inflation and to insist on the uniformity of eurozone budgetary discipline—Ms. Merkel gradually softened her stance on issues like European Central Bank interventions, which resulted in the infusion of hundreds of billions of euros into the eurozone banking system. At each crisis summit in Brussels, there was a little more give and a little more take, on both sides of Europe's fiscal divide, with creditors and debtors taking steps toward a consensus, even as they appeared on the outside to be fighting it.

The euro crisis was about a lot more than a currency. Were the euro to unravel, it would be a damaging blow to the European Project, which—for all its pomposity—had helped cork and stuff away many of the nastier tendencies in Europe.

The single currency was a symbol of how far the Continent has come from its bloody past. Its destruction would at best be a major dent to Europe's prestige, and at worst, spark social unrest on a large scale. Given its history of civil strife and destructive ideologies like fascism, Europe cannot afford to take trends like the appearance of far-right parties and rising xenophobia, coupled with spiraling youth unemployment and economic stagnation, complacently.

But the art of eurozone maintenance is a tricky one, requiring fewer bazookas and more summits. Of course, summits in themselves solve nothing, and despite a surfeit of summitry, the euro was still far from in the clear. What was clear was that going forward, Germany was going to have to lead more from the front than from behind, as had been its practice.

It is not easy to be German in Europe today, if it has ever been so. But for many countries it is also not easy to have Germany in charge of Europe. For the eurozone, and indeed the European Union as a whole, the real challenge might not turn out to be fixing the design of the currency union as much as adjusting to a new and austere boss, Germany.

And as if that isn't a tough enough challenge, the region has to contend with a new boss on the global horizon as well. Germany's Asian doppelganger: China.

SIX

Chateau Chongqing

A THICK LAYER OF SNOW BRIGHTENED THE TYROLEAN night sky as the streets of Kufstein fell silent. Tired out by a busy day on the ski slopes, the tourist throngs were turning in for bed. But within the usually placid interiors of the Thaler Hotel there was pandemonium. Great gaggles of ten-year-old Chinese kids swarmed the corridors, their chatter echoing loudly.

"Hi," one of them called out to me boldly. Her friends clustered around, giggling. "Ni hao," I replied. "Have you had a fun day?" Three years after having left Beijing, my Chinese was rusty but adequate. The kids looked nonplussed and fell momentarily silent.

"Are you Chinese?" asked a bespectacled boy with braces flashing silver across his teeth. "Do I look Chinese?" I countered. "You speak Chinese," he said cautiously. A girl with smart, bobbed hair and a very grown-up expression sighed at his ignorance. "Don't you know?" she said, turning toward him with a slight frown. "These days it's normal for foreigners to speak Chinese. It's no big deal."

What has, in fact, become increasingly normal is the sight of hordes of Chinese children hitting Europe's ski slopes, fanning through the Continent's shopping malls and filling up its chocolate shops. If it is school vacation time in China, it is study-tour time in Europe.

I was joining one of six groups of kids that a German company, European Culture and Studies (ECS) Tours, had brought over to

Europe for the Chinese New Year break in late January 2012. ECS was run by a young couple, a German lawyer Rudolf Reiet and his Chinese girlfriend Xing Li.[1]

They were new players in the lucrative market for study groups in Europe. Parents in China paid up to RMB 60,000 ($9,500) to send their kids on a two-or three-week whirlwind tour of the Continent's sights. But in addition to holiday pictures, the kids were also expected to bring home skills like eating with a fork and knife and learning the appropriate time to clap at a Western classical music concert.

Europe might have been battling multi-pronged challenges from the need to slim down bloated welfare states, address issues of identity in an increasingly multicultural landscape and locate a new and effective logic for the European Project in the face of the euro currency's crisis, but the popularity of the continent for tourists from rising Asian powers like China was unabated.

ECS Tours had only been able to make inroads into the already saturated market for European study tours by focusing on the western city of Chongqing, Xing Li's hometown. "Beijing and Shanghai are impossible," explained Rudolf over dinner on my first night in Kufstein. It was the less traveled paths of relatively impoverished provinces like Henan and Guizhou that they were looking to tap into.

"We are cheaper than the companies focusing on the big cities," said Rudolf. The kids from Chongqing were paying "merely" RMB 36,000 ($5,700) for their ongoing ten-day trip to Europe. Winter tours were shorter and cheaper than their summer equivalent because parents only let their children travel after they had celebrated the Chinese New Year (which usually fell in late January or early February) together at home.

Chinese tourists who, like the Japanese before them, had taken to visiting the Continent by the busload, had already remade the traditional European Grand Tour according to their own tastes, history and consumer culture.[2] They congregated by a willow tree in the extensive grounds of Cambridge University's King's College, flocked to the obscure German city of Trier and, perhaps most perplexingly, stood snapping pictures in front of the Berlaymont—the mammoth spawn of 1960s modernist architecture that served as the European Commission's headquarters in Brussels.

At Cambridge, the tree in question makes an appearance in a 1928 poem by Xu Zhimo, a poet who had studied at King's. Battalions of

Chinese children are forced to memorize the verse in school, which explains the arboreal attraction. In Trier, the draw is Karl-Marx-Haus, the birthplace of the communist revolutionary whose "thought" is still drilled into every Chinese student.[3]

The Berlaymont was a tougher puzzle to solve. I put it down to the Chinese identification with bureaucracy. The Chinese "Party State" was after all one gigantic mesh of officialdom. In Europe, the European Commission, with its faceless technocrats and byzantine regulations, suffered from a deficit of love, but for many Chinese it must have struck an affectionate, familiar chord. And so come fine weather or (more usually for Brussels) drizzle, it was a rare moment that a Chinese tourist was not to be found posing among the phalanx of blue European flags that lined the Berlaymont.

More typical stops included Paris for the romance and Louis Vuitton; Austria for mountains and Swarovski; and Italy for canals, gondolas, Gucci and Prada.

Chinese travelers have emerged as the European tourism industry's knights in shining armor, riding to the rescue of otherwise stagnant economies. A hefty proportion of the region's luxury goods sales are now made to the Chinese even though tourists from the mainland remain a tiny fraction (less than 1 percent) of total travelers to Europe.[4] A report by the School of Oriental and African Studies in London projects a ballooning of Chinese tourists to Europe from around 3 million to over 8.5 million by 2020.[5] But what is lost in these statistics is just how recently Chinese travelers, outside of official delegations, had begun to visit Europe at all.

I had been living in Beijing for two years when in 2004, 12 European countries were given what the Chinese authorities called ADS, or approved destination status, making it possible for Chinese tour groups to obtain visas for holidays to the region. Back in 2002, a mere 645,000 Chinese tourists had visited the European Union.[6]

It wasn't only the huge increase in numbers of travelers over the last decade that stood out for me, but also the fact that they definitely did not spend their time in Europe gawping at the advanced, capitalist, democratic West at work. Many Chinese instead appeared to treat Europe like a cross between a museum and a shopping mall. And the Chinese ten-year-olds I was following proved to be no exception.

The kids were getting a truncated rendering of the typical version of the Chinese Grand Tour with a few days each in Germany,

Switzerland and Austria. By the time I met up with them they'd already been to Switzerland and had spent a day in Austria. I was traveling with them to Innsbruck, Salzburg and Munich.

There were 35 children in my group, all from a single primary school in Chongqing. Rudolph, the organizer, explained that there were three types of kids on the tour. The largest group comprised the children of high officials of China's ruling Communist Party. "It's really easy to tell who these are. They talk just like little *lingdao* [leaders], ready to launch into a politically correct speech at the asking."

Then there were the kids of entrepreneurs. "You can spot these pretty easily too," smiled Rudolph, telling me about a child from the previous summer's group who brought extra packets of instant noodles along with him to sell to classmates fed up with the European fare on offer, at the inflated price of 5 euros each.

The third category of students was the smallest: children of parents of modest means who had obviously saved up to give their kids the opportunity of visiting Europe. "They have less money to spend and their clothes are shabbier than the others."

The next day we set off early. It was icy cold, but the children were warmly dressed in wool-lined boots and Gore-Tex jackets. Our coach driver was a beefy, mustachioed Hungarian. Drivers from Hungary were cheaper and more flexible regarding work hours compared to their Austrian counterparts, Ge Qingfei, the young tourist guide accompanying us, informed me. Guide Ge was from Shanghai and had the kind of chocolate-box good looks of a Taiwanese pop star. He'd lived in Germany since his student days and was in charge of all the logistics for our group.

I sat up front next to Zhang Qi, the group's "cultural instructor." It was Teacher Zhang's job to play DVDs relating to the cultural particularities of the country we happened to be passing through. After the video was screened, quizzes were handed out to the kids and the teacher talked them through these.

Teacher Zhang was only 30 years old, but her face was lined and tired. Originally from China's northeast Liaoning province, she now lived in Germany where she worked as an interpreter. This was her second time taking kids from China around Europe. I asked her what she thought of the children. Were they different from how she'd imagined they would be?

"Oh! They are very lucky," she replied. "We didn't have the kind of opportunities they have when we were kids. They're so confident, so knowledgeable." Many had already traveled to foreign countries with their parents. I noticed over the next few days how the kids were rarely impressed with Teacher Zhang's tidbits about European culture. "So tell us something we don't already know," their expressions seemed to suggest as she launched into a lecture about appropriate table manners.

As we pulled up by the ski slopes just outside Kufstein, Guide Ge clapped his hands to get everyone's attention. "We're going to spend two hours learning how to ski, followed by lunch," he announced.

"What's for lunch?" yelled one of the kids from the back of the bus. "I'll die if it's schnitzel again," moaned a podgy lad sitting behind me. The children cracked up. "We hate schnitzel," many of them called out. "That's enough," said Guide Ge and herded them out of the bus.

Half an hour later everyone was kitted out with skiing boots, sun visors and gloves. I took the ski lift up the slopes with the two English girls who were to be the instructors for the morning. They'd been teaching groups of Chinese children all week, they told me, so many that they'd seriously begun contemplating taking a Chinese-language class.

"Do you ever get any Indians?" I asked them. They shook their heads. Never. I was about to find out why. It was my first time out on a ski slope and the cold was brutal. It took around a minute before I realized that this was not my element. Indians are made for gasping at snow, chucking a few snowballs, and then retiring for chai and samosas. Chai stalls being scarce in the Austrian Alps, I opted for the second-best option and headed off for a coffee at the restaurant we were to have lunch at later, leaving the kids to their skis.

I was almost thawed by the time the children came trooping in, breathing heavily from their exertions. Three girls and two boys slid in at the table next to me. Almost immediately, the iPads and mobile phones were out. How was the morning, I asked them, my voice raised so as to be heard over the beeps of video games.

"Not bad," Lei, a tall 11-year-old girl, replied with studied nonchalance. And the trip so far? Was Europe meeting expectations?

She took her time thinking before answering. "Well, the traffic seems really confusing here. So many rules to follow on the road. I'm not sure who gets right of way. It must be scary to drive here!"

Lei's father was in real estate, she said, and her mother worked for the Chongqing municipal authority. Sitting next to her was Zhao, whose dad was an engineer and mother a housewife. In China's communist heydays, "housewives" had virtually ceased to exist as a category, with women almost always holding jobs out of the home. But they were making a comeback in the context of the country's expanding nouveau riche.

"Also, I don't like the breakfast here," added Zhao, continuing from where Lei left off. "All that ham," she muttered darkly. The Chinese usually ate hot buns stuffed with pork or a bowl of congee (a rice porridge) in the morning. Bread, cold ham and butter did not seem to be going down too well. "But," Zhao continued, "it's a lot more peaceful out here than in China. Quiet."

I thought about where the kids were coming from. Chongqing, a municipality in China's southwest, was one of the largest urban agglomerations in the world. It was home to 32 million people, four times the size of Austria's 8 million-strong population.

What I remembered most from my visit to the city a few years ago was the ceaseless aural assault. The churning of cement mixers, the sizzle of spicy noodles at roadside stalls, the spluttering of exhaust pipes and the heavy thud of wrecking balls: everywhere the sounds of trade and movement, of the old giving way to the new.

"You mean it's a lot more boring out here," giggled Lei, and Zhao grinned back in agreement. The Austrian countryside boring compared to Chongqing? It was tough to disagree.

Later, I sat between the two children on the way down the ski slope. Guide Ge and two other girls were opposite us. The girls flirted with the guide, teasing him about his messy hair. Guide Ge was indulgent, enjoying the attention, until he suddenly burped loudly. The girls burst into peals of laughter.

Ge decided to turn the embarrassment into a teaching opportunity. "In Europe, you must cover your mouth and say sorry when you burp," he said solemnly. "Shouldn't you do that in China too?" shot back one of the girls.

It is still common in China for groups of tourists visiting abroad to be handed out instructions on how to behave, including injunctions not to spit, litter, or burp at meals. But these kids were of a different generation.

Guide Ge's already cold-reddened cheeks flamed a deeper color. "You must pronounce the 'r' in sorry clearly," he said, doggedly pedagogic. "Try practicing 'rrrrr. Sorrrry.'"

"Rrrrrr. Sorrrrrry," the girls growled in unison all the way down.

Back on the bus it was DVD time. An animated video provided all kinds of useful information such as the Austrian passion for apple strudel, ice skating and coffee shops. "Austrians love to spend time in coffee shops eating cake," ran the commentary.

Afterward, Teacher Zhang led the group in a pop quiz. "Name three famous Austrian people," she demanded. "Swarovski," chanted the bulk of the students in reply. "Very good. Any more?" There was a long silence. "Anyone at all?"

"Beethoven?" replied the rotund schnitzel-averse lad. "He's German," corrected Teacher Zhang. "Haven't you all heard of Haydn or Schubert?" But no one bothered answering her. They were all agog, staring out of the window at a giant statue of Daniel Swarovski. We had arrived in Wattens, another essential stop on any Chinese tour of Europe, headquarters of the Swarovski crystal empire.

We had ostensibly come here for educational purposes, to take a look at the Crystal Worlds museum, an exhibition center for Swarovski-crystal-inspired art installations. But the kids zipped through the museum in 15 minutes flat until they broke upon the vast shop at the end. This was where the serious business for the day began.

China's per capita GDP might still have been a fraction of that of the EU average,[7] but these were the mainland's children of privilege, and their behavior and opinions were evocative reflections of the shifting scales of global power. What I found particularly interesting was how the professions of many of their parents—including policemen, municipal government officials, army officers and investment department bureaucrats—were not ones usually synonymous with wealth, certainly not in Europe.

But then, despite decades of economic reform, China's state-led capitalism has created a murky world of entrenched corruption, where the line between government officials and entrepreneurs is distorted. Even as I accompanied the children on their tour of Europe, Chongqing, their hometown, was in the news, with allegations emerging of egregious abuse of power on the part of the city's Communist Party chief, Bo Xi Lai. Over the next few months, Bo, once a rising star of Chinese politics, was abruptly dismissed from his post and later expelled from the party, his wife convicted of murdering English businessman Neil Heywood, and his right-hand man, police chief Wang Lijun, sentenced to fifteen years in prison for abuse of power and bribe-taking.[8]

As China headed into its once-in-a-decade leadership transition at the end of 2012, a slender spotlight on the usually opaque private lives of the country's powerful officials was revealing some information about the nexus between politics and business.[9] The children I was following were not all the sons and daughters of high-ranking officials, but their behavior hinted at the wealth that even those lower down the pecking order could amass, using their power to dispense patronage and lubricate business deals.

Back at the Swarovski shop, the credit cards came flashing out. Calls were placed on mobile phones. A quick check with their parents back home and the kids began snapping up Swarovski like candy. Eleven-year-old Chen picked out a crystal-encrusted watch that cost a cool 2,800 euros. "It's for my auntie," she said.

The shop staff insisted on speaking to her parents before making the sale. They got her father on the phone, and he gave them the green light. Chen's dad worked in the Chongqing public security bureau. He was a cop. Her mother was a manager in a state-owned enterprise. Over the course of the next hour, Chen blew a total of 4,200 euros on gifts for her family.

Chen and the other kids were assisted in their shopping by a battalion of Chinese sales staff. The shop employed six Chinese salespersons, half the total number of the shop floor staff. Jackie, a sales assistant originally from mainland China, had worked in the shop for ten years. "It used to be Taiwanese and Hong Kongers, but now it's busload after busload of mainlanders," she said, before scurrying off after a ten-year-old demanding to see every model of crystal bunny available.

At the cash counter, a blonde Tyrolean beauty called Terese dealt with the long queues of Chinese kids. "*Mima* [pin code]," she instructed one child who was swiping a card in the reader. "*Men piao gei wo* [Give me your entry ticket]," she told another.

"I've had to learn a few sentences in Chinese," she said. "Although some of these kids can speak some English." Terese smiled fondly at the boy in front of her and asked, "Do you speak English?"

"How much?" he replied in English, revealing the perfection of his transactional vocabulary.

The boy was called Yao, and he was a naughty one, always playing pranks on the other kids. His father was another public security bureau official. His mother worked in the municipal department in charge of attracting foreign investment to Chongqing. "What have you bought?" I asked. He held up a crystal dog. "You know what I like about this?" he grinned. "The fact that it's not 'Made in China!'"

The orgy of shopping went on for some two hours. I sat in the middle of the store and chatted with a few of the kids who were done with their buying. Yuan, a girl whose mother owned a store that sold the somewhat unlikely combination of Maotai (an expensive brand of Chinese liquor) and pizza was less than impressed with what she'd experienced of Europe thus far.

"It's OK, but I must say I prefer Chongqing. The food is so much better there." What about the pollution, I asked her, thinking back to the perennial throat-scratching haze I recalled the city draped in. "It's not so bad," Yuan said. "Our roads are clean. It's just that China is so much more *re nao*." "Re nao" literally translates as "hot and noisy," but with a positive connotation of excitement.

That night at dinner the conversation at my table was all about money. "Do you know how much cash her father gave her for this trip?" grinned Fan, a plump, jolly-looking 11-year-old pointing at her friend, Xue. "Stop it, stop it," gasped Xue as she tried to put a hand over Fan's mouth to prevent her from speaking, but Fan shrugged her off. "Four thousand euro! Can you believe it?"

"How much did your dad give you?" I asked. "Me? Two thousand," she replied happily. Not for the first time I was amazed by how comfortable the kids were talking about money. Ask them a question about politics, even something as innocent as whether their parents were party members, and they immediately became stiff and uncomfortable. But ask them about money and they answered with ease.

Not the third girl at our table, though. Fan's outburst had caused Zeng's lips to press so close together that they'd almost disappeared. "How much did your dad give you?" demanded Fan of her. "I'd rather not say," she replied primly. "What does he do?" I intervened. She appeared reluctant to answer even this. But she finally revealed that he was the head of a major local bank. Fan let out a whoop of appreciation. "You must be really rolling in it!" she laughed.

"So, girls, how've you been enjoying Europe?" I asked to help alleviate Zeng's obvious discomfiture. It was Zeng who replied first. "The hotel rooms are rather small here. But still I think it's better than America because it has so much more history and they've protected their environment well."

Zeng was obviously a member of the little *lingdao* group that Rudolf had told me about. I asked Zeng what she thought of China's own efforts at environmental protection. "Not so good at the moment because we have too many people. But we also have the one-child policy, so I think it will only get better and better," she answered pat.

"Well, I think the one-child policy is terrible," interjected Fan. "My mother went to Hong Kong to have a second baby, so I have a younger brother." "I have a younger sister too," Xue chimed in.

"Shhhhh, be quiet," Zeng hissed at them, a finger on her lips. "Didn't your parents have to pay a fine for breaking the one-child policy?" I asked. "I'm not sure," shrugged Xue. "Not mine, because my brother was born in Hong Kong," explained Fan. By this time, Zeng had given up trying to shush them. "Well, there's only one child in my family," she said firmly.

The next day we were off to Salzburg, and after a quick march through the gardens of the Schloss Mirabell, it was time for more shopping in the city's pedestrianized center.

The group met up later at a Chinese restaurant for lunch. I sat at naughty Yao's table, with three other video-game-playing boys. They were passing on the buffet lunch in favor of the McDonalds burgers one of them had bought from down the road. They passed on the hot tea as well. "I don't like hot water," explained Yao. "I prefer cold drinks like Coke." My association of the Chinese with tea was so strong that I found myself quite shocked by Chen's attitude. But then, these kids were born in 2000, I reminded myself not for the first, or last, time.

In the afternoon we paid a quick visit to the Salzburg Toy Museum. There were some displays of old-fashioned Austrian toys, teddies and dollhouses from the nineteenth century. But the museum's pride was a special traveling exhibition of toys from China. The kids took this ubiquity of China—Chinese-speaking assistants in shops, China-related exhibitions in museums—in their stride. It only seemed to confirm their sense of China's superiority. Once again, it made me recall how these were children born at a time when China's ascent to superpower-dom was pretty much taken for granted, an assumption that would have been laughable for the generation before.

In the late afternoon, we attended a specially organized concert by a local string quartet that played bits of Mozart and Haydn. Much emphasis was placed on teaching the kids not to clap between movements. Given that half of them fell asleep during the concert, clapping was not that much of an issue. Teacher Zhang took advantage of one of the lulls in the music to yell at the sleepers for their rudeness. "This is Europe," she said severely. "This kind of behavior will not do here."

The chastened slumberers made an effort to keep awake for the rest of the performance, but sometimes they clapped in the wrong places and drew a dirty look from Teacher Zhang.

The next morning we were back on the bus, heading for Munich. A new DVD was playing. "Germans love potatoes most of all," we were told. "They eat boiled potatoes and roast potatoes and mashed potatoes and potato salad." And just in case the point hadn't been driven home yet: "The Chinese like rice, but the Germans like potatoes."

The German predilection for sausages was also touched upon before the commentary moved on to non-culinary Germanic enthusiasms, such as the displaying of garden gnomes.

Later, when Teacher Zhang conducted the pop quiz, the one question all the kids got correct involved matching the logo of various car companies to their names. BMW, Audi, Mercedes, Volkswagen—the children knew them all.

The quiz ended with a trick question. "Which is bigger," asked Teacher Zhang, "Germany or Chongqing?" The kids took a while to think about this, but most plumped for Chongqing in the end.

The children were scheduled to spend the morning at the Deutsches Museum in Munich, but I said good-bye beforehand. "Bye, bye, Auntie Journalist, come and see us in Chongqing soon," they chanted as I took my leave.

On the train journey back home, I felt peckish and headed to the restaurant car. It didn't take me long to decide what to order. What else, but a plate of potatoes and sausages?

AS I DUG IN, I thought about the backdrop to the kids' visit. In the months leading up to it, China had been splashed across the pages of the region's news media. It was the one country that appeared to be on the mind of every European country's leadership from careworn Greece and anxious Spain, to stern Germany and muddled France.

It wasn't Chinese spending on luxury goods in Europe that was exercising their minds, although Chinese money was at the core of this preoccupation. Europe, after all, was in desperate need of cash, and the Chinese were sitting on a foreign exchange reserve mountain that was over $3 trillion high.

In late October 2011, a high-profile eurozone summit in Brussels ended with a decision to boost the bailout fund, the European Financial Stability Facility, to about a trillion euros by leveraging existing guarantees. The ink wasn't dry on the agreement before then French president Nicolas Sarkozy was on the phone to China's Hu Jintao to ask for China's help in investing in a new special investment vehicle. A day later, the chief executive of the bailout fund, Klaus Regling, was on a flight to China, cap in hand.

It was an astounding turnaround. The days when Europeans went to China in gunboats, extracting concessions and dictating terms, may have been long gone, but during my years in Beijing it was still pretty standard for European leaders to lecture their Chinese counterparts on "proper" economic management and political reform. In the space of two or three years, with China being projected by some as the lender of last resort to Europe, the scales of power had shifted with a thump.

Speculation that China might be the only country with pockets that were deep enough to ultimately pull Europe out of the financial quagmire it was sinking into had become commonplace. A surfeit of (mostly implausible) ideas was floating around the mediasphere. One involved the creation of an EU-China bond that, unlike an EU-only bond, would rope cash-rich Beijing into the deal by offering a better interest rate than it was getting on, say, the US treasury bonds. Others, including journalist Fareed Zakaria, suggested bribing China to help out by offering Beijing a bigger role in the international financial system such as pledging that a Chinese candidate becomes the next head of the IMF.[10]

The sense of superiority evident among the children from Chongqing as they zipped around Europe was therefore not just the result of childlike self-centeredness. It was underpinned by a more profound change in the center of gravity of global power.

One of the most often misquoted Chinese adages involved the assertion that the character for crisis and opportunity were the same, or in another variant, that the character for crisis comprised those for danger and opportunity. Neither was true.[11] Nonetheless, Beijing appeared to have embraced the idea. It had been playing the eurozone crisis like a particularly tuneful erhu, dangling potential lifelines at Europe's peripheral nations and creating the impression of crucial support for the euro, without committing to any concrete numbers.[12]

As matters came to a head in the first half of 2010, with Greece within a hair's breadth of defaulting on its capacious debt, the divisions that were to plague the European Union for the next few years began to harden. It took months of wrangling before a recalcitrant Germany agreed to the first bailout package for Athens.

But in June of that year, only hours after the credit agency Moody's had downgraded Greece's credit rating to junk, it was China that held out a financial carrot to the floundering authorities in Greece, in the form of a multibillion-euro investment package. While signing the deal, Chinese Vice Premier Zhang Dejiang gave the eurozone's weakest link a public vote of confidence, declaring Beijing's belief in Athens's ability to overcome its fiscal problems, an announcement that moved markets positively following weeks of turmoil.

Under the agreement, the Chinese company Cosco undertook the construction of up to 15 dry bulk carriers in Greece. It had already taken over the cargo management at Piraeus, the eastern Mediterranean's premier dockyard, on a 35-year concession worth $1 billion the year before, despite vocal opposition from trade unions. Other than shipping, tourism and telecommunications were the main sectors included in the deal.

At the time, Greek Deputy Prime Minister Theodoros Pangalos praised China in an interview to the *Daily Telegraph* newspaper, echoing sentiments often expressed by African nations indebted to Beijing. "They are not like these Wall Street people pushing financial investments on paper. The Chinese deal in real things, in merchandise. And they will help the real economy in Greece," he said.[13]

A month later, as fears of the Greek contagion spreading to Spain gathered momentum, the Chinese once again stepped in, buying 400 million euros worth of Spanish bonds, a move that helped prop up investor confidence so that a subsequent Spanish bond auction was actually oversubscribed. Over the next couple of years, Chinese leaders appeared to be on a continuous conveyor-belt-like tour of troubled European capitals, magnanimously promising unspecified "support" to the euro and asserting their trust in the leadership of Europe to sort out the mess.

The benefitting countries lapped up this Chinese munificence with what at times appeared to be slobbering gratefulness. When Chinese Vice Premier Li Keqiang visited Spain early in 2011, he was hailed by the local media as a modern-day "Marshall," a reference to the American secretary of state after whom the post-war reconstruction program in Europe was named.[14]

During Mr. Li's Spanish tour, Chinese companies announced plans to buy shares in European petrochemical ventures, and tens of thousands of cars with a few million euros' worth of Spanish wine and ham to top it off. But once again it was the vice premier's promise to keep buying (indeterminate numbers of) Spanish government bonds that grabbed the headlines.

Crucially, there was no way of verifying the hard figures behind Chinese bond purchases, since the composition of Beijing's foreign reserves is a state secret, while Europe publishes no aggregate data on foreign buying of debt and few member states reveal this information either.

Europe's troubles also allowed China the opportunity of investing directly in the region, snapping up cheap assets and even getting contracts for public infrastructure projects by offering low prices to governments struggling to rein in spending.

Aggregate Chinese investments in Europe remained small, but the crisis certainly helped speed them up. In 2006, China's total investment into Europe stood at 1.3 billion dollars. By contrast, in 2011 each one of a slew of acquisitions, including a Hungarian chemical company, BorsodChem, and a major Norwegian silicon unit, Elkem, exceeded that amount.[15]

That year, the Chinese invested $10 billion in Europe, triple the amount of a year earlier, according to a study by the economic consultancy Rhodium Group and the Chinese bank CICC.[16] A year earlier in 2010, Chinese carmaker Geely had taken over Ford's ailing Volvo unit for 1.8 billion dollars, making it the largest acquisition of an overseas carmaker by a Chinese company.

China's Europe-crisis strategy was thus a two-pronged affair. On the one hand, Beijing made gestures of goodwill that cost it little, like public pronouncements of support, while on the other, private and state-owned Chinese companies used Europe's straitened circumstances to secure commercially interesting deals and access to technological know-how.

The latter was usually built into the deals struck by Chinese corporations. For example, the Greek package announced in June 2010 included an exchange of know-how between China's Huawei Technologies and the Greek telecom's organization OTE.

Crucially, it was not only debt-laden southern European countries that found themselves in Beijing's thrall. Even European powerhouse Germany's relative economic buoyancy owed much to its exports to China. For example, the country's recovery from the 2008 crisis was due in substantial part to its exports of cars and advanced machinery to China.[17]

It was increasingly evident that Berlin and Beijing had developed a distinctive relationship, decoupled from broader EU-China ties. In some ways, Germany had emerged as the China of Europe: an export-oriented, manufacturing heavyweight accused of undervaluing its currency and creating economic imbalances by enjoying a trade surplus at the "expense" of the deficits of its neighbors.

In China, the admiration most people seemed to feel for Germany was often untinged by the negative connotations that the Third Reich had left in the minds of many around the world. I remember cringing when a German friend, who worked as the China correspondent for a leading British newspaper, told me about how, on ascertaining his nationality, a Beijing taxi driver had flashed him a thumbs up sign while approvingly asserting, "Germany. Good country! Hitler. Strong leader!"

Hitler adulation is not a common phenomenon in China, but the parallels between Germany and the Chinese mainland are numerous. Engineers and scientists are venerated in both nations. German Chancellor Angela Merkel's educational background is in physics, while President Hu Jintao had trained as a hydraulic engineer. Germany and China both practice variants of state capitalism.[18] And it is Germany that China looked to for models when developing many of its current legal standards, patent protection being one example. It is as if China wants to be Germany when it grows up.

Nearly half of all EU exports to China originate in Germany, while close to a quarter of all EU imports from China are destined for Germany.[19] Germany is China's number one trade partner in the European Union and China the top foreign investment destination for German companies.

Trade between the two grew by 400 percent in the first decade of the new century, and Germany sold billions of euros' worth of technology to China every year.[20] More than 7,500 German enterprises were operational in China. German engineering heavyweight Siemens alone had some 80 companies and entities with more than 40,000 workers located in China, 98 percent of whom were Chinese nationals.[21]

When Chinese Premier Wen Jiabao visited Germany in April 2012 at the height of the eurozone's troubles, it was his sixth visit in eight years. The same year, German Chancellor Angela Merkel visited Beijing twice, even as she failed to visit the epicenter of the region's fiscal woes, Athens.[22]

In the meantime, the European Council on Foreign Relations, a think tank, published a report titled "China and Germany: A New Special Relationship?"[23] The authors answered the question in the affirmative. The two countries were for the moment in a perfectly symbiotic relationship, with China providing the market that Germany needed, while Germany supplied the technology that China was still lacking. Moreover, Chinese companies bought German equipment to produce the very goods that were then sold back to Germany. It all seemed virtuously circular. But for how long?

When I had visited Germany to meet with the mittelstand, China had been an inescapable presence. In Cologne, the talk was all about Sany, the Hunanese heavy machinery-manufacturing giant, which had set up its European headquarters there.

In an inversion of the usual pattern of German companies moving manufacturing operations to China to take advantage of lower labor costs, Sany was busy building a massive manufacturing facility close to Dusseldorf. But the real shock waves had been created earlier in the year with Sany's acquisition of a top-tier mittelstand: concrete pump manufacturer Putzmeister. The move gave Sany access to the kind of world-beating technology that had kept Germany's nose well ahead of China's in the high-value-added, technologically sophisticated sectors.

The deal was described by some German media as *Götterdäm-merung*, a term that meant the twilight of the gods, signaling a violent downfall of the system.[24] Excited journalese aside, it was clear that the Chinese had come a long way from the days when they were mocked for buying nearly bankrupt no-hopers, like hi-fi maker Schneider or regional jet maker Fairchild Dornier.

Putzmeister was a hidden champion, part of the economic backbone of Germany. It had long been the global market leader in its sector. But the 2008 crisis had proved a tough hurdle to cross for the venerable German pump maker, with sales plunging from a billion euros to 440 million euros.[25] In contrast, Sany's fortunes, like China's, were on the up. Flush with cash, the Hunanese heavyweight closed the deal with Putzmeister in early 2012, at 525 million euros.

A few months later, Sany was in the news again. This time, for acquiring Intermix GmbH, a German truck mixer maker, the third-largest manufacturer of truck mixers in the world.[26]

By 2011, China had in fact become the biggest foreign investor in Germany, with 158 greenfield investment projects, ahead of the United States with 110 and Switzerland with 91.[27] In 2012, Sany's potentially game-changing acquisition was accompanied by a raft of other Chinese takeovers, including Xuzhou Construction Machinery group's purchase of a majority stake in another German concrete pump maker, Schwing.

The world of concrete pumps may sound unexciting, but it could be a powerful symbol of the new Chinese hand in Europe. Schwing's pumps were being used to build the new European Central Bank tower in Frankfurt, for example. The ECB's new home would now be built using Chinese equipment.

Other Chinese investments in Germany that year included Hebei Lingyun's acquisition of German car-parts maker Kiekert and LDK Solar's buyout of German solar group Sunways. Acquisitions like these gave Chinese companies access to a number of high-end markets in Europe, in addition to technology and a skilled work force.

China could no longer be dismissed as "merely" a low-end, low-cost manufacturing destination. Putzmeister, for instance, had lost its global leadership to Sany in recent years, which with its 70,000-strong labor force dwarfed the German mittelstand in scale.

Nonetheless, the people at the German firms I visited seemed almost breezily self-assured in the face of China's rise. Young Tim

Dolezych, the heir apparent to the eponymous Dortmund-based lifting and load-securing equipment company, Dolezych (mentioned in the previous chapter), admitted that his main competitor was China's Juli Sling. But he was confident of the company's China strategy, which involved setting up an "independent daughter company" in China, employing 130 workers. "We have our own Chinese competitor within our group," he laughed, adding that the Chinese were "proud to work for a German company."

Germany's confidence sprang from its anomalous economic strength at a time of generalized weakness across Europe. But the European Union as a whole was less complacent about China's expanding footprint in Europe. Think tanks and business lobbies serially produced reports and papers urging Brussels to take protective action against the Chinese "invasion." A report called "The Scramble for Europe" by the European Council on Foreign Relations made parallels between the European colonization of Africa in the nineteenth century and China's current activity in Europe.

"China is buying up Europe," it claimed, adding, "Crisis-hit Europe's need for short-term cash is allowing China not just to strike cut-price deals but to play off member states against each other . . . replicating a strategy it has already used in the developing world."[28]

In another paper by a Brussels lobby group, Business Europe, titled "Rising to the China Challenge," a gloomy scenario was painted of a China that was increasingly competing successfully against hapless European companies, both in Europe itself and in third country markets. It argued that by direct and indirect state subsidies, forced technology transfers, restrictions on raw material exports from China and threats of retaliatory measures, Beijing ensured an unfair advantage for Chinese companies.[29]

Both reports called on the European Union to put pressure on China to open up its services and public procurement markets to European firms, as well as to lift restrictions on export of rare earths and other raw materials. There was also an increasing clamor for instituting a system for vetting direct foreign investment in key sectors in Europe, targeted at the Chinese.

The EU commissioner for trade, Karel De Gucht, made periodic threatening noises aimed at Chinese investment throughout his tenure. At one point, he proposed a move to block Chinese companies from participating in Europe's public procurement market until Beijing lifted restrictions against European companies' access to the Chinese public procurement market.

He was joined by EU Industry Commissioner Antonio Tajani who in late 2010 openly warned against China's growing influence in strategic sectors of the European economy, stating that important European businesses should be protected from possible takeovers by Chinese firms. Tajani floated the idea of an agency, along the lines of the Committee on Foreign Investment in the United States, to examine whether "an acquisition by a private or public foreign company represents a danger or not."[30]

Anti-China sentiment was not restricted to eurocrats. It was widespread in Europe. I ran up against it almost every day. I would go to buy bathroom fittings, and if I expressed surprise at the high cost of a towel rack, I'd be stiffly told that this product was "not Made in China" after all.

During book talks centered on my China memoir, *Smoke and Mirrors,* regardless of whether I spoke of how dynamic China's economy was, the commendable work ethic of Chinese people, or the surprisingly pragmatic policy-making of the Chinese Communist Party, the question-and-answer sessions would involve aggressive old ladies asking how "the Chinese" could countenance kidnapping children and selling them into slavery, or why Chinese immigrants insisted on living in ghettos in Europe instead of embracing the local culture.

The latter question always put me in mind of European expat ghettos in Chinese cities where ladies-who-lunch sipped their Starbucks lattes before picking up their kids from American international schools and rarely spoke even basic Mandarin. The reluctance to embrace local culture was certainly not a Chinese-specific phenomenon, yet Europeans always seemed to pick out China as abnormal.

I am not an apologist for the Chinese Communist Party. Years of working in the country as a journalist had left me depressed with the censorship and thought-indoctrination that was part and parcel of the contemporary Chinese state. The country faced large-scale corruption and grave environmental destruction. But there was also cause for optimism as millions of people were lifted out of poverty and were living better lives than ever before. From an Indian perspective, China's strides in basic education and primary health care were commendable. China's reality was as messy and contradictory as "truth" tends to be.

But popular opinion is often more black and white than truth, and the general view of China from Europe was black. The Chinese were not beloved. But unfortunately for the Europeans, the Chinese had the cash, and money is well liked, even if those that have it are not.

The locals might carp, but given that investors from China were increasingly the messiahs of distressed European assets, they were also increasingly able to reshape trends in taste and business.

EVEN THE HALLOWED French landscape of wine-growing Bordeaux was not immune. Names like Zhang and Li had begun cropping up among the list of the region's wine barons. Rocketing figures for wine consumption in the Chinese mainland, combined with the reputation enjoyed by Bordeaux wines, had made owning a French vineyard, or two, an increasingly attractive proposition for some Chinese with cash to spare.

China is not a traditional wine-drinking nation. Still, in 2011 it surpassed the United Kingdom to become the fifth-largest consumer of wine by volume, according to the International Wine and Spirits Research group. The mainland's wine market had experienced more than 20 percent growth every year since 2006, and by 2012, around 20 percent of Bordeaux's exports were destined for China.[31]

Purchases by the Chinese in Bordeaux began in 2008, when a trading company from Qingdao city bought Chateau Latour Laguens, a 30-hectare vineyard. By 2011, more prestigious estates like Chateau Laulan Ducos, classified as a Cru Bourgeois, began passing into Chinese hands. Another significant acquisition in 2011 was the 10-million-euro deal whereby COFCO, a state-owned oil and food giant, became the owner of Chateau Castel Viaud.

During the Bordeaux *en primeur* tastings in 2011, when thousands of wine professionals from across the world traveled to the region to assess the year's offerings, the estates offered vintage reports in three languages—French, English and Chinese.[32] Bordeaux winemakers also recently published a recipe book pairing wines with Chinese dishes, suggesting, for example, a Saint-Emilion for pig's feet.

On one typically chilly Brussels summer morning in June 2012, I boarded a train from the Gare du Midi bound for Bordeaux. I was dashing off to meet Zhang Jin Shan, the new owner of Chateau du Grand Mouëys, a middle-sized estate in the picturesque Entre-Deux-Mers area.

The meeting had not been easy to organize, given that Zhang lived in northern China's Ningxia province and was only occasionally in Europe. I'd been in touch with Aline Moineau, the chateau's long-standing manager, to arrange the interview, and much time was lost as she tried to pass messages between me and Zhang through his French interpreter back in China.

A month of persisting had yielded a two-hour slot with the Chinese entrepreneur on one of his lightning-quick trips to his new French chateau. As the train neared Bordeaux, I sent Aline a text message alerting her of my imminent arrival.

"Don't worry," she texted back cheerily. "There will be someone waiting at the train station with a big shit with your name on it."

In the gaffe department, Franglish was pretty much head to head with Chinglish. In China, it had been quite common to visit public toilets where signs politely reminded users to "flush after finishing shitting and pissing." In Brussels, it was quite standard to show up for a meeting with someone only to have their secretary apologize that their boss "was retarded."[33]

At Bordeaux train station, the promised "big shit" of paper with my name on it materialized, and I was whisked off to the chateau. Grand Mouëys, a neo-Gothic pile of stone, was located along the banks of the river Garonne, surrounded by a 170-hectare expanse of vineyards and forest. Florid turrets flanked its crenellated walls, bringing to mind a medieval world of knights, damsels in distress and romance. But seated within the Grand Mouëys' genteelly dilapidated dining room, the estate's new owner did not cut a romantic figure.[34]

Zhang Jin Shan was dressed in an ill-fitting pinstriped suit, with rimless glasses framing his mottled face. His bravado attempt at a comb-over did little to disguise his balding pate. It was eight in the morning when we met, and the 49-year-old Chinese entrepreneur was chomping, somewhat forlornly, on a croissant.

I asked Zhang how he'd been enjoying the local French food. The lord of the chateau glanced at his croissant dispiritedly. "*Hai xing*," he replied with a shrug, using a phrase that in Chinese signifies only the faintest of approval. "I've got used to it," he continued, unenthusiastically.

Aline Moineau pursed her lips so tight that they almost disappeared. But Zhang didn't appear to notice. He'd perked up talking about his plans for a "luxurious" 50-seat Chinese restaurant; the intended pièce de résistance of the high-end hotel and spa into which Zhang meant to convert the chateau.

The food will be upscale Chinese, not the kind of sweet-and-sour gloop served up by the average takeout joint in Europe. "You know what I mean," he said. And I did, instantly conjuring up a feast of bullfrog's ovaries and shark fin soup set out under enormous chandeliers and a ceiling slashed with red and gold.

I asked why he'd want to open a Chinese restaurant in a French chateau. Wouldn't a French restaurant make more sense? "No," he replied emphatically. "In France there are many French restaurants, but very few Chinese ones. The guests in my hotel will mostly be Chinese, and the fact that they can find good food here will be attractive for them."

"But perhaps they would want to try French food," interjected Aline primly. "Please let Mr. Zhang talk with the journalist first and ask your questions later," snapped Sophie, the young Chinese woman who served as Zhang's French interpreter.

There was an obvious clash of cultures on display here. And one that fed into larger resentments against Chinese investments in Europe, even as these were actively being courted.

Thanks to the explosion of Chinese wine consumption, the price of Bordeaux wines had risen in recent years, even though wine consumption in France itself (where 50–60 percent of the region's wines are sold) had been falling. Chinese consumers of wine had played an important part in ensuring Bordeaux continued to flourish despite the economic slowdown in Europe and aggressive competition from new world wines.[35]

When Zhang bought Chateau du Grand Mouëys, it had been languishing on the market for over five years. Its then owners, the aristocratic German Bomer family, had been hard pressed to find takers for the chateau's 12 million euro price tag. Although the final price that Zhang bought the estate for is not public, he is believed to have paid a fair price.

Later in the afternoon, I met Karine Lemaitre, Chateau du Grand Mouëys's enologist, in charge of all wine production. She was excited about the possibilities opened up by Zhang's investment in the vineyard. "With a big capital injection, we can really try to push up the quality of the wine produced here," she said.

But although she was eager to experiment and happy with the opportunity, she remained wary of the challenges presented by a Chinese boss. Being unable to communicate directly with Zhang was the biggest difficulty, she said. Something was always lost in translation, and decisions were taken too late.

Aline joined in the grousing. Much of the discussion centered around Sophie, the young Chinese woman who had acted as translator during my interview with Zhang. Sophie was the first Chinese staff hired to work at the estate full-time. She was to be the estate's accountant and had taken up residence a few days prior to my visit.

"But she [Sophie] misunderstands basic numbers in French. If you say 10,000 she thinks it's a million. This is very dangerous in an accountant," said Aline, her eyes round with censure. I asked if they had brought this rather critical lacuna to Mr. Zhang's attention.

Aline and Karine exchanged solemn looks. After a pause, Aline revealed that they had tried to say something, but the genial Zhang had turned ferocious at the first hint of criticism and asked them to "stop complaining." That Sophie was the only person through whom the French staff could communicate with Zhang couldn't have made matters any easier.

I could also well imagine that Zhang was a lot more aggressive than his mild appearance suggested. He may have been a newcomer to the world of French wines, but he was not a beverage virgin. As head of the Ningxiahong group, he was in fact China's emperor of goji berry drinks. Goji, a small, red berry, is believed to have medicinal properties by many Chinese, and Ningxiahong produces every year 30 million bottles of *gouqi,* a berry alcohol that it sells in its 300,000 sales outlets countrywide.

What Zhang lacked was any pretensions to sophistication. His Mandarin was earthy, his mannerisms rustic. The only French he could muster up was a barely recognizable "Oui!" As with many Chinese entrepreneurs of his generation, he was a self-made man with a checkered past.

Born in 1963, a few years before the start of the Cultural Revolution, Zhang grew up in the hardscrabble of an obscure town in one of China's poorest provinces, Ningxia. His mother was a peasant working the fields, while his father had a small-time job in the local railways.

Zhang never made it to university, but a technical diploma landed him an accounting job with a state-owned enterprise in 1983. By 1996, he had somehow made the leap to running a *baijiu* (a popular Chinese spirit) factory, and in 2000 he bought Ningxiahong, then a struggling factory, and transformed it into the successful, diversified business it is today. Other than goji-berry-related products, the company's activities currently also include real estate, printing, catering and a travel agency.

Zhang did not want to dwell on the past. During our interview, it was the future he was all fired up about. He was dismissive about the wine produced at Chateau du Grand Mouëys in its current avatar and oblivious to any hurt French feelings his curt assessment might engender, despite Aline's presence in the room. "It's no good," he said, of the wine. The taste, he claimed, was *mama huhu,* mediocre. Everything must change, including the packaging, he continued, because it was of "low quality."

"It's not a question of low quality, but a difference in tastes between China and Europe," Aline interrupted. "No!" Zhang retorted sharply, showing some claws for the first time. "It's got nothing to do with cultural differences in taste. The quality is bad." He looked pointedly away from Aline. Argument over.

That afternoon, Karine and Aline revealed that Zhang had plans to bottle the estate's wine in heavy glass, embossed with gold lettering and stoppered with a red cork, in keeping with Chinese aesthetic preferences. "All of them try and do this," Karin said, referring to the other Chinese investors in the region. "There is some kind of bandwagon effect. Everyone wants a certain kind of packaging and has the same plans. Sell all the wine produced here back in China and set up a hotel on the estate."

Karine told me of another small estate, Grand Branet, just two kilometers from Grand Mouëys, with the exact same business plan as Zhang's. "It's crazy," sighed Aline. "Two chateaux in the same village, in the middle of nowhere, planning to set up big hotels for Chinese tourists. Will it work?"

I made vague sympathetic noises while trying to look non-committal. "I am not thinking so," she replied to her own query.

What I was in fact thinking was: *two* Chinese-owned vineyards in the same small village. Was talk of a Chinese takeover of the area not as exaggerated as I had assumed?

What I discovered was that the Chinese acquisitions of French vineyards had thus far all been of small or middling estates. The mighty Grand Cru, the most prestigious and expensive of wine classifications, had eluded investors from the Chinese mainland. And to put the investments in perspective, only an estimated 20 estates out of around 9,000 in Bordeaux were in Chinese hands by mid-2012.

Nonetheless, Zhang had big dreams and said he would work toward acquiring a Grand Cru estate, "like Chateau Lafite," within the next ten years. It was a challenging ambition. But who was I to say that to someone like him. "When I was a child in Ningxia, I couldn't even dream of going to a city like Beijing," he chuckled. "And now here I am."

He waved his hand at the chateau's imposing interiors. "All this," he beamed, "it makes me feel like a prince. It's good."

But what may have been good for Zhang was not necessarily good for everyone. One effect of Chinese investments in the region was the potential destabilization of the centuries-old *négociants* system, upon which the Bordeaux wine trade had flourished for so long. Under the system, a group of merchants, or *négociants,* parceled up the majority of chateaux production between them and controlled the distribution of the wine globally, ensuring controlled supply as well as price stability.

Consequently, the region's thousands of chateaux depended on a few hundred merchants to actually sell their wine and lacked direct relations with customers. Given that many chateaux did not have the resources or in-house expertise to build their own sales channels, the *négociants* served a useful role, and the system has been fairly successful in achieving harmonious relations between its parts.

Enter the Chinese upstarts. Chinese vineyard owners tend to exclusively sell all the wine of their estates to China. Moreover, they rarely go via *négociants,* relying on their own distribution systems back home instead.

It was unsurprising that there was talk in Bordeaux about the market getting overly dependent on a single country: China. Giving the *négociants,* for long powerful purveyors of the trade, short shrift was bound to ruffle complacent feathers.[36]

In a telephone interview, Alain Sichel, the president of the Union de Maisons de Bordeaux, an association of *négociants,* pooh-poohed the notion that the Chinese represented any kind of threat. Only 75 percent of Bordeaux wine was in fact traded through *négociants,* he said. "We do not have an exclusive right over wine produced here." The Chinese investors in the area were looking to sell wines to their contacts and friends in China and wanted total control of the process. "It's understandable," he continued quite reasonably.

But suddenly his tone turned a tad threatening. "It will, however, never happen to a Grand Cru." The statement had the ring of a Gypsy's curse. What did he mean, I asked. "The Grand Cru will never pass to the Chinese. The Grand Cru will never be sold exclusively in one market. So the Grand Cru will always need us," he intoned with semi-religious fervor.

And then he slipped back to the suave, almost languid, tenor he'd begun on. "In the end, we welcome the Chinese. China has been a fantastic outlet for our wine. There is room for everyone here."

Sichel may have downplayed any nervousness at the new, Asian face of the region's wine barons, but the fact was that the idea of hordes of loud-mouthed Chinese tourists tramping around the Bordeaux countryside, quaffing wine from red-and-gold-patterned bottles while scarfing down chicken feet à la mode at opulent Chinese restaurants was not a thought that warmed the cockles of the hearts of many locals.

CLEARLY, CHINA'S ENGAGEMENT with Europe is a complex matter, and it is this complexity that made a European response to China's growing clout difficult.

It was tough for European leaders to play hardball with their Chinese counterparts despite the clamor from business and human rights groups. Every year as the annual EU-China summit rolled around, the daily press conferences at the Berlaymont would reverberate with questions about what the European Union would be demanding from China.

Much was made of "reciprocity," a reference to the idea that Beijing should reciprocate the market openness purportedly demonstrated by Europe. The most concrete call was reciprocity in public procurement, since European companies were denied access to government procurement projects in China.

But the chilly truth was that the European Union was hardly in a position to "demand" anything of Beijing. Not only had the eurozone crisis exacerbated the region's divisions, allowing China to play member states against one another, but Brussels was playing a particularly weak hand given that the member states remained unable to agree on any carrot to offer Beijing as an incentive.

Reciprocity was a two-way lane. But in Brussels, it seemed to mean a one-way street of China giving European companies greater market access. Over the three summits I covered in Brussels, not even hesitant steps were taken toward meeting any of China's main concerns.

What Beijing wanted was for the European Union to offer it Market Economy Status (MES), a technicality that would make it harder for Brussels to initiate and win anti-dumping cases against Chinese firms at the WTO (World Trade Organization). Under the terms of its accession to the WTO in 2001, China will automatically be granted MES in 2016 in any case, making it an "easy" sop for Europe to grant—one from which they could potentially extract much mileage.

But the bloc's 27-member states remained deadlocked on any move. Similarly, China's demand that Europe lift the arms embargo placed against it in the aftermath of the Tiananmen Square killings of 1989 languished on the European Council debating table. Individual member states in bilateral meetings with the Chinese occasionally made statements indicating their openness to an end to the embargo, but no consensus was ever reached at an EU-wide level.

As an Indian, I had always been struck by how much of a cheerleader for the European Union China was. Unlike India, which consistently gave Brussels short shrift, Beijing had systematically wooed the European Union for years, motivated by the idea of having a single negotiating partner on issues like MES and the arms embargo.

Visits by EU potentates, such as European Commission President José Manuel Barroso and European Foreign Policy Chief Catherine Ashton, attracted much state-directed media attention in the Chinese mainland. By contrast, in India, the European Union's high and mighty visited in an obscurity that remained unimproved by the Lisbon Treaty and other EU efforts to improve its foreign policy profile.

India's embassy in Brussels, which tripled as New Delhi's mission to Belgium, Luxembourg and the European Union, was staffed by a handful of officers who spent much time complaining about being bored when they were not moaning about the European Union's inability to make decisions. There was a total of one Indian foreign correspondent based in Brussels: me. And I was there because of my husband's job, not because a newspaper had thought it necessary to post someone to report on the European Union.

From New Delhi's perspective, allocating precious diplomatic resources to an entity that lacked either the will or the way to address any of its major strategic concerns was a luxury it could not afford. From India's desire for a permanent seat on the Security Council of the United Nations, to support at the Nuclear Suppliers Group for the historic civilian nuclear energy deal New Delhi had struck with the United States, the European Union had repeatedly been unable to formulate a united stance.

The free trade agreement the two entities had been negotiating since 2007 was the only really substantive bilateral engagement. But political constraints at both ends had hampered progress. Moreover, the Indians complained that on the one issue of real interest to New Delhi—the facilitation of visas for Indian professionals in Europe—member states retained the final say, making the European Union a less-than-authoritative interlocutor.

India's somewhat lackadaisical attitude toward the European Union was oft bemoaned in Brussels. Eurocrats rarely lost a chance to berate me about it. They appeared to consider it a self-evident fact that countries should spend more time and effort in cultivating Brussels. But they didn't appear to consider the underlying question of why it would make sense to do so. Given the current contours of the European Union's competences, it was in fact more puzzling to come across a country, like China, which did extend itself Brussels-ward.

Beijing's mammoth embassy in the Belgian capital boasted over 100 officials, including seconded researchers from think tanks, universities and an array of ministries, all focusing on the further development of EU-China relations. A battery of Chinese journalists, including 35 reporters for the state-owned Chinese news agency Xinhua alone, covered the workings of the European Union in detail, religiously taking notes at every daily press conference.

In part, the discrepancy between the Indian and Chinese presence was explained by the substantial difference in their economic engagement with the European Union. Sino-EU trade in goods in 2011 was worth a whopping 428.7 billion euros, with China enjoying a surplus of 156-odd billion euros.

In contrast, EU-India economic ties were much less muscular, despite the European Union's being India's largest trading partner. At around 80 billion euros in 2011, EU-India trade was less than one-fifth that of Europe's trade with China.[37] European companies invested only 3 billion euros in India in 2011, compared to 17.7 billion euros in China that year.

The differential attitude toward the European Union was, however, not only the result of divergent economic ties. For years, Beijing had pinned its hopes on the European Union emerging as a strong, one-stop negotiating partner that could address its concerns swiftly and more effectively than the 27 disparate member states could. Moreover, the idea of Europe as a global power with the potential to balance the United States also had traction among some Chinese thinkers.[38]

The same European officials who castigated me about India's indifference were always quick to point to China as a contrasting model that New Delhi should follow when it came to investing in the European Union. But I always felt rather sorry for the Chinese. It seemed to me that they had got the short end of the stick. After all that lobbying and wooing that went on in Brussels, Beijing had very little to show for it in terms of having had any of its strategic priorities met.

If anything, the mood in Brussels was more anti-Chinese than ever before, with China regularly held up as the bogeyman the European Union needed to defend against. As the eurozone crisis deepened, Brussels seemed to feel the need to get more, not less, aggressive in its China policy. From 2010 on, a slew of proposals sought to challenge alleged subsidies to Chinese manufacturers—from telecommunications equipment makers to solar panel producers.

Small wonder then that the Chinese were becoming disenchanted with the European Union, an attitude that was reflected in the series of summits held in Brussels during the period I lived there. EU-China relations were clearly at a stalemate, with no give or take on the concerns of either side. Summit takeaways consisted chiefly of public relation announcements of cultural and youth exchanges.

Brussels's insiders revealed that Beijing was increasingly bypassing Brussels to deal directly with national capitals, often snubbing the European Commission and even ignoring requests for meetings.[39]

When my friend and EU-China expert Jonathan Holslag, a researcher at the Brussels Institute of Contemporary China Studies, returned from a field trip to Beijing in late 2011, he had a notebook full of quotable, but disparaging, quotes. He told me how during a series of meetings he held with officials in the Chinese capital, the great and the good of Europe were repeatedly mocked.

Then French president Nicolas Sarkozy was referred to as "a naked little emperor," the European Commission president José Manuel Barroso was described as being "as unconvincing as a rag vendor," while the European Unions's blustering trade chief, Karel de Gucht, was "a crying monkey that watches the river flow by."

There was a profound crisis of Europe as a role model, Jonathan said. And given the mess the eurozone had landed itself in, this was hardly unexpected. In an interview to Al Jazeera in late 2011, Jin Liqun, the supervising chairman of China's sovereign wealth fund, accused Europeans of sloth and indolence, pointing the finger at a "worn-out welfare society."[40]

CLEARLY, EUROPE'S PREDICAMENT and the manner of its handling had only served to confirm to China its own position on a range of issues, from the "risks" of democracy, the importance of stability and the limitations of the welfare state to an economic model that promotes saving over consumption.

"If a small country like Greece with an economy that only accounts for three per cent of the EU's economy can derail the whole union . . . it says a lot about the deficiency of the EU's political and economic integration," analyst Xia Wenhui said in a commentary in Xinhua, elaborating a common Chinese interpretation of the goings-on in Europe.[41]

The lack of control over events that Europe's leaders had displayed epitomized the kind of nightmare scenario that was the stated aim of the Chinese authorities to avoid at all costs.

China might have been a rising power but the country faced pressures and contradictions that made governing Europe feel about as onerous as choosing between waffles and cake for afternoon tea. Chinese leaders had to battle eye-watering inflation, catastrophic environmental degradation, a yawning rich-poor divide and major health epidemics every day. To them, the inability of Europe's authorities to make their school teachers retire at 62 or government employees forgo a thirteenth month's pay every year was proof, if it was ever required, of the dangers of walking down the Western-liberal path so often urged upon them.

The other outcome of European factional wrangling was Beijing's increased ability to exploit these divisions. Europe might have effectively employed the strategy of divide-and-rule during its colonial adventures of yore, but China was proving a dab hand at the twenty-first century version of the same game.

This oriental version of divide-and-rule had some notable successes. For instance, an investigation by the EU trade chief on China's dumping of solar panels in mid-2012 was undermined when the powerful German chancellor Angela Merkel came out in support of resolving the dispute through a negotiated settlement during a visit to Beijing.[42] Merkel's announcement caught Brussels entirely by surprise, given that it was German solar panel producers that had led the anti-dumping demands.

Analysts pointed out that her support for the Chinese position on the matter came barely a week after an announcement of large Chinese orders for German products.[43] Clearly, even from an individual country's perspective, China's growing influence was resulting in conflicted goals and outcomes. In Germany's case, Chinese imports of German products at a time when European demand was flagging served to boost the economy as a whole. But this had to be weighed against the interests of a specific sector, like that of solar panel makers—a sector that had strategic implications for Berlin, given its interest in the renewable energy industry as a source of jobs and growth.

Add the contradictions between national concerns and the interests of the European Union to the mix, and the stew only thickened. The tension between Brussels and national capitals, so evident in the unfolding of the eurozone crisis, clearly extended to other areas as well. The "rise" of China was a case in point, highlighting the inherent difficulties in balancing the trade and foreign policy needs of the sum and the parts of the European Union.

In the solar panel case, Karel de Gucht went ahead and launched the anti-dumping probe, barely a week after Merkel's comments.[44] But several other European Commission proposals targeted at China sank faster than one could say "ni hao," either because they lacked industry backing or because member states saw their economic interests best served by carrots rather than sticks.

For example, Brussels's proposition to challenge alleged subsidies to China's telecommunications equipment makers won no EU industry support, while its calls for EU-wide scrutiny of inward investments—with an obvious eye on China—went nowhere either.[45]

Europe's China-shaped challenge is formidable. On the one hand, China can help provide a much-needed raison d'être for a continuingly strengthened Europe. With the specter of war fading into historical oblivion and the appeal of the battle against climate change dimming amid the economic crisis, China has emerged as a rallying cry, a rousing bogeyman, a twenty-first century existential test for Europe. One that leaders credibly claim is best met united rather than divided.

But saber-rattling from the position of weakness that the euro crisis had engendered will do Europe no good either. Utilizing the China "threat" constructively to give the European Union purpose, but without descending into protectionism and alienating a powerful Beijing, is no easy task.

Europe needs to realize that the rules of the game have changed. China cannot be wished away, shut out by protective fences or beaten out by punitive hits. This is no longer a world in which EU-China relations equals Europeans lecturing China on its human rights violations. Europe's ability to dictate terms is sharply circumscribed, even if the eurocrats in Brussels have not yet come to grips with this changed reality. Ultimately, Europe needs to work with China as much as it needs to ensure that China does not play the bilateral agenda to its unilateral advantage.

What is called for is a united European China policy: smarter, sharper and more strategic than what has gone thus far. This is a tall order for a creature of European Union's nature—sprawling, shifting, process-focused, consensus-seeking at the best of times. And for Europe, these fiscally straitened days are possibly the most difficult times in recent history.

But the European Union needs to find it within itself to rise to the China challenge or suffer the ignominious consequences. This much is as clear as if there were a big "shit" with China's name emblazoned on it planted firmly atop the European Commission headquarters in Brussels.

What's more, China isn't the only "Asian" flavor that Europe is having to get used to. Gherkins from India are having some success in tickling European taste buds as well.

SEVEN

The Global Gherkin

AS THE ONLY JOURNALIST REPRESENTING AN INDIAN newspaper in Brussels, I spent many a day speeding between offices in the Indian embassy in Brussels and the various directorates at the European Commission. I soon began to feel I was developing a strange form of tinnitus—the same sentences echoed in my ear, with phrases like the inability to deliver "meaningful outcomes," and the failure to develop "clear negotiating mandates."

It struck me with some force how in many ways the Chinese were the Americans of Asia, while the Indians were the Europeans. As players on the international stage, the United States and China are both goal-oriented and able to act decisively in their national interest. Despite the existence of internal divisions, they are coherent entities that speak with a unified voice. Backed by hard power, their strategic planners take a long-term view of evolving rivalries and alliances.

In contrast, the Indians, like their European counterparts, are notable for the glacial pace of their decision making. Constrained by the workings of coalition politics, both the 27-member European Union and India valorize plurality and argumentation over actual outcomes and performance. They often appear unable to articulate a clear vision of their core interests, with internal factiousness hijacking unified, long-term agendas. Unlike the Unites States and ironically, "communist" China, the political mainstream in both Europe and India is Leftish and characterized by a distrust of unfettered markets.

Polyphonic (both boast over 20 official languages) and seemingly chaotic, the European Union and India are the world's two most populous democracies. The commonalities between them are underscored by the fact that their governments use an identical catchphrase to describe their union: "unity in diversity."

But despite the similarities, or perhaps because of them, neither India nor the European Union is particularly engaged with the other. Rather, the United States and China form the twin poles of their (once again) common strategic fixations. Ultimately, both India and the European Union are in essence soft powers, beguiled by and envious of the hard muscle shown by the Americans and the Chinese.

The relatively thin economic interlinkages between the two do not help either.

The European Union shares the world's biggest bilateral economic relationship with the United States. Transatlantic flows of trade and investment amount to around $1 billion a day and account for nearly a third of world trade. Total US investment in the European Union was three times higher than in all of Asia. And EU investment in the United States was around eight times the amount of EU investment in India and China put together.[1] But China's trading might was substantial, too. And it had emerged as Europe's primary source of imports.

In a 2011 report produced by the Center for Transatlantic Relations at John Hopkins University, which investigated the European Union's relationship with key parts of the non-European world, the chapter on India was titled "The EU and India: Surprisingly Weak Links."

India accounted for only 3 percent of EU goods exports and 2.1 percent of EU goods imports.[2] EU trade with China was six times greater than with India. The European Union's FDI into India was a mere 40 percent of the equivalent investment in China and less than 2 percent of its FDI in North America. And despite India's much-touted service industry, the country only accounted for 2 percent of the European Union's services exports and imports.[3]

This went a long way in explaining the sizable difference in the level of EU-India engagement compared to that of Europe's with China. European commissioners were in Beijing almost every month of the year. Since having taken over as trade chief, Karel de Gucht, for example, traveled to China five times in his first three years in office, more than double the two trips he made to India.

Almost every major think tank in Brussels had a slew of China experts. Remarkably, there was not a single India specialist to be found. The asymmetry in India and China's diplomatic and media presence in Brussels was mentioned in the previous chapter.

But even though at first glance the Indian presence in Europe was lightweight, scratch a bit deeper and another picture emerged. In Belgium alone, India was embedded in the unlikeliest of places. From the pickled gherkins in grocery stores to the largest offshore wind energy farm in the country; from the sandstone exterior of the new city museum in Antwerp to the algorithms of the IT systems of the country's largest banks and supermarkets; from the sizzle and steam of the old world industry of iron and steel that had once formed the backbone of the Belgian economy to the last-ditch hopes of salvation for venerable local brands like the crystal makers Val Saint Lambert, the invisible hand of the market in Belgium was often an Indian one.[4]

DAYS AFTER MEETING WITH Antwerp's Indian diamond merchants, I'd headed to the obscure Flemish town of Aalst on the outskirts of Brussels to report on a product that was distinctly less glamorous: the gherkin, a relative of the mundane kheera.

In the Indian business landscape, IT and pharma are the equivalents of what are known as charismatic megafauna in the world of wildlife conservation. They grab all the attention. But just as even the tiniest bugs can reveal novel secrets of the natural world, there are hosts of less "sexy" products fundamental to understanding the new global economic architecture and India's role in it.

My first encounter with one of these business world "bugs" had been a few years earlier in China, where I'd discovered that the most successful Indian company on the mainland was not one of the usual suspects like Tata or Reliance. It was, in fact, the laminated tube maker, Essel Propack.

Essel's tubes had revolutionized the cosmetics and pharmaceutical industries, almost single-handedly transforming the toothpaste tube market in China from one dominated by metallic, aluminum tubes to one where the plastic-laminated tube ruled as king. Following the company's entry into the mainland in the late 1990s, the majority of the domestic toothpaste industry switched to using laminated tubes, of which Essel supplied around a third, making it the most successful Indian manufacturer in China.[5]

In Aalst, another successful business bug awaited discovery. The town was best known for its three-day carnival celebrated around Lent and involving men dressed up in fishnet stockings, fur coats, and plastic breasts, as well as plenty of onion throwing.[6] But it was gherkins rather than onions that had taken me there. In particular, the millions of gherkins that traveled the long road from south India to Belgium every year.

From almost zero in the early 1990s, India today grows some hundreds of thousands of tons of gherkins annually and has emerged as one of the world's leading producers and suppliers of the vegetable. Pickled gherkins are consumed in large quantities in Europe and the United States as condiments, but in India they remain an alien food. In fact, gherkins grown and pickled in India are almost wholly exported, there being no domestic market for them.

For farmers, they have spelled a silent revolution. Tens of thousands of small-and medium-sized farms across Karnataka, Tamil Nadu and Andhra Pradesh have been converted to growing gherkins, a cash crop that has emerged as possibly the biggest success in India's agro-export story.

In Aalst I found myself face-to-face with millions of jars of pickled condiments, the contents of many of which were produced and packaged in India, lined up in a warehouse that belonged to Intergarden. This Aalst-based company had been bought in 2006 by the Indian food major Global Green.

Part of the Avantha Group, Global Green was the largest global supplier of gherkins outside the United States and the third-biggest gherkin processor in the world.[7] With seven processing facilities in India, Hungary, Belgium and Turkey, Global Green had emerged as a multinational to be reckoned with, its customer base extending to over 50 countries.

As a result, whenever a customer reached for a jar of pickled vegetables in a supermarket in Europe, be it Tesco in the United Kingdom or Carrefour in France, there was a fair chance that it would have been grown and bottled in India by Global Green or one of its local competitors.

Aalst was Global Green's European hub, and the warehouse I was visiting in this medieval town epitomized the truly global nature of the business. I walked past capers grown in Turkey, silver-skin onions produced in Holland, and sour cherries and sweet corn from Hungary, interspersed liberally with the Indian gherkins. From this nerve center, they then spread out all across Europe and to over 27 countries.

Still at the Aalst headquarters, I had a telephone chat with Vineet Chhabra, the managing director of Global Green at the time, who was speaking from his office in India. "We have shown that Indian farming can be competitive against western European and North American suppliers. Our growth has been such that we have displaced suppliers in these markets," he said.

The reasons for India's success? Chhabra believed that in the agro business, India's edge came from climate and surplus labor. While gherkins, for example, could only be harvested in Europe during the short summer season, in India, year-long harvesting was possible. Moreover, as a labor-intensive activity, gherkin production was far more cost-effective in India than in the labor-deficit West.

The echoes from the diamond cutting and polishing industry, a story I had reported just a month earlier, were loud.

Although Global Green comprised only 4 percent of the world-wide market for gherkins, it had grown by 53 percent over the last five years, and there was certainly room for expansion in the gherkin business.[8] But it was not gherkins where the serious money lay for the Avantha group, of which Global Green was a part.

Tracking the group's main business operations in Belgium took me only a few dozen kilometers away from Aalst to the city of Mechelen, once the center of the lucrative continental European cloth trade in the late Middle Ages. My taxi drove me to the outskirts of the city, where it pulled up outside a row of neat concrete buildings, surrounded by manicured lawns.

The name Pauwels was emblazoned on various edifices prominently, with a discreet CG added on occasion. As in Aalst, there was little to reveal the plant's Indian links, until I spotted a tricolor fluttering in the distance. We were waved inside by the Flemish guards. One of them folded his hands in a namaste, embellished with a quick wink.

I had arrived at the Belgian headquarters of Indian electrical engineering heavyweight Crompton and Greaves (also part of the Avantha

Group). I'd arranged to interview the company's managing director, S. M. Trehan, the man who had been credited with turning CG around from a primarily domestic, loss-making, debt-laden company into a profitable global player.[9]

Trehan was to have flown in from India that morning, but a flight delay meant he was running late. I passed the time browsing through the corporate literature strewn around the office.

It proved to be a lot more interesting than I had imagined electrical transformers could be. Among other trivia, I learned what the world's highest wind turbine and the Paris Metro had in common with millions of sweaty Delhi residents sheltering under ceiling fans. The answer, unsurprisingly given the circumstances, was Crompton Greaves (CG): an Indian company that had in a period of a few years become a transnational entity to be reckoned with.

Beginning with its 2005 acquisition of the power transformer maker Pauwels (where I was seated), CG had undertaken a seemingly inexorable march across Europe, buying up companies in the power systems sector in Hungary, Ireland and France, all in consecutive years. And now its signature SLIM transformer was being used inside a 160-meter-tall wind turbine, the world's highest, in Brandenburg, Germany. It had also recently supplied two hundred 25 KVA to 1000 KVA transformers to RATP, the operator of the Paris Metro.

The brochures I thumbed through featured the name Pauwels-CG, a hyphenation that was used during a transition period to allow the change of ownership to be digested by the locals.[10] The company had been a mainstay of the area since 1947 when its founder, Mechelen resident Emmanuel Pauwels, began building transformers in a small workshop.

Crompton Greaves's acquisition of Pauwels did not attract the kind of xenophobic brouhaha that had greeted Indian drinks tycoon Vijay Mallya's (failed) 2006 bid for the French champagne house Taittinger or, most famously, Lakshmi Mittal's (successful but fraught) takeover of Arcelor.[11]

Partly this was because electrical transformers did not excite passions like either champagne or iron and steel could. The former was charismatic, and the latter, industrial megafauna. Cultural icons and national champions being taken over by companies from a Third World country with malodorous levels of poverty did not sit well with many in Europe. Middling companies that made electrical parts inside complicated machinery that no one was even aware of made for an easier target.

Articles were written hailing the CG takeover of Pauwels as a strategic template for other Indian companies to follow in Europe. Khozem Merchant, the *Financial Times*'s Mumbai correspondent, argued in a piece that the CG acquisition, made at a price tag of 32.1 million euros, epitomized the win-win benefits that Indian and European companies could offer each other. CG got access to European markets, allowing it to go global, while the application of sound Indian-led management helped turn Pauwels's 3-million-euro loss into a 17-million-euro gross profit, within a year.[12]

Many middling European companies lacked capital, management focus and the ability to compete globally. For Indian firms hungry to expand their footprints internationally, these were relatively affordable propositions that gave instant access to markets and client bases in the West.

But despite the business sense that such Indo-European mergers and acquisitions might have made, they were always sensitive, in a continent where a protected job market was an integral part of the social contract. Pauwels, for example, had employed well over 2,000 people at the time of its acquisition, making it a substantial economic player in the area.

Although most of these jobs were preserved following the CG takeover, the uncertainty of being bought out by an alien company from a faraway country that most people had long consciously or implicitly thought of as inferior must have been unsettling.[13] The world was changing, and it was the status quo powers like Europe that were understandably least happy about it.

It was a couple of hours before Trehan finally blew in, rumpled from his long journey but clear-eyed nonetheless. He was short and dark, bespectacled and balding, and stuck out like a sore Indian thumb on a white Flemish hand, among all the beefy, light-haired employees who scuttled alongside him. We spent some time talking about CG's decision to expand beyond India's borders.

"There came a point when we decided that it was better to be a small fish in an ocean than a big frog in a well," Trehan said, sinking into a leather chair set behind a Flemishly proportioned table that all but dwarfed him. "By 2004, it was clear to me that the Indian market for any product that Crompton Greaves made was only around 3 percent of the global market for that product. So, there was a 97 percent market we were not tackling. But to make a dent in this 97 percent, we realized that we would have to move outside. We needed customers, financing, employees, factories, all outside of India."

The results of the decision to go global had been dramatic. In 2005, the company was exporting a mere 5 percent of its wholly India-manufactured products. By 2009, when our meeting took place, 41 percent of its products were made and sold outside of India, in addition to the 25 percent of domestically manufactured products that were exported. In that period of time, CG had grown from a $500 million firm to a hefty $2 billion one.

Although the power distribution market in Europe had suffered in the wake of the 2008 financial crisis, Trehan said the power transmission sector had continued to grow. Moreover, the replacement demand for transformers remained high. Europe's climate-change-inspired embrace of renewable energy had also opened up new avenues for the company, and CG was increasingly converting the distribution transformers it made to fit the needs of wind turbines.

Given Indian entrepreneur Tulsi Tanti's company Suzlon, the world's fifth-largest wind turbine manufacturer with a major European presence,[14] wind energy's association with India was already well established. But CG was taking this connection beyond the turbines themselves, to transformers, and even the most cutting-edge developments in offshore wind energy—onshore's more expensive, but potentially game-changing cousin.

Offshore wind farms performed the seemingly utopian transformation of a free, non-polluting resource—wind—into the electricity that was needed to feed the power-hungry contemporary world, without the entanglements in land-use disputes common in densely populated regions. Offshore turbines, moreover, enjoyed the higher and more consistent wind speeds available over the sea.[15]

A year after my initial interview with Trehan, I met him again, this time in the company of his boss, Avantha Group Chairman and CEO Gautam Thapar. We met on a wind-blown, charcoal-sky day at the port of Zeebrugge, on the North Sea. There was a group of around 20 people, all associated with the Belwind project—Belgium's largest and most ambitious offshore wind farm.

Our eyes were drawn to the gloaming horizon, but the object of all that peering—the offshore wind farm—remained obscured, living up to its reputation. Belwind was located 46 kilometers off the coast of Belgium, making it the furthest offshore wind farm in Europe and thus invisible from the coast. Nine hundred million euros had been invested in the project, backed in part by the European Investment Bank. When completed, it was to power the equivalent of 350,000 households with 330 MW of electricity.

Belwind was notable not just for its size or location but for the fact that it was an attempt to tackle one of the chief technological challenges that plagued offshore wind. Offshore wind farms cost more than twice as much as their onshore counterparts. One reason for this was that turbines at sea are harder to set up and maintain. Accessibility for even routine servicing is a major concern, and during the harsh winter months an entire wind farm may be unapproachable for long periods of time.

The Belwind project was hoping to reduce greatly the expense of the maintenance of offshore parts by miraculously (it seemed to me) enabling this servicing to take place on shore—a solution that could potentially revolutionize the renewable energy sector.

And it was not one of the cohorts of usual suspects like Siemens or Areva that took the credit for this innovation, but India's own CG. Trehan, who was as perky as ever, tried explaining this engineering abracadabra in layperson's terms.

"In conventional offshore, there are lots of moving parts in the offshore substation. This substation is likely to break down and need maintenance," he said slowly, giving me the chance to scribble it all down in my notebook. "What we have done is devised a way to move all the moving parts from the substation and put them onshore where maintenance is much easier and cheaper, dramatically improving the reliability and cost-effectiveness of the offshore farm."

CG was participating in Belwind as part of a consortium consisting of steel fabrication firm Iemants, installation and maintenance services major Fabricom and CG's system division. The design, procurement and construction of the high-voltage substation was CG's sole responsibility, as was connecting it to the electricity grid.

This was all pretty cutting-edge stuff. Following its European acquisitions, CG already accounted for 30 percent of the transformer distribution market for renewable energy in Europe. But as Gautam

Thapar, the big boss, explained, the Belwind project was a "major milestone that marked an Indian company's ascent into the high-value solutions and systems segment."

For more than 200 years, Europeans had dominated the engineering world, accounting for the great majority of technological breakthroughs. CG's Belwind solution epitomized the slow but steady swing of the pendulum of economic and technical prowess back to the East: the headline story of the new century.

Our group was meant to have taken a helicopter ride out to the farm for close-up inspection. But the stormy skies, so common to the North Sea, meant we were asked to wait until the weather settled. I passed the time fruitfully by interviewing Thapar.

He admitted that Europe's financial crisis had been an opportunity for companies like his, by allowing acquisitions at lower prices than might have been possible at fiscally healthier times. But he also insisted that there was enough growth within Avantha in India for it not to need to go out and buy that growth. Acquisitions in Europe were not about buying growth, he stressed, but getting access to technology.[16]

"Our focus outside India has always been on technology because in India you are still not there when it comes to many industries as far as innovation, consortium working, etcetera are concerned. So for CG, going global has meant access to talent and knowledge where it is available rather than having to create it in our own environment."

We ate lunch. I chatted with some Flemish bankers from KBC Bank who were involved in the financing of Belwind. They asked me whether I'd been made to have an arranged marriage. They asked me about the caste system in India. They asked me if I'd ever met Lakshmi Mittal: all the standard stuff that many Europeans consider while making chitchat with an Indian.

After several hours of waiting, we were told that the planned helicopter ride was off. Waves near the farm were crashing in at four meters high and it was deemed unsafe. There was disappointment but also a sense of vindication for CG's solution of onshore repair and maintenance of the substation. "You can imagine what the weather conditions are like in the winter, if it's already so bad now," said Trehan. "Imagine trying to repair the offshore substation. It would be impossible."

I returned to Brussels that evening feeling vaguely disoriented. Belwind was a nationalist project in Belgium, and it was a tad weird to find all these Indian links to it. It might have been hard for Europeans to accept India's new role in the global economy, but it could be difficult for an Indian, too, to come to terms with it. Americans or Germans probably strode around the planet expecting their home country's footprints to be stamped across the face of it. Indians of my generation had certainly not when we were growing up in the 1980s and 1990s. And even now in the emerging BRIC worldscape, it sometimes took me by surprise how I could accidentally turn up a stone in small, oddball Belgium and find a familiar name or logo or accent from my childhood.

I had first met that feeling—a minorly thrilling, raised-eyebrow kind of "really?" feeling—when as a student at the London School of Economics, I discovered that the iconic British Tetley tea that I drank every morning had just been bought by "our" very own Tata.

Indian manufacturing titan Tata's sweep across Europe, and in particular the United Kingdom, is the stuff of business legend. By 2012, Tata in Europe had grown to comprise 19 companies with a 45,000-strong work force spread across the region. It owned Jaguar Land Rover in the United Kingdom. In Spain, Tata Hispano churned out thousands of the bus-and-coach cabins that dotted the continent. In early 2007, Tata Steel took over the Anglo-Dutch steelmaker Corus (the European Union's number two steel company), transforming it into a significant industrial presence in Europe.

BUT IN BELGIUM IT WAS NOT TATA but mighty Mittal that resonated the loudest. Lakshmi Mittal was an Indian national whose Mittal Steel, a company described by the *Economist* magazine as being "from everywhere and nowhere,"[17] bought European giant Arcelor in 2006, to emerge as the world's largest iron-and-steel company. It dominated the industrial landscape of Europe thoroughly. Headquartered in Luxembourg, it has several plants littered across Belgium where iron and steel was once the blood and guts of the industrial economy.

In China, whenever I revealed I was Indian, the response was usually a rapturous rendering of a Raj Kapoor-era Bollywood song. In the United States, the same statement elicited talk of IT and software.

But in Belgium, the word "India" was mostly coupled with steel and Mittal.

In economically depressed Wallonia, the southern part of the country, I visited the workshop of the once world-renowned crystal makers Val Saint Lambert. "You're from India? Perhaps your article can persuade Mr. Mittal to come visit our shop," said the company's marketing head, gesturing in the direction of the nearby ArcelorMittal plant in the city of Liege.

A day later, I was up north in the Flemish city of Ghent, talking with the port authorities about their plans to expand cooperation with counterparts in India. "We specialize in steel," said the port's commercial director, "and we should be the natural choice for any Indian steel company." He paused briefly and frowned before quickly adding, "Although I don't want to offend Mr. Mittal. Perhaps we shouldn't encourage the competition."

The port's concerns were rendered intelligible by the fact that the single steel plant of ArcelorMittal in Ghent accounted for one-third of its business. One of the largest private employers in the country, with close to 5,000 people on its payroll, ArcelorMittal Ghent was a goliath that straddled the local economy. It was Europe's largest integrated steel plant with a capacity to produce several million tons of flat carbon steel a year.

It loomed over the Ghent port's skyline like a gnarled, steaming creature, fed fat on fire and coal. Reverberating with the grime-and-iron clang of old-style industrial production, it was a universe away from Europe's dominant office-based, white-collar environs.

It took me several weeks to arrange a visit to the site, and I'd had ample time to read up on it. But nothing prepared me for the elemental fury and heat of the experience. The plant held within it blast furnaces, coking plants, steel shops, hot strip mills, cold rolling mills, sinter plants, coating lines and vast areas to store the hulking hills of raw materials shipped in every day.

A plant supervisor talked me through the technical processes. Iron ore was heated up in sinter plants to separate the oxygen from the ore, converting it into sinter. In the coking plants, it was coal's turn to be heated into coke before it was mixed with sinter in the blast furnaces at temperatures as high as 1200 degrees Celsius. Here the carbon in the coke worked to remove the oxygen in the sinter, and the resulting hot iron or pig iron emerged, comprising 96 percent iron and 4 percent carbon.

It was a curiously exhilarating process to watch. Steel was so much a given of everyday life. The constituent element of everything, from the keys with which we locked our doors, the trunks in which we folded away clothes, to the knives with which we cut our bread. And yet, rarely had I paused to consider the formidably inventive and complex process through which it was cast into this world.

Inside the steel shop in the Ghent plant, steam rose up in gigantic, balletic puffs. I felt the searing heat coming off the liquid iron as it was constituted into slabs, even from several stories up. The slabs burned with a bewitching intensity, their molten glow highlighted by the gloomy, mechanical surroundings in which they were born.

The steel industry had, however, been struggling in the aftermath of the 2008 crisis. Global shipments had fallen, and tapering demand from the automotive and other steel-intensive sectors had led to serious belt-tightening. At the time of my visit, the Ghent plant had been running at half-capacity for several months. One of its two blast furnaces had been closed and only recently reopened. People had inevitably been sacked.

By mid-2013, when this chapter was being written, matters had not improved much. The protracted economic trough had more or less killed the demand for steel in western Europe. And ArcelorMittal, which accounted for around 6 percent of global steel production, manufactured more than a third of its worldwide crude steel in Europe. Nearly 100,000 of the company's 260,000-strong global labor force worked in the region.

The slowing of once-burgeoning markets like India and China only worsened the situation. Production and share prices for ArcelorMittal were sharply down and the company was running huge losses.[18] By November 2012, the credit rating agency Moody's had cut the company's ratings to junk status, following a similar downgrade by Standard and Poor's.

Throughout my stay in Europe, ArcelorMittal was firefighting, trying to return to profitability by shutting down excess capacity. However, curtailing production and jobs while simultaneously placating unions and governments did not make for an easy task. By 2012, nine of its 25 European blast furnaces had been idled.[19]

But it was the company's decision to shut down two furnaces at its plant in Florange, in eastern France, that brought the potentially fraught relationship between powerful "Indian" businesses and a troubled European economy in the process of adjusting to a changed global political economy into focus.

Mittal insisted that the furnaces were not viable and that they had in fact been slated for closure by former owners Arcelor, well before his company became involved in 2006. But the newly elected socialist government of Francois Hollande demanded that they be kept open, even threatening a temporary nationalization of the plant.

Hollande's position was unenviable. He had come to power in a country in desperate need of boosting its competitiveness, whipping its public finances into shape and convincing would-be investors that it was open to business. France, the eurozone's second-largest economy, had been stripped of its treasured Triple A investment rating by two credit rating agencies. And it had not balanced its budget in almost four decades. Public debt stood at more than 90 percent of the GDP and public spending at 57 percent, a eurozone peak. Unemployment was above 10 percent, with youth unemployment at a steep 25 percent.

Protecting jobs had consequently been a key promise that had helped get Hollande elected. The two blast furnaces in Florange together employed about 630 workers, out of a total of 2,700 workers at the site, and 20,000 ArcelorMittal employees across France. The Elysée was not happy with Mittal's decision to downsize, and within weeks of the announcement, Mittal was embroiled in an ugly, public spat with Industrial Recovery Minister Arnaud Montebourg.

What stuck out was how quickly the French political elite rounded on Mittal, with Montebourg accusing him of "not respecting France." Mittal had never been liked in France. His takeover of Arcelor in 2006 had elicited nakedly racist comments such as a description of Mittal shares as "monkey money" by the then chief executive of Arcelor. And despite six years at the helm of one of France's manufacturing mainstays, Mittal remained suspect as the Indian guy who was taking over French companies and cutting French jobs.

It is noteworthy that in 2012, PSA Peugeot Citroen announced its intention to close down the Aulnay plant near Paris, a move that was to result in up to 8,000 job losses, compared to the 600-odd jobs at stake in Florange. And yet, Montebourg explained these as being "unavoidable" because the carmaker's existence was at stake.[20] In the same year, a slew of other major companies in France announced decisions to downsize, including Alcatel-Lucent, Air France and Sanofi. Yet, their CEOs got far less public and political flak than Mittal.

It was Mittal, the Indian, who became the scapegoat for a French sense of insecurity at a time of uncertainty. It was, after all, easier to blame big business and rapacious "foreigners" for France's troubles instead of turning the spotlight on the French voters' unwillingness to accept structural reforms or the trade unions' bid to protect their privileges to the detriment of the entire country's well-being.

Eventually, talks between Mittal and the French government yielded a last-minute deal under which ArcelorMittal agreed that there would be no forced layoffs in Florange in addition to pumping a further 180-million-euro investment into the plant. The furnaces would remain idle but kept in working order for possible future use.

It sounded like a great deal for Florange to me, but Philippe Tarillon, the local mayor, told French media, "I understand the workers would have preferred to get rid of Mr. Mittal. And I will share a secret with you. Me too."

Clearly, the crisis afflicting Europe was a double-edged sword for Indian businesses. On the one hand, it had opened up opportunities: the prices for acquiring European companies that would bring valuable technological know-how and distribution networks were more interesting than before. On the other hand, the slump in demand combined with the high costs of doing business in Europe with its especially "sensitive" social sector, a.k.a. trade unions, could make life very difficult and unprofitable. For example, by the end of 2012, it was clear that the slowdown in Europe had left the formerly profitable electrical engineering company Crompton Greaves's Belgian operations in serious trouble. Weak demand and overcapacity in the transformer market resulted in a plummeting of earnings for the company.[21]

For Europe, the crisis begat equally contradictory needs and responses. Witness the French advertising campaign, "Say Oui to France," aimed at attracting foreign investors,[22] even as the Elysée threatened ArcelorMittal's Florange plant with forced nationalization. Mittal in France, and other Indian manufacturers in Europe, could not be magicked away with threats or insults. And even if they could, Europe would probably be in a worse shape as a result.

AS ARCELORMITTAL CONTINUED TO FIGHT its battles, my reporting on Indian business began to take me away from manufacturing to the new economy focused on information technology. This was the area that had most closely come to be associated with India globally. If China conjured up visions of massive engineering projects, India brought to mind software parks and buzzing call centers.

But although historically Europe may have been of the Old World, when it came to IT-related offshoring, it was the new frontier for Indian companies. For years, while the likes of Tata Consulting Services (TCS), Wipro, HCL and so forth had inveigled their way into the US and UK markets, gobbling up substantial portions of those countries' generous outsourcing pies, continental Europe had remained a closed fortress.

There were language barriers, with many Indian firms unable to operate at their best in a non-English-speaking environment. But more than language, it was the continental European mindset that proved difficult to surmount.

"In Europe, the social sector is very sensitive," explained the mustachioed Hemakiran Gupta, country manager for the outsourcing company TCS's Belgium operations.[23] We were sitting in the TCS office, located a stone's throw from Brussels's busy Montgomery Square. Spotting the TCS logo as I drove past the broad avenue that ran in front of the office sometime during my first week in the city had been another one of those surprise "recognition" moments for me.

Sensitivity to job losses due to offshoring is much stronger in continental Europe than in the United States or Britain, Hemakiran continued. "They are used to doing things a certain way here and they need to be convinced that an Indian company can adapt to their way." Europe's strong trade unions tended to equate even outsourcing with downsizing, so offshoring evoked adverse reactions.

Indian companies, moreover, remained at a disadvantage compared to their local European or North American competitors because of the mountainous barrier erected by visa restrictions. It could take months for an Indian employee of an IT firm to get the requisite work permit to join a project in a European country. Given the type of deadlines involved, the project could on occasion have finished by the time a work permit came through. Visas were also restricted to a single European country, although the nature of IT projects was often cross-border.

The cumulative result of these hurdles, according to Quantum Advisory, an outsourcing consultancy, was that only some 10 percent of the continental European IT market was being outsourced strategically, and even less offshored, that is, outsourced to foreign locations that enjoy a cost advantage, like India. I was chatting with Sridhar Vedala, the founder of Quantum, in the lobby of one of Brussels's business hotels. Quantum, which was set up in 2009, billed itself as the first and only IT outsourcing advisory firm based in Europe with a focus on offshoring to India.

Over the course of three years, I met Vedala several times, mostly in a hotel lobby, sometimes in an airport coffee shop, as he dashed between meetings and countries. He seemed to divide his time between London, Brussels and Bangalore. He carried his office in his laptop. He had a backpack. It was all very informal and untidy and very IT.

"In Europe, IT is still thought of very much as a core function of a company and there is continued reluctance to outsource it," Vedala explained, identifying companies like the German pharma giant Bayer and the chemical major BASF as examples. Operationally, these companies may have been very globalized, but they still retained IT services in-house, employing upward of 20,000 people for the job.

But the very fact that Europe had remained so anti-outsourcing for so long was the next big opportunity for Indian IT, he claimed. Because the US and UK markets were saturated, the growth going forward had to come from the Continent.

Some of the companies I spoke to agreed. "Look at France," said Abhinav Kumar, the marketing and communications director for TCS in Europe, bubbly with excitement. Seventy percent of France's $30 billion IT market remained controlled by local companies. If Indian firms could take over even a small percentage, it would signal significant revenues.

Everyone agreed that the economic crisis had negatively impacted the fortunes of Indian IT firms who counted banks among their major clients in certain ways. But counter-intuitively, the slowdown was turning out to be a positive for outsourcing as a whole.

"We see a change from the belief that offshoring is a temporary phase whose advantages are not sustainable, to a mindset that sees it as an emerging trend that will continue to expand further," TCS's Hemakiran Gupta said. TCS had been operational in Belgium since

1992 and had gradually been able to capture some 7 percent of the country's IT market.

The company had 700-odd consultants working with Belgian clients—200 located locally. Out of Belgium's top 20 firms, several were TCS clients, including the telecom major Belgacom, retail giant Colruyt and the world's largest maker of beer, InBev.

Hemakiran explained that the financial crisis had also forced companies to look at new models of operating and saving costs. "Companies are increasingly convinced of the cost-effectiveness of a project-mode rather than of a staff augmentation-mode," he said. IT jargon was unfortunately unavoidable when talking to IT types.

He claimed that it was only post-crisis that TCS had begun to see smaller companies become interested in outsourcing. The impact of the economic crisis on the banking and financial sector played a role in explaining this.

Almost half of TCS's revenues came from this sector, which was also the area worst hit by the crisis. However, the regulatory and organizational changes forced on the sector following the downturn had actually created a range of opportunities for IT services.

"The way in which banks manage risk means a change in their processes, in which IT can play a crucial role," said Hemakiran. He cited a recent EU directive that split up bancassurance companies, or insurance companies that use the sales channels of partnering banks to sell their products. This was a move that had affected almost every major bank operating in the Belgian market, from ING to Fortis. "It used to be the case that one division handled both sides [banking and insurance] with one system. But now, the IT systems involved have to be duplicated."

Quantum Advisory agreed. "Offshoring" was gradually losing its status as a swear word, Ali Toure, Vedala's Malian-German partner in the firm, told me (also seated in a hotel lobby, mobile, laptop and backpack in clear sight). Vedala and Toure had teamed up while working together at the IT consultancy EquaTerra, in Shanghai. The two were as geography-free and networked as the products their clients developed.

Toure said that the economic crisis had forced businesses to look to bottom lines. In fact, the biggest challenge that Indian IT companies were beginning to face in Europe was that their global competitors like IBM and Accenture were increasingly being pressured by their clients to offshore in India.

"The scene is changing very quickly. Look at any of the big companies, whether it's BMW or Daimler, they are now asking their IT vendors to offshore at least 50 percent or more of their operations."

Ironically, he explained, the resistance was not from the clients anymore, so much as from the global IT firms for whom offshoring in India spelled less profit.

And it was not only piecemeal outsourcing that European firms were looking at but long-term "strategic outsourcing" that moved beyond "body shopping" (more IT jargon) where five or ten people were hired for a week for some small job.

Toure gave as an example the three-year offshoring deal between Mahindra Satyam and the German chemical company BASF, a notoriously outsourcing-shy firm.[24] We also talked about the latest European heavy to have joined the offshoring trend at the time: ArcelorMittal. (I loved the way ArcelorMittal morphed alternatively into a European or Indian company, depending on the context.)

But the fact was that despite the Indian roots of its founder, ArcelorMittal had behaved in very European fashion in being chary of outsourcing for years. At the time of my meeting with Toure in early 2011, however, ArcelorMittal was looking for a company to help consolidate its IT infrastructure across Europe, a $600-million contract.

In any event, Indian companies lost out to the US-headquartered Computer Sciences Corporation (CSC), but one reason given for CSC's winning bid was its large presence in India, where it employed upward of 25,000 people. CSC was therefore seen as bringing the cost advantages of offshoring to their clients while simultaneously enjoying a greater cultural proximity to companies in Europe.[25]

Nonetheless, Toure observed that European firms were coming to be more interested in hearing about offshoring from Indian mouths rather than from European ones, belying the conventional wisdom that had until now led many Indian companies to hire European employees to head their sales operations.

TCS Belgium's Hemakiran Gupta agreed. "Europe is coming to grips with the fact that there are no such things as truly local companies any more, or at least that these local companies can have no growth."

Globalization's inescapable logic was such that since almost every profitable firm worked with markets outside Europe and with an increasingly international employee base, the local-foreign distinction, once of paramount importance in the continent, was beginning to blur.

TCS Marketing Director Kumar pointed out that even in the notoriously domestic firm-dominated French IT services market, the large "local" players were increasingly employing Indians. For example, French heavyweight Capgemini had revealed that it would soon have more staff in India (upward of 21,000) than it did in its home market of France (about 20,000).[26]

And despite the challenges, Kumar was bullish about Indian IT's future in the European continent. "There's just so much space to grow in this market," he said, alluding to Germany and France in particular. Indeed, the European market only accounted for about 20–25 percent of India's total IT export revenues. Everyone I spoke to agreed that France, Germany, Belgium and the Nordic countries were the places to watch.

Of course, the mere fact of the existence of space to grow did not mean that growth would automatically follow, but there was some substance to the optimism. "Big deals" for outsourcing were finally taking place in Europe, Toure said, lowering his voice conspiratorially. However, despite the newfound appetite for contracting out IT processes, outsourcing remained a ticklish issue and was often shrouded in secrecy, like a dirty family scandal.

Toure told me that a common tactic of his European clients was to hire Indian firms through local partners rather than directly: a move that allowed them to distance themselves from the "outsourcing" word.

"Look, everyone is doing it, but no one will talk about it. There is a wall of silence," claimed Ulrich Bäumer, a nattily suited lawyer with Osborne Clarke, as we sat in his office, a few kilometers from the Rhine, in the German city of Cologne.

Bäumer, who headed his law firm's "India practice," talked about the difficulty he had in finding German companies willing to discuss their experiences in outsourcing to Indian firms at an event he had recently organized. "With the exception of Deka Bank or Deutsche Post, they were all like, 'no thanks.'"

But despite the reluctance to go public, Bäumer claimed that there had been a noticeable change in German attitudes. Five years ago, only a handful of big companies would consider outsourcing. Today, even the mittelstand came to him seeking advice on finding the right company in India to outsource to. And increasingly, the outsourcing involved offshoring. Of the top 30 companies in Germany, 25 are offshoring, Bäumer said.

The main reason for this shift was that the Germans had finally understood that "outsourcing and offshoring are a necessity, like it or not, because of demographics."

Bäumer revealed that according to Bitkom, German IT's representative body, the country had a shortfall of 45,000 engineers in 2012. The German engineering federation VDMA said another 70,000–80,000 engineering posts remained unfilled. "What else are you going to do but outsource?" Bäumer asked with an expressive shrug.

And while the German market may be a tough nut to crack, once opened, it was likely to stay that way. "By culture we are conservative. Germans don't like change, so it's tough to get a new German client. But once they agree to take you on, they are likely to stick with you. That's the plus side of being risk averse," chortled Bäumer.

Indian companies, on their part, were making some changes as well, tailor-making their front operations and hiring Germans as their local managers. Infosys and Wipro both had a sales team in Germany fronted by a German.

Hemakiran Gupta added that Indian companies had found it tough going in the region partly because they were "very revenue-focused and so don't prioritize getting into the social fabric." But TCS at least has come to the conclusion that its Europe strategy would have to differ from its formula for success in other markets.

"Pure offshoring like in the US can never work here. On the other hand, pure localization, which is feasible in Latin America and other emerging markets, is not appropriate for Europe either, due to financial reasons. In Europe, we need a middle path between localization and offshoring."

Quantum's Vedala agreed. He said that until recently, Indian IT firms tended to base themselves in the United Kingdom with the idea that they could just send a few people across to the Continent as and when needed for projects. "Indian companies focus on verticals but are not regionally focused. That's not good enough. You don't just need a guy who knows banking; you need a guy who knows France."

This was something the bigger players in India seemed to have cottoned on to, with TCS's Belgium operations and their dedicated country team being a case in point.

But negative perceptions and mental barriers to working with Indians were a long way away from disappearing from Europe. A survey that Quantum carried out among some of the top 35 companies in Europe revealed wide-ranging and persistent discomfort with the way Indians ostensibly operated.

Companies in the Nordic region pointed to the "awkwardness" with which Indian men interacted with women. "Often, the Indian teams that are sent to make a sales pitch don't include even a single woman," Vedala said. "But the people they are pitching to are commonly women."

Another complaint listed was the difference in the way Indians were perceived to behave toward their European clients and toward their own Indian subordinates. "Europeans often feel that when they visit India, the manner in which their counterparts talk to subordinates is quite rude. Something they are uncomfortable with," said Vedala.

Moreover, across the Continent, survey respondents felt that Indians displayed a reluctance to disagree, a tendency to over-commit and a lack of transparency in sharing information. A final point made had to do with the perception that Indians working onshore in Europe made little attempt to integrate with local employees, preferring instead to socialize and live with other Indians.

I had heard this last point made about the Chinese as well. It always confused me somewhat, given the historical and contemporary manner in which European communities abroad operated almost entirely free of the local context to a far greater extent than Indian, Chinese or other immigrants to Europe did.[27]

But Vedala appeared unperturbed. "Our guys have got to change," he concluded. And everyone from Hemakiran to Bäumer concurred, as they did on the fact that this "change" was already underway.

Vedala pointed to his own company as evidence. "The idea of an Indian software programmer has been acceptable to the Europeans for a while now, but it's only very recently that they have been able to accept Indians in the IT consultative or advisory space." Winding down our interview, he stuffed his laptop into his bag and smiled.

"We are competing directly against the likes of Gartner and McKinsey, and we are making a go of it."

The chief villain in the Indian-IT-in-Europe tale, the consensus suggested, was visas. It was "ridiculous" how difficult it was for Indian IT workers to obtain visas, Bäumer stated flatly.

"People here [in Germany] are blind. They don't understand that our IT companies have to pay Indian engineers bush money to come here to work." I interrupted, asking for a clarification of the term "bush money." He snapped his fingers to jog his memory. "What do you call it in English? When you have to give a bonus to persuade someone?" "A hardship allowance?" I asked.

"Yes! That's it. Indians are often given a hardship allowance to come here because they don't like the climate and find the language difficult. German firms still think they can dictate the terms of transaction, set the price and have no problem in getting people to come in swarms over here from India."

"But," Bäumer paused dramatically, "50,000 engineers in Bangalore are not just waiting for the chance to come here." The lawyer claimed that in the 13 years he had worked in the India practice of the law firm, he had come across perhaps five Indians who had stayed on in the country for more than two to five years.

I thought back to the European Economic and Social Committee hearing I'd attended in Brussels on the European Union's proposed intra-corporate transferee directive that would have eased some of these visa woes.[28] If only Bäumer could have testified. Although, given their entrenched positions, the majority of those fearful of "social dumping" would likely have remained unswayed. Their vision of a Europe destabilized by underpaid, overworking Indian IT drudges did not seem particularly susceptible to reason or facts, as the hearing had demonstrated.

BUT FOR INDIAN IT, as indeed for other services, there was another parallel glimmer of hope for visa succor: the free trade negotiations between New Delhi and Brussels that had been launched in 2007. A Free Trade Agreement (FTA) between India and Europe had long been tom-tommed in certain quarters as the key to unlocking the vast potential that the bilateral relationship held.

I came across a 2006 piece by Kumar Mangalam Birla, the chairman of India's Aditya Birla Group, claiming that an FTA with India could be the answer to Europe's economic woes (and this was years before fiscal crises threw these woes into the spotlight they are in today). "If Europe relaxes its restrictions on labour movement and signs a free trade agreement, India could be the magic bullet that will solve the economy's shrinking labour pool and welfare state problems," he wrote.[29]

FTA negotiations were duly started, but as the years kept passing, these discussions floundered in a quagmire of technicalities. There were a few false slivers of hope along the way (in part due to the excitable Indian Commerce Minister Anand Sharma's penchant for premature declarations of the agreement being on the verge of readiness), but in reality, the talks remained deadlocked, with both the Indians and Europeans predictably blaming foot-dragging on the part of the other side.

The fault was actually quite evenly distributed, even if the negotiating tactics differed. A senior EU official familiar with the ins and outs of the discussions summed it up thus: "The Indians are playing low to settle higher and we [the Europeans] are playing high to settle lower." But while this may have been an accurate description of strategy, the problem was that despite all the "playing," there appeared to be scant signs of any "settling."

After decades of elevating autarky to the status of state religion, India's post-1990s economic reforms meant that New Delhi was more open to trading with the world than would have been conceivable at the time the country gained independence in 1947. In India, colonialism had been directly linked to European imperialist wolves in "free trade" sheep's clothing.

That the twenty-first century saw India actively seeking out and negotiating FTAs was therefore path-breaking in the Indian context. In August 2009, for example, New Delhi signed two significant trade deals with South Korea and ASEAN (Association of Southeast Asian Nations) in the space of two weeks.

The successful conclusion of these deals was in sharp contrast to the negotiations the same two entities had with the European Union. Negotiations between the European Union and ASEAN that began in May 2007 had completely broken down over the non-trade issue of Brussels's censure of human rights violations in military-ruled Myanmar, one of ASEAN's ten member nations.

Trade agreement discussions with South Korea had fared better (and were eventually concluded), but the European Union found that it was unable to close the deal for months. Almost an entire year passed between the initialing of the agreement and its formal signing in 2010, with Germany and Italy stalling under pressure from their automakers.

When it came to trade deals, the European Union certainly did not have it easy. Protectionist trade unions, a coalition of 27 member states with divergent priorities, and a convoluted internal decision-making process did not make for quick results. In this regard, India was Europe's twin with its cumbersome coalitions, powerful civil society organizations and conflicting interests among political constituencies.

Nonetheless, India had two FTAs under its belt with the very same places the European Union was struggling to close deals with. To an extent, this put paid to the charges with which EU officials disparaged India.

"Unlike the Chinese, the Indians do not go to negotiations with a firm goal," one European negotiator told me. "They are great at debating but lousy at practical give and take." But it was India, not the European Union, which had actually managed to conclude trade accords with South Korea and ASEAN.

"Aha!" countered the European official. "But that's because India's deals lack ambition." "Ambition" was the European Union's mantra of choice when it came to trade negotiations, and its purported lack on the part of negotiating partners was the inevitable reason trotted out for stalled or failed discussions. In Europe's thinking, India's FTAs with South Korea and ASEAN lacked "ambition."

For example, while the India–South Korea Comprehensive Economic Partnership Agreement (CEPA) only included the phasing out of duties on 85 percent of Korean goods and 93 percent of Indian products, the EU–South Korea FTA would banish duties from 99 percent of Korean imports in Europe and 96 percent of European exports to Korea. The contentious item of "cars" was moreover kept out of the India–South Korea deal.

But what many in Brussels did not seem to grasp was that import duties in Europe on most products were already negligible, and so the road that the European Union had to travel to meet its FTA targets was considerably shorter than the one India had to go down to meet its own.

"Ambition" in the Indian and European context meant different things. It was a relative term. Yet, the European Union kept holding on to the term as some kind of categorical imperative, with the result that India's offers at the FTA negotiating table were consistently dismissed as lacking in the kind of ambition that was apparently non-negotiable for Europe.

The two sides had agreed to eliminate tariffs on 90 percent of all tradable goods at the outset of the talks. What they were at loggerheads about in the ensuing years was in an upping of this figure. But the fact was that in any FTA with India, the European Union would be the greater beneficiary. Given the European Union's already low duties, most of the elimination of tariffs would necessarily come from New Delhi's side.

Over the course of the discussions, the key EU demands that emerged were for New Delhi to remove cars, wines and spirits, and dairy products from its negative list. While India was reportedly amenable to the request on dairy, it only offered a middle ground on cars and alcohol.

My sources for these details have to remain anonymous, given that the discussions were not public. But people involved in the negotiations on the Indian side told me that cars were a particularly sticky point.

The Indians had hoped that a proposal whereby tariffs on high-end luxury cars in India were abolished, while small and medium carmakers retained a degree of protection, might pass European muster. But while this compromise was reportedly acceptable to some of Germany's upscale auto manufacturers, small carmakers in France and Italy were loath to agree to it. Of course, the long-protected Indian auto industry wasn't happy either.

And while the Europeans remained frustrated by India's stance on tariffs related to certain categories of goods, the chapter on trade in services remained even more intractable. The European Union was asking for greater access to a range of sectors, including insurance, banking, legal services and retail. But New Delhi was firm that any demands necessitating legislative changes in India, such as greater access in the insurance and legal services sectors, were red lines that could not be crossed.

In the meantime, the Europeans appeared unable to develop a clear position on the one area in which the FTA would have a clear benefit for India: visas. India was hoping that any potential deal would include a clause to facilitate the temporary stay in the European Union of highly skilled Indian service providers.

But given that visas and immigration were a member-state competency rather than one that the European Commission could directly negotiate on, the European Union made no clear offer on the matter. The specter of an army of "cheap" Indian labor marching into Europe and taking away local jobs, raised as an argument against the European Union's intra-corporate transferee directive, was also frequently brought up in connection with the FTA.[30]

The European Union's blue-card scheme and the ICT directive, discussed in Chapter Two, were parallel attempts to have the FTA address some of India's labor mobility concerns. Similarly, the Indian government's independent push to liberalize the retail sector addressed some European demands. These moves by both governments ran into a mountain of domestically mounted challenges as the global economic downturn slowed growth and hurt jobs.

The 2008 and 2010 crises had led to a renewed contestation of the putative benefits of globalization and liberal economics in both India and Europe. The free trade and investment agenda promoted by an FTA were not an easy sell to citizens in the post-crisis environment.

Nonetheless, in September 2012, India was finally able to push through its opening up of the retail sector, albeit after extended delays and at the cost of losing one of the governing coalition's main allies.[31] The European Union's ICT directive, conversely, continued to ping-pong across the discussion tables of the European Parliament and Council. Once again, despite the European tendency to denigrate India's ability to act decisively, it was New Delhi rather than Brussels that was able to deliver a politically tough outcome.

But while retail liberalization in India might have been a meaty bone to throw Europe's way, it was insufficient to satisfy the EU criterion of "ambition" in the FTA. A host of issues apart from tariffs and services contributed to the negotiations gridlock.

The European Union, for example, wanted any trade agreement to include a chapter that would entail a commitment by India to adhere to certain labor, child-protection and environmental standards. For New Delhi, the inclusion of non-trade issues such as these in an FTA was almost insulting. It was strongly felt that this European demand was rooted in a world of superior, prosperous Europeans hectoring former colonies about their backward levels of social development.

The European Parliament, the chief supporter of the proposal, was unable to appreciate such a reading, instead insisting that an "ethical" European trade policy necessitated that FTAs include "human rights" clauses.

The fact was that a lot of India's labor, child rights and environmental protection failings were inextricably linked to poverty rather than legislative lacuna. In effect, the European Parliament was berating India for being poor, rather than considering how an FTA might help generate the economic growth in India that would in turn have a beneficial impact on the lot of labor, children, and the environment.

With an out-of-touch, inflated sense of self, the European Parliament continued to insist it would not approve any trade deal without human rights clauses attached. European Commission officials privately expressed frustration with the attitude of these politicians, as technocrats often do. But it was clear to me that much of the European discourse surrounding the deal was anachronistic, a throwback to the days when Europe could set the agenda and dictate terms, smug in its superiority and insulated from its own hypocrisy.

The cold contemporary reality, however, was that the European Union was scarcely in a position to bully India into anything, least of all a trade deal that enjoyed very little political support domestically. An FTA with Europe had few vocal supporters and extremely loud detractors in India.

Ever since returning to power for a second term in 2009, the UPA (United Progressive Alliance)—a coalition of parties led by the Congress—had been under siege, accused of massive corruption and growth-deflating incompetence. The prime minister, Manmohan Singh, had emerged as a lame duck of spectacular proportions.[32]

Were he to expend his scanty political capital on pushing through a free trade deal with the European Union, everyone from trade unions and farmers' lobbies, to carmakers and prohibitionists, would lambast it. From New Delhi's point of view, the political fallout of not signing the deal was in many ways more beneficial than that of concluding it.

And yet, the Indians remained at the negotiating table with offers, as in the case of cars, which would lead to substantial benefits for European industry. Under the circumstances, it might have been best for the European Union to water down its insistence on "ambition" and take what was on offer even if this would have meant a partial rather than complete reduction on tariffs for certain categories of products.

An FTA between Europe and India would have significant symbolic importance beyond the technicalities that would bring their own profits to the industry and economy of both partners. It would help vitalize a bilateral relationship that was lackluster between entities that were good fits. Europe needed India's markets. India needed European technology and know-how. Both were committed to maintaining diversity and democracy despite significant obstacles.

Concluding a big-ticket trade deal with the European Union would also likely shift India's attitude toward Europe away from its current indifference to a greater enthusiasm and sympathy. If the European Union could get its act together and help facilitate the short-term labor mobility of Indian service professionals, which would ultimately only help Europe's own economy, it would signal to New Delhi that Brussels was a player that could in fact address and deliver on issues of interest to India.

But the European Union looked set to cling to its ideas of "ambition," even if this meant shooting itself in its dogged, bureaucratic foot. The notion persisted that it was somehow self-evident that other countries like India should be spending political capital on courting Europe.

"We are the world's largest economy," my eurocrat friends repeated, even as the eurozone sank into a recession. "We lead in technology," they boasted, as China and India developed their own high-tech industries, from pharmaceuticals to renewable energy. "We are a model for regional cooperation that India should learn from," they intoned, as the Greeks pilloried Germany's Angela Merkel as a Nazi. "We are the leaders on climate change," they insisted, their words so much hot air as the United States and China ignored their entreaties.

And so, Brussels and New Delhi continued to sniff at each other contemptuously, the potential exemplified by south India's Europe-crossing gherkins sealed into assembly lines of jars.

EIGHT

Disunity in Diversity

DURING MY STUDENT DAYS IN LONDON, I SOMETIMES visited a restaurant called Belgo. This Belgian eatery always provoked mild hilarity among my friends as we took up the challenge outlined on the restaurant's place mats: Name six famous Belgians.

Someone would invariably call out: Jean-Claude Van Damme. Then a furrowed-brow hush would descend, interspersed with the odd giggle, until someone else ventured, "Hercule Poirot?" Or on another occasion, "Tintin?" But these suggestions were disqualified for being fictional. We never made it to six "real" people before the game ran out of steam amid the arrival of *moules* and *frites*.

When I became a resident of Belgium, almost a decade later, I discovered that the inability to name famous Belgians had a lot more to do with my ignorance than their non-existence. One of my favorite surrealist painters, Rene Magritte, whom I'd always assumed was Dutch, was in fact Belgian. The toothy, guitar-strumming Jacques Brel, who'd conjured up romantic visions of Paris for me, also turned out to be Belgian. As was the painter of baroque extravaganzas, Peter Paul Rubens, not to mention the creator of the little blue people, Pierre Culliford, of Smurfs fame.

Some of those on this list might not have been earth-shatteringly "famous" in a Brangelina fashion (although Jean-Claude Van Damme was in the vicinity), but the broader point is that Belgium is not a country writ large on the imaginations of most peoples. If anything, it tends to be dismissed as boring and damned as insignificant. So much so that it's even been suggested that if Belgium did not already exist, no one would bother inventing it today.[1]

It is these two misconceptions that I learned to take issue with. First off, the country may indeed have been small, but it was anything but boring. The travel writer Harry Pearson suggests that Belgium's "boringness" is only a camouflage to make sure it doesn't get invaded by one of its neighbors, so that any marauding troops are cleverly tricked into marching right through to somewhere that appears more exciting.[2]

"Belgium" in its various historical avatars had, after all, been invaded and annexed and split and stitched up again, with blood-soaked regularity. Small wonder that the French historian Jules Michelet called it "the meeting place of wars, where the plains are fertile because the blood does not have time to dry."[3]

This might not have been the kind of slogan that the Belgian tourist authority was in a hurry to adopt, but the country was "exciting" for less gruesome reasons as well. It was the birthplace of pigeon racing, French fries, and the saxophone. It was the place that gave the world the English word "binge," from the bacchanalian revelry in the town of Binche, where an annual carnival sees a parade of people wearing huge headdresses made of ostrich feathers pelting spectators with oranges to the beat of frenzied drumming.[4]

No, Belgium could only be called "dull" by the badly informed.

Nor was it unimportant. In fact, Belgium, and its earlier incarnation as part of the Low Countries, has always been at the center of European affairs and an effective barometer of the great shifts and churnings of the Continent's fortunes. It was the area's busy port towns like Bruges that enabled Europe's flourishing medieval cloth trade and saw the creation of the first stock exchanges. The religious upheavals of the Reformation and Counter Reformation found center stage here. From Napoleon's march across Europe to Germany's twentieth-century expansionism, Belgium was always at the forefront. It may have been a part of the buffer zone between the Continent's warring powers (the French president Charles de Gaulle reportedly claimed the country had been invented by the British to annoy the French), but it was almost always a reliable microcosm of the larger state of play in Europe.

The country was officially born in 1830, a mere fifteen years after Napoleon's defeat at Waterloo led to the creation of a United Kingdom of the Netherlands (incorporating present-day Holland, Belgium and Luxemburg). The idea was to maintain the region's ever-precarious balance of power and keep any rekindled French militaristic ambitions in check. I found it interesting how so much of the twentieth-century and—now, with the euro crisis—twenty-first century discourse in Europe, was dominated by the idea of German expansionism, as though militarism was something unique to the Prussian DNA. In fact, for so much of Europe's history it was the French who had been associated, not with the berets and accordions of today, but with pillaging troops intent on conquest.

Belgium was detached from the United Kingdom of the Netherlands following revolts by Catholics who resented Protestant interference in clerical matters, and French speakers in the south (Wallonia) who chafed against the dominance of Dutch as the language of governance and education. The linguistic battles of present-day Belgium, which this chapter will explore later, had roots that stretched well back to before its creation, although the form and intensity of these was to mutate considerably over the decades.

The result was a new state that has been described as the product of an "arranged marriage between spouses who had little in common [Flanders and Wallonia], following a nineteenth-century compromise among the Great Powers interested in creating a neutral buffer."[5]

A king needed to be rustled up to preside over this new entity, which didn't prove easy. Louis, the Duke of Nemours, one of the French king Louis-Philippe I's sons, turned down the offer. Eventually, Prince Leopold of the house of Saxe-Coburg-Gotha was installed on the Belgian throne. Given that King Leopold I, as he became known, was German, a British royal by marriage (indeed, an uncle of Queen Victoria, who was German too),[6] a Protestant and a freemason, he was a rather odd choice, at least by the standards of today. But he made a go of it until his death in 1865.

Over the course of the latter half of the nineteenth century, Belgium's second king, who with the dull predictability of European monarchical nomenclature was called King Leopold II, took Belgium into the realm of colonial powers, having acquired the Congo in Africa as a private fiefdom. The goings-on in this tiny country during that period open a window onto the wider brutalities and hypocrisy of colonialism.

In the first half of the twentieth century, Belgium was literally on the front lines of the two world wars, Michelet's description of its blood-fed plains never more apt, as hundreds of thousands died fighting in Flanders's fields in the north and in the Ardennes in the south.[7] Fast forward to the post-war rubble of Europe, and once again Belgium provided the pulse for the creature that emerged phoenix-like from the wreckage: the European Union.

THE HEADQUARTERING OF THE EUROPEAN UNION in Brussels means that it is in Belgium that the heads of state and government of the Continent's big and small nations converge, to wrangle and bargain, plead and hector, and give shape to the historically unprecedented, technocratic institutional arrangements that have taken the place of the bloodshed and conquests that governed the relations between them for centuries.

Small and "boring" Belgium today remains as important a gauge of where Europe is and where it is heading, as it has been throughout the Continent's convoluted, sometimes shocking, sometimes inspirational, history. But what the current state of play in Belgium reveals about the larger state of affairs in Europe does not give cause for exuberance. It is a country deeply divided and perennially on the verge of crisis, albeit a managed crisis that does not involve violence. It is, as always, Europe's Mini-Me.

The divisions that plague Belgium have an epic quality that is at odds with the surface serenity of this green and pretty country. Knowing very little about the place, as evidenced by my lack of success at the "name six famous Belgians" game, my first few weeks in Brussels were befuddling.

People would tell me to meet them at the Arts Lois metro station, but when I exited the subway, the signs proclaimed it to be the somewhat abusive-sounding Kunst-Wet. I would go to the central train station to buy a ticket for Courtrai and come back with one for Kortrijk. I would try to input the name of the street we lived on, Avenue De L'Opale, into my car's GPS navigation system and only find an option for the vowel-heavy Opaallaan.

The source of all this confusion was that Brussels was officially a bilingual city, with all street and direction signs displaying names in both French, the language of the country's southern Walloon region, and Dutch, the language of the country's northern region of Flanders.[8]

Brussels, the conflicted child of the marriage between Flanders and Wallonia, was geographically situated in Flanders and had historically been a Dutch-speaking city. Having emerged as the capital of Belgium post-1830, it was, however, gradually acculturated to the French side of things. In the nineteenth century, 80 percent of Bruxellois spoke Dutch. Today, it is French that is spoken in about 80 percent of homes in the capital city, with Dutch predominant in only around 15 percent of the households.[9]

Usually a statistic like this would suffice to clarify the linguistic status quo of a place, but Belgium is a country wracked by language, wrought by language, possessed by language. And so the statistics were endless, carefully collected and hoarded and brought out at emotional moments, by all sides of the linguistic debate. In 2006, 28 percent of those living in Brussels had a good-to-excellent knowledge of Dutch, while 96 percent had a good-to-excellent knowledge of French, I was told. And so it went on. And on. Every Belgian I met seemed to be an amateur bean counter. I only need mention the curious linguistic status of Brussels and they would begin to babble irrepressibly like an uncorked bottle of champagne, but without the sweetness. And so I also learned that between 2000 and 2006, the proportion of monolingual Dutch families shrank from 9.5 percent to 7 percent. And also that while 50 percent of businesses in Brussels use French for internal communications, only 32 percent use both French and Dutch.

In Belgium, statistics like this, far from inducing the soporific stupor that might be expected, lead to outrage, grief and political rampaging. Linguistic sensitivities are such that language impartiality in Brussels has been pushed to absurd extremes. For example, there was much kerfuffle about which should come first on public transport signage, the Dutch or French name? Bus companies cunningly solved the problem by using rotating signs so that offence was avoided. It got even sillier. Because it proved impossible to find the exact equivalent number of Dutch songs to French, only neutral English, Spanish or Italian songs were piped through in Brussels's metro stations.

I read this humorless explanation in a local news website:

An experiment in April [2011] involved a playlist with a selection of the international hit lists. This accidentally included a couple of songs by Brussels or Walloon artists in French. Immediately, the MIVB [the transport authority] received dozens of complaints from angry commuters arguing that there should also be room for the better Flemish songs. In order not to set the cat among the pigeons, the MIVB has now decided not to continue the experiment. The company will continue to apply its old formula, which includes 70 percent English-speaking songs, 15 percent Italian-speaking and 15 percent Spanish-speaking records. According to the MIVB, this formula creates the least problems.[10]

But the linguistic angst of Belgians was not a joking matter. In April 2010, about a year after I'd moved to the country, the five-party federal coalition government collapsed over what sounded like a particularly nasty virus: the Brussels-Halle-Vilvoorde problem. This very same affliction had caused an earlier collapse of the government in 2007, which had left the country without a government for 194 days.

At the time, some had suggested that Belgium was best off being put up for sale on eBay.[11] "For sale by auction: Country of ten million with well-established royal family, good reputation in chocolate and beer industries—and boasting a history lasting 177 years. May need some refurbishment: Government has been missing for three months now, but seems to have managed anyway. Linguistic and cultural divisions persist and debts of 300 billion euros have to be reckoned with," the spoof read.

Belgium had managed to avoid being auctioned off, although between 2007 and 2010 it featured no less than three prime ministers. But now, Brussels-Halle-Vilvoorde had reared its ugly head again and we were to see an even more spectacular absence of government. It was to turn out to be a world-beating, belief-bending, absence of 541 days, lasting until December 2011.

The term "anarchy" tends to be associated with war-torn nations in lawless parts of the developing world rather than the genteel, waffle-scented environs of a prosperous western European country like Belgium. Yet, taken in its literal sense of the absence of government, Belgium was as anarchic as it gets.

Nonetheless, it was no failed state; or at least it was a uniquely successful failed state. While politicians spent hundreds of fruitless days wrangling over arcane minutiae like the boundaries of certain voting districts, the garbage was collected on time, the post arrived every day, and the average Belgian (or Indian) resident was able to enjoy her afternoon biscuit and coffee with little sense of crisis.

In fact, the country managed the whole of its six-month presidency of the European Union in the second half of 2010 with a caretaker government. When questioned by foreigners, many Belgians affected a jovial attitude toward it all, as though their non-governmental state was an exasperating but harmless national quirk.

But beneath this cheeriness, deep emotional scars lay etched. Belgians did not take their language politics lightly at all, and the problem of Brussels-Halle-Vilvoorde (BHV) was a case in point.

The reader is now about to become familiar with what few in the wider world would have any knowledge of, but in Belgium has led to the downfall of two governments and a staggering 735 government-less days between 2007 and 2012.

BHV was an electoral district where voters had the choice of plumping for either a Dutch-or French-speaking politician. That's it. Nothing more dramatic.

To understand why this fact should have such earth-shattering consequences for Belgian politics, we must first come to grips with one of the most bizarre political systems in the world. Belgium, with all of its 10 million people and 30,500 square kilometers of territory (by contrast, the single Indian state of Madhya Pradesh is spread over 308,000 square kilometers and houses well over 60 million people), had a dual federal system with multiple loci of authority.

The Belgian Constitution divides all powers between governments at the Center, and three territorially based regions, Wallonia, Flanders and Brussels, which have separate, directly elected, parliamentary-style legislatures, a legislatively accountable executive body, and broad *exclusive* policy authority in specified areas like environment, agriculture, housing, transport and public works. But in addition to the regions, there is a further separation of powers between three disparate *communities,* which are defined linguistically rather than territorially, comprising Dutch-, French-and German-speaking groups. It is the communities rather than the regions that have the authority to legislate over areas like education and culture.

As a result of all this segregation, I found myself unable to take public transport to my son's gymnastics class, which, although 15 minutes away from our home by car, was located in what was officially a Flemish region and therefore unconnected to Brussels, a city that operated on all things practical in splendid isolation from either Flanders or Wallonia.

It was really very difficult to get one's head around. It helped to think of my history lessons in school in India and how under the British Raj separate electorates were instituted for Muslims and Hindus, so that Muslims could only vote for Muslim candidates and the equivalent for Hindus.

Political life in Belgium is effectively entirely segregated along linguistic lines. There is no national, pan-Belgian constituency. Since the 1960s, all the country's political parties had split into separate French-speaking and Flemish entities. As a result, Dutch and French speakers are unable to cast a "national" vote, even if they would like to.

A citizen can only vote for the candidates on the electoral list linked to her place of residence. So a person who lives in Flanders is in practice unable to choose a French-speaking candidate, with the reverse holding true for a resident of Wallonia. Brussels is the only region where voters are offered candidate choice from both sides of the linguistic divide.

But all of this is to overlook that troublemaker, the infamous Brussels-Halle-Vilvoorde. BHV is a voting district that while technically in Flanders had a substantial number of French-speaking residents. In other words, it was an example of an area that belonged to the Flemish *territory* but that had a substantial French *community* resident in it. The electoral lists for the district did not offer French-speaking candidates, and so francophone residents of the region had been permitted to vote on the electoral lists of nearby Brussels.

So, what was the problem?

Well, the Flemish didn't like it.

Why?

Because they believed such permissiveness would only lead to the creeping Frenchification that had already claimed Brussels as francophone (despite its official bilingual status), by allowing French speakers to reside in Flemish areas but vote for francophone politicians in Brussels who had little stake in representing Flemish interests.

It was over the inability to decide how to split BVH into politically acceptable, linguistically divided voting regions that Belgium's federal government kept collapsing. The compromise finally thrashed out in 2012 was of such mind-boggling complexity and dullness that even a researcher as keen as me found it difficult to unpick. Suffice it to say that most of the area encompassed by the district was divided along language lines, but the residents of some parts were given language "facilities," that is, the ability to stroll the few hundred meters it took to get to "Brussels" and vote on the capital's bilingual electoral lists.

But despite the horrendously complicated challenges that such a decentralized federal system provoked, regional autonomy was also part of the reason that the country functioned quite well on a day-to-day level despite the governmental lacuna at the Center.

Belgium was clearly an example of the European Union in miniature, where complex institutional arrangements allowed a culturally distinct, even antagonistic, north and south to coexist in a union, if not exactly harmoniously, at least without the gore of yore.

On the downside for Belgium (once again mirroring Europe's dilemmas more broadly), the crisis of the federal government meant that difficult policy decisions like budget-cutting (the country's public debt was just under 100 percent of the GDP) or scrapping the country's automatic wage-indexation[12] proved hard to push through. The effect on investors of a virtually continuous political stalemate was less than salubrious. Through the euro crisis, Belgian bond prices remained volatile, with Belgium and France seen as next in the firing line should fiscal contagion spread north of Spain and Italy.

Now, despite what many Europeans thought, Belgians were not inexplicably bizarre. There was a method to their madness and underlying reasons for their seemingly irrational politics. Like all peoples, they were handcuffed to their history, and it was in this history that the embittered roots of all this linguistic acrimony lay.

FROM ITS INCEPTION, a language apartheid was applied in Belgium, where a French-speaking elite in both the southern and northern parts of the country sought to impose French as the sole language of education and government. French, the language of the Belgian aristocracy, came to symbolize everything refined and intelligent, while Dutch, the language of the northern peasants, was treated as a coarse, country-bumpkin cousin to be kept out of earshot.

It wasn't until the Belgian state was 50 years old that the first speech in Dutch was heard in the Parliament building in Brussels. The discrimination against Dutch speakers sometimes had tragic consequences. For example, in 1873 a murder trial ended with the wrongful conviction and execution of two Flemings. After their heads had been offed, another person confessed to the crime, and it was subsequently found that the defendants could not understand French, that their attorney knew no Dutch, and that the francophone judge had relied on a mistranslation of a conversation overheard by a jailer. Public outcry eventually led to a change in the law, permitting both Dutch and French to be used in criminal trials in Flanders.

Over the following decades, Dutch speakers painfully clawed back linguistic equality for themselves. But it wasn't a privilege easily conceded by the haughty French-speaking elite. It was only in 1893 that Dutch was recognized as Belgium's second language (although 60 percent of Belgians used it). In the 1920s, when the University of Ghent was debating becoming exclusively Dutch speaking, a Walloon MP claimed in all earnestness that replacing French culture with Flemish culture was like "replacing a lighthouse with a candle."[13]

This linguistic inequality was reinforced by an economic asymmetry between Belgium's north and south. With large coal reserves, Wallonia was among the earliest regions in Europe to industrialize, and it experienced rapid growth during the nineteenth century. Flanders, conversely, relied on subsistence agriculture. It had no modern industry. Crop failures led to a famine and contributed to massive unemployment and hardship.

The Dutch language's fortunes began to really pick up after the Second World War, when a dramatically inverse economic landscape in Belgium emerged. Once-prosperous Wallonia began a long and steady decline in the wake of the collapse of the coal and steel industries. But Flanders zipped ahead with industrial modernization. The Flemish port of Antwerp prospered, and industries like car assembly and shipbuilding took off. Foreign investment poured into the region. By the mid-1960s, the Flemish GDP per capita surpassed that of Wallonia for the first time and has remained well ahead ever since.

Today, the per capita GDP of Flanders exceeds that of Germany, France and the United Kingdom, while that of the Walloon region is similar to the level of the poorest regions in France and Italy. The unemployment rates and the high-school dropout rates in Wallonia are both twice those of Flanders.[14]

Belgium's francophone south is moreover overwhelmingly socialist, its politics driven by strong trade unions, in contrast to Flanders's relative fiscal conservatism.

Quoting from a 1917 pamphlet by G. de Waele, titled "Flamands and Wallons," the Belgian memoirist Luc Sante has this to say about the difference between the two: "Whereas the Fleming is a silent and obstinate worker . . . whose taciturn soul perhaps cedes to the vigor of the body, the Walloon . . . is more cheerful than the Fleming, maybe less serious . . . he may show less application in his work but his motion is livelier."[15] The stereotypes apply equally today.

But despite having achieved almost complete segregation, political and linguistic, between the two regions by the 1960s, taxation remains a federal affair, as does the business of paying the country's generous welfare benefits. The result is large cash transfers from north to south, with richer Flanders essentially subsidizing the social security benefits of Walloons to the tune of some 10 billion euros a year.

The Flanders-Wallonia rift approximates a diminutive version of the larger north-south divide of Europe that pits the fiscally conservative Germanic north against the socialist Mediterranean countries of the south. As the Flemish rail against paying for the benefits of "lazy" Walloons, so the Germans resent bailing out "indolent" Greeks and Portuguese.

BELGIUM FINALLY HAD A GOVERNMENT by the time I pulled up outside Flemish politician Eric Van Rompuy's modest home in Sterrebeek, a Flemish village fifteen minutes north of Brussels (as usual I had to take a taxi, there being no public transport connecting Brussels to the Flemish regions). Eric was the brother of European Union President Herman Van Rompuy, a former Belgian prime minister and a writer of haikus.[16] The Belgians, I discovered, did dynastic politics almost as well as the Indians. Eric's nephew, the son of Herman, Peter Van Rompuy, was Belgium's youngest federal senator. And Tine Van Rompuy, the third of the Van Rompuy siblings, was also a politician, who belonged to a different political party.

Eric opened the door while attached to some kind of heart-monitoring machine, which struck me as an apt metaphor for Belgium given its near perennial state of cardiac arrest. But the elderly Fleming assured me he was well enough to talk and ushered me into his drawing room. He seemed excited, if also surprised, that an Indian journalist was interested in matters like the Brussels-Halle-Vilvoorde issue.

I asked why the Flemish were so reluctant to help out their economically straitened southern compatriots. They were all Belgians, after all. What about that vaunted European principle of solidarity?

It wasn't so simple, he replied, in a measured, dry, Flemish way. "Flanders produces two-thirds of Belgium's GNP. We pay more than 60 percent of income tax. And we pay two-thirds of social security contributions, even though Wallonia has double the unemployment."

But Flanders was part of the same country as Wallonia, I countered. What was the point of Belgium existing if Flanders wanted nothing to do with its southern sibling?

Eric seemed thrown by the question before offering a rather weak, "Well, Belgium is a fact now." He brightened as he thought of something else to add. "And it is the capital of Europe. It would be anti-historical to split the country when the European Union is all about bringing the continent together."

"Um, and that's it?" my expression must have asked, because he hastened to add ever more anemic reasons. "If we were to split, what would happen to the airport?"

"So, Belgium is being held together by an airport?" I asked incredulously.

"Well, and the national debt too. We have a 340-billion-euro national debt. Who would take it on? How would this be divided?"

Eric sighed. "We are Siamese twins. We cannot be separated or we will die." In fact, medical science had advanced enough for some successful Siamese-twin separations. But it didn't feel appropriate to mention this at this juncture.

Eric was honest. "Most Belgians are not emotionally linked to the country. You must understand our history. It is very painful." And there followed a typical half-hour spiel of all the wrongs the Flemings had historically suffered, including the one that most often brought tears to the eyes of my grown, male interviewees: the story of the Flemish soldiers in the First World War who died because they couldn't understand the orders given by their exclusively French-speaking officers.

Interviewing Belgians was sometimes similar to talking to the Chinese. At the start, it would be all blank stares and denials of anything amiss. "The Chinese Communist Party is very good. They have helped China become much richer," was the standard line in Beijing. And here in Belgium, the first response to how a Fleming felt toward a Walloon was usually, "We are all Belgians. We have no problems with the French-speaking. It's the politicians who blow matters out of proportion."

But probe ever so gently and the genie would come whooshing out of the bottle. In China, people would abruptly start complaining about demolished homes and rapacious real estate developers in cahoots with corrupt local government officials. In Belgium, the digging would more often than not end with that old story of dying Flemish soldiers in the First World War unable to comprehend their callous French-speaking officers. Another popular rant involved the apocryphal three generations of Walloon families who all subsisted on employment benefits.

I was never able to actually track down these purportedly incurable spongers. But I did understand the Flemish frustration with the Walloons, who preferred to live off unemployment benefits funded in large part by Flanders's taxes, rather than simply learn Dutch and either move or commute to available work in Flanders.

Part of the problem was the strict monolingualism (with the exception of bilingual Brussels) that the country had chosen, so that in Flanders it was illegal to use French in any public space and vice versa in Wallonia. It wasn't uncommon, for example, for people to report to the authorities someone living in a Flemish village advertising a house for rent or sale in French.

In Belgium, the struggle to end the linguistic apartheid that had discriminated against Dutch had led to the establishment of monolingual territories (French, Flemish and a small German-speaking enclave), and eventually to communicative isolation between its language communities.

The residential and work segregation between the two communities were almost absolute. There were no national newspapers, television or radio stations—aimed at both the French-and Dutch-speaking communities. Each region had its own public broadcasting organization regulated by its language community, not the national government.

A friend who worked for the Flemish broadcaster VRT in Brussels told me that despite sharing an office building with their French counterparts, journalists from the francophone and Flemish TV stations rarely spoke to each other socially and never shared contacts professionally. When a bus crash in Switzerland killed 22 Belgian children on a skiing vacation in March 2012, Flemish and Walloon journalists (who worked in the same building in Brussels) rushed to the scene of the crash without any coordination between them, and once there, preferred to pool information with foreign correspondents rather than with each other.

"But that's crazy," I said, thinking back to my days as a TV reporter in India and the intense level of information exchange that went back and forth between journalists at times of national tragedy. "Yes," my friend agreed. "But you see, you have to understand our history . . ." And out came the story about the Flemish soldiers and their French-speaking generals.

The divisions that have maimed Belgium were seeded in the educational system. From elementary school up till university, the curriculum was taught exclusively in either French or Dutch, bilingual educational institutions having died out, even in Brussels.

At a party at our home in Brussels, a Flemish couple's eight-and ten-year-old children were unable to communicate with any of the other kids present, despite the youngsters having between them languages ranging from French and English to German and Spanish.

It is not uncommon for schools to punish with detention children "caught" using French with friends on the playground, if they happen to be enrolled in a Dutch school.[17] I found this so extreme that I decided to visit a school with similar rules to understand what was going on.

"I know people say we are racist," young, blonde Lies Dierckx admitted dispiritedly. Dierckx was the "language coordinator" of Mater Dei, a Dutch high school in Brussels's Woluwe-Saint-Pierre commune. The school required that all pupils who join sign a "contract" that committed them to having a "positive attitude towards Dutch." They were also asked to "swear" that they would watch Flemish TV and read Flemish newspapers. They were expected to speak Dutch while in the school at all times, including in the hallways and playground.

Dierckx insisted that the school had no other option but to adopt seemingly draconian measures in order to stem the steady decline of standards at what was formerly a leading local educational establishment.

Corresponding to the broader Frenchification of Brussels, the Woluwe-Saint-Pierre commune, once the center of a Dutch-speaking community, is today francophone. The majority of the area's

Dutch-speaking families have relocated away from Brussels to Flanders proper.

French-speaking families choose the Dutch medium school not only because of its geographical proximity to their place of residence but also because French-speaking schools in the area are perceived to have lower academic standards. In part this is chalked up to the fact that immigrant families, which comprise a large chunk of Brussels's population, tend to overwhelmingly be francophone and almost always send their kids to French schools.

Dierckx said that the change in the composition of the student body at Mater Dei had been striking over the last decade. By 2012, only 23 percent of the school's student body came from a native Dutch-speaking background, compared to 60 percent in 1999. And it was getting "worse." In the first form, a mere 8–10 percent of the students come from Flemish backgrounds.

The influx of French speakers into a Dutch school inevitably affected the academic performance of the school adversely. Teachers could not teach because the Dutch-language levels of students from French-speaking backgrounds were insufficient. "We spend all our time teaching the students the meaning of words rather than focusing on the content of the lesson," explained Dierckx. "The French-speaking children do not share the same cultural assumptions and knowledge as us [Dutch speaking]."

The language coordinator sighed. She was armed with statistics and charts. But she put them aside and looked at me with genuine distress. "The French-speaking make fun of the Dutch-speaking children's accent during French class, but at least they [the Flemish] make an effort to learn French. The same cannot be said the other way around. No Flemish child pokes fun at a French-speaking kid trying to learn Dutch."

In the hallways and playground, the Dutch-and French-speaking children almost never mixed. The Parent Teacher Association had split between the francophone and Flemish. The French-speaking parents expected the school to "accommodate to their needs, even though this is a Dutch school. It's a nightmare. We cannot run a school like this." Dierckx tapped the table we were sitting at with a pen.

I had some sympathy with Dierckx, as I did with Flemish complaints about the attitude of the Walloons more broadly. The Flemish tend to speak Dutch, English and (if educated before the strict monolingualism of contemporary schools was enforced) French, usually to a high standard. The Walloons usually speak French. Period.

BUT STEPPING BACK FROM the micro-level ins and outs of the great Belgian drama, I couldn't help feeling that the country, for all its cobbled streets and chocolates, was a dystopia. In many ways, Belgium represented an extreme failure of generosity and a complete inability to cope with what, from an Indian point of view, was pretty minimal diversity.

In India, we balance more than 20 official languages, and almost all Indians are multilingual. The diversity that citizens negotiate on a daily basis isn't confined to the linguistic. We are a country of hirsute sardars and smooth-skinned Tamils, of fish-eating Bengalis and vegetarian Gujaratis. In our "Hindu" country, there are almost as many Muslims as in all of Pakistan. With no single language, ethnicity, religion or cuisine, India's existence is immensely more complicated than Belgium's.

As much as Flemings and Walloons claim irreducible differences, to my Indian eyes they are remarkably alike. They are uniformly afflicted by terrible weather, eat the same brand of "speculoos" biscuits and share a love of grumbling about how Belgium's PR is outmatched by its neighbors. "French fries are really Belgian," moan the Walloons. "The best 'Dutch' tulips are actually grown in Belgium," the Flemings insist. Walloons and Flemings find common ground in conceiving of Belgium as a negative entity, one that is not Dutch, French or German. They are, moreover, culturally Catholic, having emerged from the carnage and chaos of the Reformation and Counter Reformation with a common ecclesiastic glue.

Yet Belgium remains undisputedly one of Europe's most deeply divided entities. The Flemish politician Eric Van Rompuy explained India's relative success with multilingualism compared to Belgium's dismal failure with mere bilingualism by suggesting that it is easier to find an equilibrium among many, than between two entities (in this case, linguistic communities) that are more or less equal in size. "When you are two and equal, there is no arbiter," he claimed.

But perhaps the real reason for India's strong identification as a nation, despite decades of Western predictions of the country's "inevitable" balkanization following its emergence as an independent state in 1947, is that India existed as a coherent civilization for centuries before it achieved political unity.[18]

Even as far back as Alexander the Great's march across the Pamirs and the Indus, there was clarity about what Harvard Indologist Diana Eck calls the "sacred geography" of the land known to the Greeks as Indika—the territory that lay beyond the Indus River. In her excellent work, *India: A Sacred Geography,* Eck points out that "considering its long history, India has had but a few hours of political and administrative unity. Its unity as a nation, however, has been firmly constituted by the sacred geography it has held in common and revered."[19] Hinduism, which was more or less commensurate with the territory of the Indian subcontinent, produced a distinct and identifiable civilization.

Belgium, conversely, lacked the kind of antique sense of nationhood that preceded the emergence of many of the political entities we call modern nation-states. It had been bartered and ripped, annexed and swapped for centuries, tacked on to one empire only to be dissolved into another. And yet, as part of the Low Countries, the areas comprising modern-day Belgium did share history. Along with the rest of Europe, Belgium was underpinned by a common civilization based on Christianity and later imbued with the ideas of the Enlightenment.

In fact, the existence of two seemingly immutable and wholly isolated entities called Flanders and Wallonia is a modern, rather than a historical, phenomenon, related in part to the development of the welfare state. Flemings and Walloons had intermarried and migrated back and forth for centuries. It was only in recent decades that social security benefits had largely done away with the necessity of intra-Belgian migration.

Walloon shopkeepers were known to move to Flanders, just as Flemish laborers headed to the factories and mines of the south, well into the twentieth century. As a result, it's not unusual to find Flemish nationalists (Flamingants) with French surnames, just as their opposite numbers (Wallingants) sometimes have Dutch names. And for centuries before the establishment of the Belgian nation, the peoples within its present-day borders were referred to by outsiders as Flemish in the field of culture (not all so-called Flemish painters were native Dutch speakers, for example) and Walloons in matters of war.[20]

Surely, Walloons and Flemings have at least as much in common as Kashmiri Pandits and Kerala Christians. And if India had successfully, albeit imperfectly, imagined and created a unified nation out of its multiplicity of peoples, languages and religions, then Belgium could be expected to do the same. There was no inevitability to the almost rabid linguistic cleansing and its attendant segregations that the two parts of the country practiced today.

I was keenly aware, however, that the major saving grace of Belgium's existence was the lack of violence that characterized the animosity of its north and south. The Flemings and Walloons might act as though they were stuck in a bad marriage, but neither had turned into a spouse batterer. A far cry from the Republic of India, which, for all its considerable political achievement, was a country where violence between its citizens—most commonly on religious grounds but also in the name of ethnicity and, occasionally, language—was a lurking, menacing presence.

In contrast, Belgium's enduring regional conflict has not witnessed any mass violence for over half a century. In place of the riots and killings that have marred much of India's history as an independent state, Belgium has negotiated a series of compromises that have stitched together a complex federal system that is somehow holding the country together, against the odds.[21]

One explanation put forward for this is a "strong tendency towards pacifism and conflict avoidance" shared across the language divide in Belgium, the outcome of the two world wars. The academics Mnookin and Verbeke quote an anonymous Belgian political leader:

> Given the history of the country, Belgians have no taste for fighting or for wars. Our land has provided the site of battles fought by others, and our people have been occupied by the French, the Dutch and the Germans. People in this country don't like the government, and don't like the army. . . . While the ties with the nation are very thin and there is little state feeling or identity, there is not taste for violence.[22]

Perhaps even more importantly, there are no historical memories of mass violence that exist between the Walloons and Flemings, unlike the Hindus and Muslims in India, for example.

BUT ANY GENERALIZATION of the Belgian "dislike" of violence has to be tempered, as with any broader reference to "European" values of tolerance and justice, by the country's vicious history of colonialism.

Europe's amnesia about its own leading role as perpetrator when talking about climate change, its naïve tut-tutting at wars and atrocities in parts of the developing world from Pakistan to the Congo, without the consciousness of the role that European countries have played in enabling and encouraging many of these horrors, are part and parcel of a politics of forgetting. One that is captured in distilled form by Belgium's willed loss of memory related to the Congo.

It was in Brussels's Cinquantenaire Park, a short walk from my home, that the country's selective, but collective, forgetfulness was brought home to me.

On gently warm summer days, crowds throng the park's generous green sprawl, located right across from the European Union institutions. The scents of vanilla and caramel float out of waffle vendor vans and the excited shrieks of toddlers running about fill the air.

But a brutal and unacknowledged history underlies this bucolic scene. The Cinquantenaire Park was built in the late nineteenth century by King Leopold II, with the proceeds from a slave state that he established in the Congo.

For almost 25 years, the Congo, an area that was almost 80 times the size of Belgium, was a private estate of the king, before being taken over by the Belgian government in 1908. During this time, and for several years afterward, forced slave labor in the Congo was used to extract rubber to feed Leopold's coffers. In his chilling book *King Leopold's Ghost,* American historian Adam Hochschild estimates a death toll of up to 10 million people in the Congo for the period between 1880 and 1920.[23]

The economics behind the atrocities in the Congo had to do with J. B. Dunlop's 1887 invention of inflatable rubber bicycle tubes, which, coupled with the growing popularity of the automobile, dramatically increased the global demand for rubber. To monopolize the resources of the entire Congo Free State, Leopold issued three decrees in 1891 and 1892 that effectively reduced the native population to serfs.

Collectively, these ordinances forced the Congolese to deliver all ivory and rubber, harvested or found, to state officers. Male rubber tappers and porters were literally worked to death. Leopold's agents held the wives and children of these men hostage until they returned with their rubber quota.[24] Those who refused or failed to supply enough rubber often had their villages burned down, children murdered, and their hands cut off. It was the Congo under Leopold that was the setting for Josef Conrad's classic treatise on colonialism in Africa and the evil that lurks in humans, *Heart of Darkness*.

Hochschild is one of the few Western historians who directly compares the devastation wrought by colonialism to that of fascism and communism, the two great obsessions of Europe. He says that while the deaths in the Congo might not have constituted a genocide, in that their primary aim was not to eliminate a group of people, they were certainly genocidal in proportion.

Yet nowhere are even traces of this barbaric story to be found in Cinquantenaire. Instead, on one side of the park a triumphalist arch cuts a gash in the sky; on the other end a recently renovated monument gleams in the sun. The arch stands, as it was intended to decades ago, as a celebration of Belgian adventurism in the Congo. The sculpture or "monument to the Congo" shows off images of a Belgian soldier sacrificing his life in the defense of the Congo and for the greater glory of Belgium. Elsewhere, another soldier is shown heroically staving off an Arab slave dealer. The scene is topped off by one of a graceful white lady, symbolizing Belgium, receiving innocent black children in her munificent embrace.

At the center of the monument, a message in Leopold II's words is carved out:

J'ai entrepris l'oeuvre du Congo dans l'interet de la civilisation et pour le bien de la Belgique.

I undertook the work of the Congo in the interest of civilization and for the good of Belgium.

There is no explanatory note setting the monument in context or attempting to explain to modern-day Belgians the hideous hubris of Leopold's Congo exploits. The only sign in evidence near the monument was one up for a few months in 2009, stating that 94,472.26 euros were being spent to restore and clean the sculpture.

Park Cinquantenaire has plenty of company in Brussels. Much of the city was built by Leopold from the spoils of the Congo, including the city's Palace of Justice, the main law courts. But the story of how these grand buildings came to be paid for is not part of the public discourse in Belgium. Not only is it absent from school curricula, but the active glorification of colonial figures also continues simultaneously.

In the suburban hamlet of Tervuren, the Royal Museum for Central Africa, established by Leopold, is considered one of the foremost collections of Central Africana in the world. Yet, until 2005, it made no mention at all about the millions of Africans who died in the region under Belgian colonial rule, although a "Gallery of Remembrance" honors the colonialists who gave their lives there.

European explorers like Henry Morton Stanley who did much of Leopold II's violent ground work in acquiring the Congo have entire sections devoted to them, but there is scant mention of the tens of thousands of porters and laborers who were killed in facilitating Stanley's "discovery" of the region.

This lacuna is all the more significant because the museum is usually the first and often the last experience of Africa that Belgian children have. A visit to the museum is a compulsory part of the Belgian school program.

Adam Hochschild's book includes a scathing account of the museum, pointing out that while it exhibited plenty of stuffed African animals, the silence about the blood spilled in the Congo, the stolen land, the severed hands, the orphaned families and the burnt villages that were also a part of the story, was loud.

In fact, until 2005, the museum's permanent exhibition had remained wholly unchanged since the 1950s, when the Congo was still a Belgian colony. Eventually, under considerable pressure to rethink its existence, the museum added a section on the Congo under colonialism in 2005. For the first time, the museum made references to the slavery and violence that were part and parcel of Leopold's and Belgian rule over the Congo. But the main message of this exhibition was to stress that colonialism was a product of its time and therefore cannot be judged by modern-day standards.[25]

Why is the same never said of Nazism or Stalin's Russia? Hochschild argues powerfully that in Europe, colonialism has either been actively "forgotten" or remembered as a largely benign phenomenon whose unfortunate collateral damage is explained by mentalities that must be understood in their context. The reason communism and fascism have been singled out as the only genocides worth writing about is because their victims were mostly European.

In Berlin, a city awash with memorials to the terrors of the Third Reich, there are no museums to the tens of thousands of Hereros slaughtered in Namibia from 1904 on by the troops of Kaiser

Wilhelm II. In Paris and Lisbon, there are no reminders of the rubber terror, forced labor systems for extracting rubber similar to those in Leopold's Congo, which slashed in half the populations of French and Portuguese Africa.

Over the years, I spoke to several Belgians about what they knew of their country's record in the Congo. Those of an older demographic had learned about the great good that the Belgian government had done in the country: the education it had brought to an illiterate and backward place, the infrastructure that the Belgians had built, the progress they had made fighting malaria.

As an Indian, I was no stranger to the hypocrisy of colonial discourse, yet I was shocked to discover what the Belgian educating of the Congolese had in fact amounted to. At the time of the Congo's independence in 1960, there were fewer than 30 African university graduates in the entire country.[26] There were no Congolese army officers, engineers or doctors. Of the 5,000 management positions in the administration, only three were filled by Africans.

In addition to what they learned from their school curricula, older Belgians usually also had some knowledge of the Congo through a member of the family who had worked there, as a teacher or missionary or administrator. Luc Sante, whose uncle Rene was employed by the Ministry of Public Works in the Congo, describes how in his household the Congo was seen as a volatile, hot, malaria-filled place that Belgians had to brave in order to help "the Africans enter the twentieth century." There was almost no thinking involved about the negative impact of Belgian rule on the lives of the Congolese.[27]

About the period of Leopold's private reign over the Congo (before 1908), very little mention is made in the Belgian educational system, except for a few platitudes about how the king had rescued the natives from the evils of the "Arab slavers." This was the very excuse used by Leopold himself to justify his surreptitious acquisition of the Congo for his own personal exploitation.

It struck me that the similarities between some of the worst communist regimes and colonial Congo were not only limited to the scale of deaths that took place under these administrations but also in the language deployed to explain the ideologies to the people. The terminology used by colonialists was as much Orwellian doublespeak as anything communism produced. Thus were Leopold's forced laborers designated "liberated" (*libéré*) men, ostensibly liberated from "Arab" slavery, when in fact they were worked to death, their families held captive and mutilated as insurance against disobedience.

In a grotesque act of censorship and thought control, all the textbooks in the Congo, throughout the half century that followed Leopold's death, continued to praise the king—as slavishly as books in Soviet Russia once praised Lenin. And so, generations of Congolese children whose parents lost their lives enslaved to Leopold's rubber-collecting gulags were indoctrinated into believing that Belgians had come to the Congo to heroically fight off Arab slave traders through dint of sacrifice and perseverance. Criticisms of Leopold's regime were dismissed as defamation on the part of foreigners and best ignored. Forgetting was, in other words, officially decreed not only in the Congo but in Belgium as well. For example, research on the commission of inquiry that was set up in 1904–5 to examine the state of affairs in Leopold's Congo was banned well into the 1970s.

As I read about the destruction of records and the deliberate obfuscation surrounding the reality of Leopold's Congo, I thought about the incessant European censure of Chinese censorship. Indeed, Beijing worked hard to suppress memories and analysis of the great political disasters under Mao's leadership, from the devastating famines of the 1950s to the deadly chaos of the decade-long Cultural Revolution (1966–76). The European Union, in accordance with its "values," rightly worked toward a redressal by bringing pressure upon the Chinese authorities to face up to their past. But why, I wondered, wasn't similar pressure exerted upon the Belgians in whose country the European Union was headquartered, to face up to their past of atrocities in the Congo? Why was it OK to "forget" about the Congo, but not about the Cultural Revolution?

It is remarkable that the discourse about white Belgians bringing light to the Dark Continent by vanquishing the evil forces of "the Arabs" persists in contemporary Belgium, without a hint of skepticism, as demonstrated by the monument to the Congo in the Cinquantenaire Park, located slap bang next to the EU buildings. But then, given the geopolitical state of play in the new millennium, with the abhorrent clash of civilizations being played out daily in the suicide bombings and drone attacks that punctuate the news with numbing repetition, perhaps it isn't. Much has changed and little has changed at the same time, as is the way of the world.

But the result of colonialism largely being consigned to footnotes in European history textbooks is that there is surprisingly little empathy for why former colonials themselves might not find it so easy to just "forget" about the past and move on. There is a breathtaking janus-facedness to the tenacity with which Europeans cling to their own history in certain contexts (witness the Flemish obsession with French generals lording it over Flemish foot soldiers in the First World War) and the easy dismissal with which they condescendingly explain to other people in the world that it does no good to dwell on the past.

Reacting to the publication of Adam Hochschild's book, the then Belgian prime minister told the *Guardian* newspaper that "the colonial past is completely past. There is really no strong emotional link any more . . . it's history."[28] But the colonial past is a hard, ugly fact with repercussions in the present that cannot be wished away simply because Belgians no longer feel an emotional link to the Congo. To the Congolese, the experience of colonization is at least as real a manacle to their present as is the Flemish history of discrimination by the francophone in Belgium.

In his speech granting the Congo independence in 1960, the Belgian king Baudouin claimed with superlative condescension, "It is now up to you, gentlemen [the Congolese], to show that you are worthy of our confidence." Few in the world know what this "confidence" actually amounted to. When the Congolese leader Patrice Lumumba became prime minister following a democratic election and sought economic independence and assistance from the Soviet Union, alarm bells went off in the West. The Congo was, after all, a treasure trove of copper, cobalt, diamonds and gold. Less than two months after his election, a US National Security Council subcommittee on covert operations authorized his assassination. In collusion with Belgium, the United States eventually ensured that Lumumba was arrested, repeatedly beaten and then shot in January 1961. A Belgian pilot flew the plane that took Lumumba to the site of his assassination. A Belgian officer ordered the firing squad that killed the Congolese leader.

The United States and Belgium then propped up an anti-communist figure, Joseph Mobutu, a former non-commissioned officer in the old colonial Force Publique. Mobutu, who staged a coup in 1965 to emerge as Congo's supreme and supremely corrupt dictator for the next three decades, looked out for Western economic interests and his own. He is estimated to have amassed up to 5 billion dollars in personal loot by the time of his death in 1997, while his own country sank ever deeper into economic ruin.[29]

There is a very real line connecting the awful human suffering in the Congo today and the assassination of its first democratically elected leader less than seven months after the country's independence. While it is impossible to know how the Congo would have fared under Lumumba's leadership, his murder and replacement by the rapacious Mobutu was a violent blow to the ideals of national unity and economic independence that Lumumba had professed.

To those still suffering in the long shadow of having been subjugated and brutalized, often for centuries, colonialism is not some distant, largely benign, regrettably racist—but understandably so, given the context—phenomenon, with no bearing on their sense of self and environment. And yet, European officials dealing with other parts of the world in multilateral fora ranging from the WTO to the UNFCCC, as well as on bilateral agreements like free trade accords, act either fed up or surprised on encountering "Third World attitudes" that treat Europe's "fair" proposals with undue suspicion.

Perhaps a little context about how "free trade" was used by European powers to make an empire of opium addicts in China or annex huge swathes of the world into the service of expanding the coffers of European capitalists, would help present-day negotiators experience a little more empathy and appreciation of where their Third World negotiating partners are coming from. Europe, and the world, would be the better for it.

EUROPE WOULD ALSO BE BETTER OFF if Belgium could get its act together, proving that differences do not have to breed enmity. That you can speak a different language and nonetheless share a common ethos. That you do not have to be identical to each other in order to identify with each other. That being sensitive to history does not preclude moving forward in new directions.

Luckily, despite all the sourness and surliness, mean-spiritedness and narrow-mindedness displayed by the kinds of people who spent their days reporting linguistic infractions to the authorities, Belgium retains enough of a sense of the absurd to rescue it from its own worst self. This country of cartoonists and surrealists can enjoy a good giggle. In 2011, when youthful protestors taking to the streets from Egypt to Tunisia grabbed the international spotlight, Belgium had its own youngsters marching up and down Brussels in protest. But instead of demanding the downfall of a government, the Belgians were, in typical contrarian spirit, asking for the creation of one.

When the country became the world record holder for the longest absence of government, students around the country organized frites, or fried potato parties, to mark the occasion. The actor Benoit Poelvoorde urged a "no-shave-until-we-have-a-government" movement, while politician Marleen Temmerman called for the wives of Belgian politicians to withhold sex from their spouses until a political compromise had been reached.

How could I not fall in love, a tiny bit, with a place like this? I became inordinately invested in Belgium's "success." I did not want the country sold on eBay. I forcefully disagreed with the jibe that Belgium should never have been invented. I dreamed of Walloons and Flemings marching down Brussels's streets, holding hands and singing Lennon's "Imagine'," or at least agreeing to stop counting the linguistic ratio of songs played on the underground.

"Belgium" is about so much more than two groups of easily dismissed, European-fringe oddities. It is about the very substance of Europe, the weft of its complicated identity politics hinting at both the achievements and the daunting challenges of an increasingly unwieldy European Union.

Like Belgium, the European Union, winner of the 2012 Nobel Peace Prize, might have ensured the end of bloodletting as an instrument of settling internal differences. But also like Belgium, the European Union is embattled, fighting to justify itself to its own citizens. Both the European Union and Belgium are in some senses supranational projects that aim to shape unity out of diversity. But while both remain held together by convoluted institutional trappings, they have largely failed in inspiring deep loyalties or the kind of emotional resonance that the modern nation-states of Europe elicit among their people.

The European Union is such a powerful idea, representing as it does a potentially renewed world, cognizant of its past sins, yet cleansed of them. A brave new order where states find strength in ditching their primordial, tribal identities and opening up once-insular borders to outside influences. An insurrectionary, post-war, post-national mosaic of composite, multicultural identities.

But if tiny Belgium with its obscure Walloon-Flemish skirmishes were to come apart, what hope is there for the 500-million-strong, 27-nation, Europe of today? If the inhabitants of Leuven have willfully begun educating their children into being unable to speak with their compatriots in Braine-l'Alleud, a half an hour drive away, what "solidarity" could we expect from flaxen-haired, snow-rolling Finns and sun-tanned, beach-bumming Greeks, who live over 3,500 kilometers away? Belgium is the sad proof of how intractable it may be to resolve the cultural gulf between north and south Europe.

Of course, Belgium counts as a success on several parameters. It is a rich, pleasant place to live and attracts considerable foreign investment and immigration. Nobel-prize-winning European Union has chalked up similar achievements. It had brought peace to the Continent and wrought a single market to emerge as the world's largest economy.

Where Belgium and Europe have failed is in creating something more elemental than unions of common customs and bureaucratic compromises. They have failed to foster a common identity: a robust, reflexive loyalty to something larger than one's parochial familiar. Perhaps this isn't a bad thing. Patriotism is an overheated emotion, separated from bloodlust by a fine line. And perhaps what this world needs is a structure like the European Union, which appeals to the head rather than the heart. Yet, without a beating heart to imbue it with life, a head is just so much mass.

I believed it was possible for a European identity to emerge. As an Indian, I seemed to believe in this possibility with greater conviction than many Europeans. After all, it was impossible to travel across the region without confronting the myriad ways in which history, religion, language and architecture had wrought this continent into a distinctive civilization.

In churches in the medieval Flemish city of Bruges, the paintings of Spanish Habsburgs, with their protuberant jaws, line the walls. The baroque excesses of the Queluz National Palace in Portugal are mirrored in Berlin's Charlottenburg Palace. Even the Dutch and French languages, those mortal Belgian enemies, share a script and numerous root words (the English word "mannequin," for example, derives from the identical French term, which in turn has its roots in the Middle Dutch word "*manneken*").

How could one deny Europe's civilizational unity? From shared roots in classical antiquity, to the glue of Christian belief; from the flowering of the Renaissance, to the transformations of the industrial revolution; from the birth of modern-day democracies, to social revolutions aimed at dismantling gender and class hierarchies, Europe's common core is evident.

This is not to reject its real and marvelous diversity, the font of all those familiar jokes: *Heaven is where the police are British, the cooks are French, the mechanics are German, the lovers are Italian and it is all organized by the Swiss. Hell is where the police are German, the cooks are English, the mechanics are French, the lovers are Swiss, and it is all organized by the Italians.* But this is a diversity of detail rather than foundation.

"Same-same" or "different," it is, as always, a matter of perspective. What looked at from without appeared the same, could differ considerably from within. When asked by friends in Brussels how I was enjoying learning French, I would reply that it wasn't so bad given its similarities to English. Eyebrows would shoot up in perplexity. *Mais, non!* How could I say such a thing?

I would explain that after years of learning Chinese, it was pretty easy going being able to read a script straight off the bat and it didn't take a genius to guess that *prospérité* meant prosperity (in Chinese, by contrast, prosperity was pronounced *fu* and written: 福). The eyebrows settled back into comprehension. No one argued with that.

I thought back to my first trip to Europe, euro-railing as a college student back in 1994. I was 17. It was in the days before Schengen visas and the euro. My passport and wallet were filled with a multiplicity of stamps and currencies. But regardless of whether I'd disembarked in Cologne or Rome, Vienna or Paris, I had been unable to cast off the exultant, electric charge of the certainty of being in Europe. What would it take to shake the Walloons and Flemings into a similar epiphany?

NINE

Celebrating the Decline of Europe?

BUBBLE WRAP AND CARTONS. IT WAS THAT TIME AGAIN.
After three and a half years in Brussels, we were about to head back to Asia, this time to the Indonesian capital, Jakarta. Though I had never been there, I could imagine the city that would soon be our home with fair accuracy: the megalopolistic scale of it all, the gaping contrasts, the heaving and steaming of life, the screeching and haze of traffic and construction. Reverse culture shock was the one certainty of our peripatetic lives, and it was readying itself to slam back in our faces.

Everything whirled: emotions, paperwork, farewells. The tart anticipation of new adventures mixed with the sweet-sourness of nostalgia. Predictably, what had once seemed provincial and boring about Brussels now took on a shell-pink glow. There was much of Belgium that I would carry tenderly in my heart: the chocolate shops of the Grand Sablon; the Sunday flea markets; the fabulous Museum of Musical Instruments; the fat, red cherries that lit up the tree in our yard all summer; the excellent day care; and the superlative root canal specialists.

But I was rescued from drowning in all this imagined nostalgia by the reality of life in twenty-first century Europe. Though we had started the cat paperwork well in advance, we had idiotically forgotten about the religion of *les grand vacances,* which saw our vet jetting off to more reliably sunny climes for several weeks. The result was a nail-biting finish to our adventures in feline-related bureaucracy—up until a couple of days before departure, we weren't sure Caramel and Tofu would be able to accompany us to Jakarta.

Canceling our contract with the telecommunications company turned out to be a Herculean undertaking. How foolish we felt afterward at our naïveté in having imagined that all it would take was a phone call asking to terminate our arrangement. It transpired you had to apply to cancel any contract online. We were, however, unable to find the link for cancelations on the company website. We called the company's helpline. The employee who answered couldn't help and claimed he would call back. He didn't. And so it went.

When we were finally able to access the online site, we discovered that we had missed, by one day, the 30-day notice period that was mandatory for a cancelation, but no one had bothered informing us about this on the phone. We would therefore be charged for an extra month despite no longer being resident in the country. When we called again to plead an exception for our case, we were told flatly that "death" was the only permissible exception.

Nothing, however, compared with the effort of disposing of unwanted possessions. We donated a solid stack of baby clothes and over 400 books to various local charities and libraries. I advertised on an expat website and managed to sell a substantial part of my DVD collection as well as some pieces of furniture that we no longer wanted to cart around the world. We pressed barely opened bottles of booze and packets of spices on various friends.

But no matter how much stuff we got rid of, a perniciously solid mountain of other stuff remained stubbornly put. There was the cats' scratching post, the slightly ripped ironing board, battalions of plastic toys, a terminally slow laptop, and a food processor with a blunt blade. And we only kept unearthing more: a tricycle here, a dented pressure cooker there. It was relentless.

We tracked down a charity that offered to take in damaged items like ours to repair and resell and that even offered to pick up the consignment. Thrilled, we quickly dialed the number listed in the advertisement and asked for someone to come around that afternoon. In a conversation reminiscent of my chats with gardeners our first summer in Brussels, I got a polite cough on the other end of the phone, followed by the news that there was a three-month waiting list for the services of the charity's van. They could, possibly, send someone around in October (this was July).

Since we would long have been in Jakarta by then, we reluctantly turned to Plan B: dump the stuff in the garbage. Except, we found, we couldn't. The things we needed to dispose of were either not of "standard" size or of the wrong "category," since they included electronic items, and the garbage collectors refused to take them away. Extensive research on the Brussels municipal website revealed a specially designated dump near the city docks where we would have to drive with our "non-standard" and electronic items.

I had grown up in a world where the neighborhood *kabadiwalla* (literally, the rubbish guy) visited our home in Delhi once a week to take away old newspapers, empty bottles, broken appliances and other household items we needed to dispose of, which he would later ingeniously recycle. He would carefully examine the week's offerings and then hand over a small fee to buy them off us. In Beijing, too, itinerant recyclers wandered the city's hutongs although, reflecting China's status as a more advanced economy, Chinese *kabadiwallas* expected to be paid for their services rather than paying the disposer for their items.

Our last week in Brussels was spent making multiple trips to the garbage dump where we joined snaking queues of cars in hour-long waits, before we were allowed into the vast cremation ground where the city's excess was on scarred, cracked display. It was a valuable and sobering reminder of the consequences of what one consumed, like being forced to witness the slaughter of animals one ate for supper without a second thought. But there is a large gulf between knowing something is good for you and enjoying it, a chasm with which Europe was becoming only too familiar.

What is good for European businesses and Europe's economy more broadly—wage cuts, later retirement, public sector trimming, immigration, investments by foreigners, outsourcing and coming to terms with a relative loss of global power—are not enjoyable experiences. They are bitter medicine, and it isn't a foregone conclusion whether, in what quantity, and with what outcomes Europeans will swallow it.

THE MOVE FROM BEIJING to Brussels had clearly entailed more than just a switch from chopsticks to chocolate. It was a move from an energetic story of rise to a tired one of genteel decline. The hard work, optimism and dynamism of China was in stark contrast to the gloomy mood in Brussels where, even prior to the euro crisis, predictions of irrelevance had rustled dolorously among the pages of newspapers. Eurocrats obsessed about the waning clout of Europe in a world of youthful and populous rising giants like China and India.

Ebbing support for the European Project only provided an additional excuse for grousing. Initially, all this hand-wringing about Europe's decline seemed akin to the neuroses of a hypochondriac, coming as it did from wealthy, healthy Europeans, suntanned from their most recent beach vacations. For Europeans to be drowning in navel-gazing pessimism smacked of self-indulgence, when billions of people lived in disease-ravaged, gut-distending poverty. Even following proposed reforms to restore economic competitiveness, Europe's health care would be more affordable, its unemployment benefits more generous, its homes more temperature-controlled, than in most places in the world.

The *zukundtsangst*—or fear of the future—that was so widespread across western Europe was in essence a response to the growing realization that life was not inevitably going to get better and better, that crises and suffering were not merely words in musty history books. Europeans were reluctantly being woken up to the fact that even maintaining the status quo would require some change, some pain, some toughness. Sacrosanct entitlements would have to be recognized as withdrawable privileges. Compromises would have to be struck. Reality would have to be reckoned with. And self-pity would have to be jettisoned.

ALL THE TALK OF EUROPE'S DECLINE that I was bombarded with as I began to report on the European Union had a corollary that was surely worth celebrating: the rise of other parts of the world that had long been deprived and marginalized. If Europe were no longer as economically or strategically dominant in the world because other nations had begun to climb the potholed path to greater wealth and clout, it was surely something that even Europeans should find it in themselves to welcome.

If Europeans had to work somewhat harder for their money, resulting in a modest leveling out of global inequalities, surely this was only in keeping with the values that Europe claimed to espouse and wanted to universalize: those of solidarity and social justice. Perhaps, I wrote, tongue only lightly in cheek, in a piece titled "Celebrating the Decline of Europe," it was time for European policymakers to uncrease their furrowed brows and raise a toast to the great benefits to humankind at large that Europe's relative decline indicated.[1]

As the economist Arvind Subramanian points out, despite the financial crisis that has plagued the rich countries of the West since 2008, the period of accelerated global economic growth that began in the mid-to-late 1990s has mostly survived. Prosperity, in fact, continues to spread across the globe at an unprecedented pace.[2] The great "divergence," whereby the living standards of a few countries in the West pulled ahead of most others following the Industrial Revolution, was finally being replaced by a "convergence," whereby the rest of the world was catching up with the standards of the developed world.

In the decade preceding the global crisis, some 80 countries in sub-Saharan Africa and Latin America as well as Asia began to converge toward developed-country living standards. Their growth exceeded that of the United States on average by nearly 3.25 percent. From a global perspective, the post-2008 period remains a "golden age of global growth."

In my first year in Brussels, I often found myself willing Europeans to see themselves as others perceived them. To me, there was something glaringly wounded about a place that spent so much energy ensuring that foreign students are sent back home the moment their studies come to an end, or banning articles of clothing that cover the head, or ensuring that shops do not decide to hold sales at the wrong time of the year. I found it hard, too, to understand Europeans holding anti-immigrant sentiments in a region with shrinking demographics or censuring India and China for their carbon emissions from heated rooms well stocked with bottled water. Or why they so resented hard work.

A moment that remained with me long after I'd written it up for a newspaper article was when Antwerp-based Pinkusewitz Diamonds boss, Abraham Pinkusewitz, had talked, eyes glowering and beard aquiver, about why Indians were getting the better of Jewish diamantaires. He'd ascribed it to their relentless work ethic, to their willingness to stay open on weekends and "work 24 hours a day," if necessary. I'd never before come across anyone spitting out the word "work" in a manner that transformed it into a term of abuse.

Across much of Europe, the greatest privilege of all, that of less work, is the one that seems to have the greatest popular support. There is deep-seated anger at the idea of allowing in economic migrants who might work for longer hours and at less pay than the local population had themselves become willing to do. The somewhat satirical conclusion that I come to in the first chapter has a real kernel of truth in it: In countries like India and China, what people really want is the right to work; in Europe, it is the right to holiday that is the goal.

Opinions, evaluations and reactions to Europe's problems from within the region naturally differ from mine, unencumbered as they are by the constant comparison with developing countries that frame my observations. But over time, I was able to understand how this First World "crisis" must feel to those experiencing it. Gradually, a reluctant empathy made pathways through my irritation with the hypocrisy and arrogance I encountered so regularly in Europe.

Comforts and privileges are normalized with remarkable ease. This is hardly unique to Europe or Europeans. It calls to mind the difference between an older generation of Chinese and current-day youngsters, the Little Emperors, born after China's economic reforms took off at the tail end of the 1970s. The former understood what it meant to *chi ku*, "eat bitterness," and were far more likely to bite their tongue and tighten their belt if circumstances demanded it. For them, the freedoms bestowed by the contemporary avatar of the Chinese Communist Party—to get rich, to choose your own spouse, to travel—were privileges they were well aware might vanish as suddenly as they had appeared.

Not so China's twentysomethings. For these young people, competitive, consumerist, globalized and ascendant China is the norm. And for them the freedoms to shop and love and study abroad are rights that they would certainly not renounce without a fight, or possibly a revolution. I wouldn't be surprised if for even younger children like those I describe vacationing in Europe (Chapter Six), ubiquitous access to a McDonald's might not qualify as an inalienable right.

FROM 2010 ON, as the euro crisis came to a boil, it was increasingly evident, even to a skeptic like me, that the anxiety in European policy circles and the protests on the streets were not just a case of the whining of a poor little rich boy. The crisis sharpened and hastened the trends that had already been set in motion by the gradual eastward shifts in economic power over the last two decades.

The pace and depth of the changes necessitated in countries seeking bailouts were more painful and abrupt than would have occurred in the absence of the constraints set by the workings of the euro, which denied member states the ability to devalue their way out of bankruptcy.

There was great debate among economists about whether the kind of harsh reforms demanded by Germany and other northern euro-using countries like Finland and Austria were appropriate. Were they exacerbating the problem and causing needless misery, or was a rude shock to the system the only way to jolt countries like Greece, Italy and Spain into accepting reforms that had long been necessary but were politically unpalatable in the absence of a gun pointed at their heads?

What was not open for debate, however, was the very real pain caused in these countries as a result of austerity measures. Youth unemployment figures of 50 percent and higher, patients with chronic diseases facing major cuts in health care funding, hunger forcing people to forage in trash cans[3] none of these were merely the self-indulgent problems of the wealthy.

The effects of the speed and sharpness of the changes being enforced in southern Europe were not just limited to a rollback in material comforts. The social and political friction consequently unleashed within the worst affected countries, as well as between the continent's Germanic north and Mediterranean south, was grinding away at the very legitimacy of the idea of Europe.

Serious questions loomed about the ability of democracies to swallow unpopular diktats from without, be it from the IMF, Brussels or Berlin, particularly since a prolonged economic trough would likely mean that no clear end to the pain of austerity was in sight.

But the moment questions about the viability of the European Union were raised, a clammy hand gripped my heart. The European Union was not an easy thing to love for a reporter covering its day-to-day functioning. Grey eurocrats and righteous parliamentarians; endless procedure and toothless resolutions; regulations standardizing the curvature of fruits and the use of incandescent lights at fairgrounds did not make for passionate attachment.[4]

And yet, the alternative is chilling. A Europe in crisis is a recipe for a smorgasbord of unsavory tendencies—from xenophobia and protectionism, to the reassertion of tribal, nationalistic identities. Ballooning unemployment, economic stagnation and eroding trust in political institutions are not developments that can be contemplated with complacency, especially given Europe's history of civil war and devastating ideologies like fascism.

Already, parties on the extremes of the political spectrum have been gaining strength across swathes of the continent, from France's National Front (FN) and the Netherlands' Dutch Freedom Party, to Greece's Golden Dawn. When people feel under siege they lash out, finding scapegoats in every corner—from immigrants to Muslims, foreign investment to globalization. In this atmosphere, tolerance and empathy are usually the first casualties.

The European Project has kept in check the fear, prejudices and violence that had characterized relations between the warring empires and states of the continent for centuries. The ideas embedded in the European Union—of inclusion, openness, peace and prosperity—are the kind that evoke rousing symphonies as imagined aural backdrops. Yes, the actual workings of the EU institutions are lacerated with duplicity and hubris and weighed down with a ponderous penchant for process. But its essence is precious. And fragile. It needs nurturing and commitment and vision to see it through the pitfalls that the euro crisis and the challenges of a more multipolar, globalized world have opened up.

It may be tempting, but it does no good for the rest of the world to indulge in *schadenfreude* at Europe's woes. A besieged Europe is not only bad news for the world's economic health, as slowing growth in India and China is testament to, but also a blow to the idea wherein rests humanity's great hope. That of the possibility of a renewed world that is not condemned to repeat history's mistakes, but able to break out of destructive patterns of exclusion and hatred and weave together that fabled unity out of diversity.

IN SOME WAYS, India is a proto-European Union, having stitched together a large region of diverse social and cultural fabric into a political and economic union. Like the European Union, it is the antithesis of the concept of the nineteenth-century European nation-state where a single religion, a single language and a common enemy form the "natural" basis for the only sustainable kind of political unit. But, as the Indian historian Ramachandra Guha points out, on traditional

European parameters of the ideal nation-state, it is Pakistan, rather than India, that should count as a success.[5]

Over the course of its 60-plus years as an independent nation, India has defied the exclusions and divisions of this ideal and is a testament to the fact that it is possible to successfully create a strong, common identity out of seemingly fractured multiplicity. Were the European Union to care enough to look, India could serve as hope, if not guide, for the European Union's own momentous project of rejecting the homogenizing tyranny of the "nation" state, and instead choosing to celebrate difference and aggregation. But with characteristic arrogance, the European Union does not care to look elsewhere for inspiration, and certainly not toward dirty, poor, teeming India.

Instead, EU officials are quick to shake their heads in despair over India's reluctance to take a feather out of Europe's cap on issues of regional integration. India's ham-handedness in its dealings with SAARC (the South Asian Association for Regional Cooperation) is the classic case in point that they raise.[6]

While I believe that by its very existence against the odds of modern political convention, India has something to teach Europe, the reverse is patently true as well. South Asia remains one of the poorest and most backward regions of the world. Revitalizing regional trade and economic links between the countries of SAARC could potentially have dramatic benefits for all. If countries like Germany and France have found a way of overcoming their blood-soaked history, it is proof that historical enmity does not have to preclude cooperation ad infinitum, that economic imperatives and statesmanship can enable a break from beggar-thy-neighbor mentalities and damaging patterns of behavior.

More recently, the European Union brought former communist bloc countries from eastern Europe under its umbrella, enabling transformative growth there. In fact, because of this eastward push, Europe has been one of the best neighborhoods for developing economies over the last decade. In Poland, for example, per capita income increased from $2,000 in 1990 to more than $13,000 in 2011. Overall, companies in eastern Europe have increased productivity faster than those in east Asia.[7]

The successes of the European Union demonstrate that regional integration can be a truly inspirational force for economic and political change. Even post-euro crisis, about half of the world's trade in goods and services involves Europe, two-thirds of which stays within the region.[8] And despite the tensions that might have surfaced between the Germanically minded north and the Mediterranean south in the wake of the crisis, the primary achievement of the European Union, in having recast historical enemies into peaceable and economically interdependent partners, holds firm.

Were Asia able to realize even a modicum of the benefits of regional integration that Europe has reaped, it would transform the lives of the bulk of the world's peoples.

THE WAY EUROPEANS TALK of "Asia" used to irk me, given how it lumps together civilizationally disparate entities like India and China with a motley collection of seemingly unrelated southeast, central and west "Asian" countries. It smacked of a persisting orientalism, whereby a European definition of the exotic "East" prevailed over the reality of how "Asians" in fact perceive each other and themselves.

It was only at an exhibition at Brussels's superb Bozar Centre for the Arts that my skepticism about pan-Asian links was first challenged. The exhibition was titled a "Passage through Asia," and via a wide-ranging collection of ancient and medieval artifacts it told a story of precious stones and revolutionary religions, fragrant spices and radical technologies that had bound the region together for centuries.[9] Historically, Asia had been much more closely and syncretically interconnected than was either imaginable or imagined today.

I learned about the arc of Buddhist grottoes from Dunhuang in China's Gansu province to Bamiyan in Afghanistan and on to the Ajanta and Ellora caves in India. I glimpsed the pathways Hinduism had forged from India across the seas to Indonesia and Malaysia and overland to Burma. And I discovered the details of the "pax Mongolica" that saw the Mongols carve out vast territories across Eurasia, from Japan to the Balkans, in the thirteenth and fourteenth centuries.

Bronze passports, on display at the exhibition, were issued to travelers along the Silk Route at the time, guaranteeing unimpeded passage. But the Silk Route, the mesh of paths that connected Antioch in the west to Chang'an (today's Xi'an) in China, was only one of the overland trade routes that connected Asia's constituent parts. Predating it by thousands of years, a number of sea and land routes had long created interlinkages across Eurasia, with India already in contact with Mesopotamia, Egypt, China and southeast Asia. There was a jade route, an animal skin route and even a lapis lazuli route via which the blue stone traveled west from Afghanistan to India and on to Japan.

European colonialism had played a substantial role in disrupting and cutting the threads that bound the region together. Humiliated and subjugated, the region's major civilizational powers, India and China, had turned inward, rupturing the ancient links that had long extended their cultural and economic influence across Asia's diverse geography.

Later, the decolonization process saw the region reduced to a quagmire of border disputes and flashpoints between nuclear-armed states. After a hiatus of 200-odd years, it is only now that the re-emergence of China and India as economic powers is once again re-creating some of Asia's ancient linkages. In southeast Asia, China has already replaced the European Union and Japan as the main trading and investment partner. And the Association of South East Asian Nations (ASEAN)[10] is expected to displace the European Union and the United States to emerge as China's top trading partner as early as 2015.[11] China has also replaced the United States as Japan's top export market and is vying with the European Union to become India's largest trading partner.

Across the Asian continent, an array of regional groupings, from ASEAN to the Shanghai Cooperation Organization (SCO), to the East Asia Summit,[12] have ignited the possibility of mutually beneficial co-operation and coordination between states that are understandably still prickly about state sovereignty, having only relatively recently gained their independence.

It is easy to lampoon these groupings and the volley of summits they have birthed. The platitudes of (mostly) men in dark suits gathered in various permutations across the region's traffic-snarled cities are not the stuff of ballads. But then, the European Union was not exactly scintillating in its origins as a coal-and-steel union either. It would have taken a prophet of exceptional abilities to foresee the force for integration and growth that the European Union would one day become, at the inception of the European Coal and Steel Community in 1951. The boring and bureaucratic hold hidden in them the potential for the transcendent.

This is not to imply that any of Asia's regional groupings are close to achieving the kind of economic integration and policy coordination that the European Union has evolved over the decades. Even the most developed of the lot, ASEAN, lacks features like a common internal market for goods.

The SCO, in the meantime, is hamstrung by Sino-Russian rivalry. As for SAARC, the unrelenting hostilities between India and Pakistan are readily and easily blamed for its lame-duck workings. Despite its almost three decades of existence, SAARC has made scant progress toward any of its basic goals, such as free trade or the free movement of people.

EUROPE AND ASIA ARE CLEARLY not in equivalent positions. The European Union evolved after the countries of western Europe had accepted democracy and the outcome of the Second World War as final. Were Germany to have insisted on demanding its old territorial borders, the European Union would have been stillborn. But across Asia, nation-states from Pakistan to India, China and Japan have not accepted borders as settled.[13] Nor do they share basic political structures and beliefs. Instead, the countries of Asia range from military dictatorships, to communist party rule, to vibrant but unpredictable democracies. In the absence of resolved territorial and maritime claims, and without shared political values, talk of EU-like institution building can seem hopelessly out of touch with reality.

It seems fairly clear that no Union of Asia, matching the European Union, is on the horizon, even in the medium term. Yet, a mesh of trade agreements, security groupings, and mechanisms for political dialogue has begun to suture together the region, even though the binding threads remain weak and insufficient. But while working toward any level of integration between the disparate polities, cultures and economies of Asia is an uphill challenge, it is a challenge that will not be served by the European Union's failure. The survival of the European Union will not guarantee the success of Asian efforts at regional integration, but its collapse will certainly do these no favor.

The current problems of the eurozone hold valuable lessons, not only for the European Union itself, but also other parts of the world. The crisis is proof, if it was ever needed, that the European Union is an ongoing project rather than an irreversible or axiomatic fact. Europe is going to have to grapple with reassessing certain attitudes that have become so common among the union's supporters as to have hardened into certainties. Is "ever deeper integration," in fact, the right path for

Europe? Does the European Project necessitate a teleological move toward complete political and economic union? Has there been an underestimation of the persistence, power and desirability of nationalism? Where should the boundaries between the powers of democratic nation-states and unelected, supranational technocracies lie?

The unfolding answers to these questions are as much anticipated in non-European countries in the process of finding their own paths to regional stability, as among the EU-27 themselves, and will be as instructive for them

The euro has swiftly transformed from one of the European Union's greatest successes into a cautionary tale, and deservedly so. The common currency was pushed through in the 1990s by its supporters despite the skepticism and opposition of many experts who had fully predicted the unhappy consequences of yoking together countries with such divergent political economies, particularly in the absence of genuine fiscal union. But much thinking in the European Union seems to be motivated by an ideological belief in the unquestionable desirability of any and all measures leading to a closer union, rather than by rational decision making. There is a widespread attitude I encountered in Brussels that bold, visionary measures should not be hampered by "petty" details pertaining to the actual mechanics of these actions.

I remember asking an official in the newly created European External Action Service (a new European diplomatic corps set up post-2009) whether it might not have made sense for the European Union to have actually agreed to a common foreign policy before establishing a sprawling foreign policy institution whose remit appeared to be vague at best and non-existent at worst. Wasn't this an example of putting the cart before the horse? The official in question had looked down at me from the end of his very long nose before patronizingly commenting that mine was a very "Anglo-Saxon question." This was how the European Union had always worked, I was told. If it remained bogged down in details, the European Project could never move forward.

But this need for constant movement forward as an end in itself has been revealed by the euro crisis as misguided. Clearly, there is something to learn from Europe about how not to go about regional integration.

UNDERSTANDING THE EUROPEAN UNION'S FOLLIES, however, should not detract from the revolutionary potential of its underlying idea. Yet, few Indians are invested in the idea of Europe—an attitude that is mirrored in Brussels, where few seem even aware of the idea of India. As a result, both India and the European Union fail to engage with the other seriously, in what seems to be a classic case of familiarity breeding contempt. As essentially soft powers, hamstrung by coalitions and the niceties of convoluted political processes, and consumed by the challenges of handling enormous diversity, the European Union and India sneer at each other's purported incompetence and arrogance. Instead, it is the hard powers of the United States and China that are the poles of their common strategic fixations and awe.

It is true that neither India nor the European Union are geostrategic players on par with China or the United States. The military spending of these titans, for instance, dwarfs that of New Delhi, Brussels or any of the European Union's member states. But, although India and the European Union are "weaker" than China or the United States on some parameters, their underlying ideas are powerful weapons that shouldn't be discounted. These ideas stand for the antithesis of an "you are either with us and agree to everything we tell you to do, or you are against us and we will shoot you" attitude. Instead, they represent attitudes like, "Look, we might disagree, but let's talk and try to find the respect for each other's differences and cultures that will allow us to build bridges, not bomb them."

These may be highly idealized, broadly sketched portraits, but then ideas are about ideals. They may not always be realized, but their lingering presence acts as a brake against the worst excesses.

And so, while I might "celebrate" the decline of Europe in the sense of such a trend indicating a gradual redistribution of global power and wealth, I cannot celebrate any decline of the *idea* of Europe as exemplified by the European Union. After all, not only has the European Union helped normalize peace, safety, health and material comfort for the region's established citizenry, it is also an enabling conception for Europe's new citizens: the millions of migrants of non-European origins who are in the convoluted process of becoming "Europeans."

SO, IS THE IDEA OF EUROPE in danger of collapse? The euro crisis has certainly focused attention on the possibility. But by doing so, it may arguably be performing a service to the European Project by compelling closer integration in the medium term.

In 2009, the European Union had been an exhausted entity, shorn of any path-breaking possibilities after having spent all its energies in pushing through the Lisbon Treaty, a new rulebook whose notable provisions were the creation of the post of a president of the European Council and the setting up of a specialized diplomatic service. Floundering to find renewed purpose, Brussels had attempted to rally European opinion around its purported "leadership" of the global fight against climate change. But neither climate change nor a generalized sense of gradual decline had been urgent enough to crank up the euro motor in the way that the financial crisis eventually managed to.

The European Union was born out of the crisis of the Second World War. Crisis, one line of reasoning went, was the moving soul of the union. Without it, there was only stasis. It was only when in mortal danger that Europe tended to find the political will to pull together and emerge stronger and more united. I believe there is some basis to this argument. It touches upon a truth that applies not only to Europe but to basic human functioning: what doesn't kill us can make us stronger. We are all forced to prove our mettle when under attack, and this has the potential to bring out the best in us, impelling us to reach for our truest, bravest selves.

But for Europe, as in life, there are no guarantees that potential will necessarily translate into fact. And not every crisis makes us stronger. Some denude us. Others destroy us.

THE LEGACY OF THE EURO CRISIS for Europe could still turn either way. We might find a more coherent Europe with greater fiscal and political harmonization emerging phoenix-like from the ashes of the eurozone's current travails. For the optimist, Germans and Greeks are creeping closer together, as the contours of a United States of Europe are fuzzily emerging. But we might also find a fractured Europe, bereft of legitimacy and direction. Year after year of recession in the peripheral countries is going to dangerously extend the capacity of people to voluntarily implement the kind of austerity measures being asked of them.

Even in the best-case scenario of the European Union riding out the crisis and making it to the other side with its constituent parts in greater synchronicity with each other, when the fiscal dust settles, the contours of world power will undoubtedly be altered. Europe is going to have to accept a smaller, more equitable, share of the global pie.

Europe's crisis is about more than just fiscal matters. It is also a manifestation of longer *durée* global trends that have been in motion for at least a couple of decades, whereby a rebalancing of economic power between East and West is under way.

When I'd first moved to Brussels after seven exciting years in China, I had naturally found it a tad dull. Everything had felt so settled and secure compared to the flux and unpredictability of rising China. The feeling didn't last long. By the time I was leaving, less than four years down the line, Europe's future was suddenly an open book whose dénouement appeared far from predictable. This made for interesting journalism. But while certain kinds of changes seemed to me to be both necessary and beneficial for the region, I worried about the baby being thrown out with the bathwater, or the very idea of Europe being discarded, along with the uncompetitive economic practices that needed to be sloughed off. I was leaving Europe at a time when there was no tidy or comforting end in sight.

A FEW DAYS BEFORE OUR DEPARTURE from Brussels, I went out for a walk. The blossoms had long gone from the trees that lined Avenue de L'Opale, but a cool wind blew through the susurrating leaves. I walked past our neighbors' homes and nodded at the various cats that pressed their faces into the windowpanes of the stately maisons de maitre, in search of entertainment to liven up their day.

Within a few minutes, I was upon Place Jamblinne de Meux, a little rectangle of green where Ishaan had taken his first few toddling steps as a thirteen-month-old. The usual assortment of babies and senior citizens burbled from the park's benches. And since it was lunchtime, clusters of high school kids were also lounging and flirting and calling out to each other in French and Arabic. At one end of the square, two prim young girls in hijabs stood waiting at a bus stop, framed by a perfume advertisement on a large billboard that featured the deep cleavage of a well-endowed woman's assets, barely held back by a wisp of red lingerie.

I continued to walk west, down Rue Franklin, passing a Chinese massage parlor on my right, where the boss, a brassy matron from Fujian, employed a young Tibetan masseur who'd grown up in exile in India and spoke a combination of Hindi, Mandarin and English that I was possibly the only person in Belgium to completely understand.

A moment later, I was at Schuman, EU-central, submerged in a sea of pale-skinned eurocrats walking purposefully to some committee meeting or the other. Amid the clatter of building machinery that was the permanent aural backdrop to the area, the indistinct shouts of a few straggling protestors was just audible. It wasn't clear what they were unhappy about but I was reasonably sure it was either about austerity at home or human rights abuses elsewhere. I kept walking, and the hulking EU flag-flanked office buildings gave way to the commune of St. Josse. In an instant, suit-and-tie clad eurocrats were replaced by pot-bellied North Africans in djellabas. Organic cafes offering cucumber and carrot smoothies were edged aside by poky shops leaking mounds of Technicolored spices. This was the area where a Chinese friend had once expressed surprise about how most Belgians seemed to be Turkish.

St. Josse was in fact a Moroccan majority neighborhood, although the bulk of the residents had Belgian citizenship. I navigated past its thronging streets and bargain basement shops to emerge at Rue De Le Lois, a broad, modern highway where cars zinged past at speed and that took a while of waiting at traffic intersections to cross. On the other side were the parliaments. In any standard country that noun would have been in the singular, but this being Belgium we are talking about not one, but four parliaments: the Belgian Federal Parliament, the Flemish Parliament, the Parliament of the French-speaking Community (as opposed to the Walloon Parliament that was housed in the city of Namur) and the Parliament of the Brussels Capital Region.

Overcome with parliamentary excess, I hurried on toward the chocolate shops of the Grand Sablon, a pleasing square in the shadow of the late-Gothic Notre Dame du Sablon church. On my way, I passed the Royal Palace, from whence King Leopold II had once controlled and exploited the vast resources of the Congo.

Tired out, I sank into a chair at one of the alluring cafés that lined the Grand Sablon and ordered a coffee. That afternoon's walk had offered it all up—Europe's pleasures, paradoxes and dilemmas: the beauty and the privilege, the disgruntled protesters and the stifling bureaucracy, the mélange of peoples, cultures and languages, the bloody history and the uncertain future. The coffee arrived and with it a perfectly bittersweet Belgian chocolate.

Acknowledgments

THIS BOOK OWES A DEBT TO A RAFT OF FRIENDS AND allies in a multiplicity of countries. In particular, I would like to thank Nawab Khan and Steven Decraene in Brussels, Marco Omizzolo in Italy, and Gero Brandenburg in Germany. Dirk Collier and Tomas Baert offered valuable advice on all things Belgian. Joerg Wuttke provided introductions and insights into all things Sino-German. The incomparable Jean Pierre Lehmann read most of the book in manuscript form. I must thank him for his feedback and much else beyond. Tuva Kahrs' precise eye caught many a straying comma and intruding split infinitive. Sukhdev Sandhu read and responded as requested despite the twin demands that leave him with little time.

Many of the stories in this book began their life as reports for the *Business Standard* newspaper. The two editors with whom I worked, T. N. Ninan and Sanjaya Baru, provided me with both an indispensible platform and personal support.

Nandini Mehta, my editor at Penguin India, coaxed, soothed and honed in just the right ways. Publisher Chiki Sarkar stuck her oar in when needed, with beneficial results. Thank you both.

A deeply felt thank you to my mother, Gitanjali, for her nurture and encouragement. My brother, Shekhar, read this book chapter by chapter as I wrote it and his advice was my constant guide. Thanks to Kiran Ganguli for shaping me into a reader, without which I could not have been a writer. And of course to my polymath father, Swami, to whom the book is dedicated.

Gratitude is owed to my boys Ishaan and Nico for sharing me, if only reluctantly, with the laptop. But the biggest debt of all is to my husband, Julio, for his magician-like ability to always make it work out for the best.

Notes

INTRODUCTION

1. See Pallavi Aiyar, *Smoke and Mirrors: An Experience of China* (HarperCollins India, 2008).
2. This was a short-lived norm, with growth in India slowing to less than 6 percent by 2012, in the wake of the euro crisis, and the ensuing slowdown in both the demand for exports and foreign investment. However, even a modest growth rate of 5 percent and more was a lot healthier than the virtual standstill that many economies in Europe were experiencing.
3. See M. Ayhan Kose and Eswar S. Prasad, "Emerging Markets Come of Age," in *Finance & Development* 47:4, December 2010 (http://www.imf.org/external/pubs/ft/fandd/2010/12/kose.htm).
4. See Minxin Pei, *China's Trapped Transition: The Limits of Developmental Autocracy* (Harvard University Press, 2008); Gordon Chang, *The Coming Collapse of China* (Random House, 2001); Will Hutton, *The Writing on the Wall: China and the West in the 21st Century* (Abacus, 2008).
5. See Brendan Simms, *Europe: The Struggle for Supremacy, from 1453 to the Present* (Allen Lane, 2013).
6. See Felice Dassetto, *L'Iris et le Croissant* (Presses Universitaires de Louvain, 2011).
7. "A Tale of Two Expats," in *The Economist* (December 29, 2010).
8. See Amartya Sen, *The Argumentative Indian: Writings on Indian History, Culture and Identity* (Picador, 2006).

CHAPTER 1: ADVENTURES IN OCCIDENTALISM

1. Lest I trigger a stampede of diamond smugglers at the Brussels airport, I should point out that on subsequent trips I always found customs properly staffed.
2. It would have served us well to have taken a look at the Brussels Federal Police website beforehand, where under a lengthy section on advice to tourists, people are warned against giving help to those who appear to have car trouble. "Be cautious," you are told and if "you do decide to help, keep the doors of your own car locked and only roll down the

windows slightly. . . ." Then it continues: "At airports be wary if someone approaches you or in the occurrence of an unexpected event."

3. See Bryan Roberts, *Cities of Peasants: The Political Economy of Third
World Urbanization* (Sage, 1979).

4. See Felice Dassetto, *L'Iris et le Croissant* (Presses Universitaires de Louvain, 2011).

5. An extremely popular brand of cinnamon biscuits in Belgium.

6. See Felice Dassetto, *L'Iris et le Croissant* (Presses Universitaires de Louvain, 2011).

7. See, for example, Néstor García Canclini, *Hybrid Cultures* (University
of Minnesota Press, 1995).

8. Data collated from the Belgian prison authorities by sociologist Jan Her-
togen (www.npdoc.be).

9. This was the Xiaotangshan hospital built in the northern suburb of Beijing to accommodate SARS patients. For more, see Pallavi Aiyar, *Smoke
and Mirrors: An Experience of China* (HarperCollins India, 2008), 64.

10. See James Fallow, "China Makes, the World Takes," in *The Atlantic
Magazine* (July–August 2007).

11. Lest the dear reader suspect me of inventing a grotesque caricature of
the francophone, here are the details of the textbook in question: Miquel
Claire, *Vite etBien-1* (CLE International, 2009).

12. See "Le conducteur de la Stib a frappé le premier," in *Le Soir* newspaper
(February 15, 2011).

13. See http://www.time.com/time/business/article/0,8599,1925163,00.html.

14. See http://www.nytimes.com/2009/10/06/business/global/06milk.html.

15. About 42 percent of children under age five in India suffer from malnu-
trition and are "wasted" (low weight for height). Nearly 59 percent of
Indian children under age five are "stunted." The figure comes from the
Hungama survey of 73,000 Indian households conducted by the Naandi
Foundation (http://www.naandi.org/CP/HungamaBKDec11LR.pdf).

16. See "Taxi Services: Competition and Regulation 2007," in OECD Policy
Roundtables (http://www.oecd.org/dataoecd/49/27/41472612.pdf).

17. See Peggy Hollinger, "'Dockers' Strike Worries Sarkozy," in *Financial
Times* (October 14, 2010).

18. See "Marseilles Falls in European Port Rankings," in *Baird Maritime,*
February 2, 2011 (http://www.bairdmaritime.com/index.php?option=co
m_content&view=article&id=9210:marseilles-falls-to-fifth-place-in
-european-port-rankings&catid=68&Itemid=59).

19. See Eurostat (http://epp.eurostat.ec.europa.eu/statistics_explained/index
.php/Unemployment_statistics). A two-tier system was not unique to
European countries like Spain and Italy; it was also a hallmark of both
the Chinese and Indian labor markets. For all its newly found capitalist ways, the work force in China, even in state-owned enterprises, was
divided into those who were *"tizhinei"* (inside the system) or members
of the Communist Party and the *"tizhi wai"* (outside the system). Those
who were *tizhi wai* were subject to different, discriminatory rules when
it came to matters of payment, promotions and other perks. They could
also be fired with ease. The complexity of India's labor laws and the
injustice they perpetuate between a protected "organized sector" that
only accounts for 20-odd percent of manufacturing employment and a

vastly more numerous "unorganized sector" is well documented. See, for example, *Reshaping Tomorrow: Is South Asia Ready for the Big Leap?* Edited by Ejaz Ghani (Oxford University Press, 2011).

20. In 2011, Belgian papers were all agog when a clothing store, Zeb, decided to take the law into its own hands and offer discounts on its products even during the six-week "respite" period leading up to the official sales. Zeb was taken to court, and at the time of writing the European Court of Justice was mulling the vexed issue of whether Belgian retail law prohibiting discounts prior to sale was in contravention of EU law. Scintillating stuff. See http://www.flanderstoday.eu/content /no-more-sales.

CHAPTER 2: A HALL OF MIRRORS

1. See Summit Khanna, "Jain Temple Is New Symbol of Culture in Antwerp," in *DNA*, October 4, 2010 (http://www.dnaindia.com/india/report _jain-temple-is-new-symbol-of-indian-culture-in-antwerp_1447304/); see also "Into the Next World," in *Flanders Today*, September 1, 2010 (http://www.flanderstoday.eu/ content/next-world).

2. See Melvyn Thomas, "Biggest Diamond Robbery Spreads Fear amongst Indians in Antwerp," in *The Times of India*, March 6, 2010 (http:// articles.timesofindia.indiatimes.com/2010-03-06/surat/28130914_1_in dian-diamantaires-antwerp-diamond-trade).

3. A shorter version of the description of Antwerp Indians in this chapter appeared as an article in the *Business Standard*. See Pallavi Aiyar, "The Shahs of Sparkle" (June 27, 2009).

4. See Pallavi Aiyar, "Cricket May Have Roots in Belgium," in *Business Standard* (September 13, 2009).

5. I was told that a few specially invited dignitaries from the Antwerp government had been present earlier in the day, but they weren't in evidence by the time I joined the devotees. In subsequent PR videos of the temple, the propensity of the Antwerp Jains to appropriate rather than integrate was given away. "We would like to take the liberty," intoned a disembodied narrator, "to call your (Belgian) dignitaries like Nobel Prize winner Maurice Maeterlinck, King Albert I and (painter) Peter Paul Rubens, Jains, as they strictly followed vegetarianism" (http://www.youtube .com/watch?v=i_p0vjz9SxA).

6. See Geoff Pingree, "Chinese Work Ethic Tires Spaniards," in *Christian Science Monitor* (October 19, 2004).

7. Ibid.

8. See Luc Sante, *The Factory of Facts* (Vintage Books, 1998), 76.

9. Ibid., 116–17.

10. Ibid., 125.

11. See Alex Hudson, "Are Jobless Brits Scared by Hard Work?" in BBC News, February 24, 2010 (http://news.bbc.co.uk/2/hi/uk_news/maga zine/8533172.stm).

12. The proportion of foreign-born residents in Italy grew from 0.8 percent in 1990 to 7 percent in 2010, a huge turnaround for a country that had been exporting large numbers of Italians for a hundred years since the third quarter of the nineteenth century.

13. See Marco Omizzolo, *Transnationalism in International Immigration: The Case of the Sikh Community in the District of Latina*, PhD thesis (University of Florence, May 2011).

14. See Elisabetta Povoledo, "In Italian Heartland, Indians Keep the Cheese Coming," in *The New York Times* (September 7, 2011).

15. See Steven Erlanger, "French-German Border Shapes More Than Territory," in *The New York Times* (March 3, 2012).

16. See Economist Debates: "This House Believes Immigration Is Endangering European Society" (http://www.economist.com/debate/overview/210).

17. See "In Greece You Get a Bonus for Showing Up for Work," Reuters, April 28, 2010 (http://www.thestar.com/business/article/802042—in -greece-you-get-a-bonus-for-showing-up-for-work). The absurdities of the special allowances that Greece's 1.3 million civil servants received didn't end here. For example, railway employees received a 420-euro bonus a month for hand hygiene. See http://www.thepeakeffect.com/2011 /10/greece-absurd-bonuses.html.

18. See http://pewresearch.org/pubs/1461/italy-widespread-anti-immigrant -sentiment.

19. Ibid.

20. See http://www.ipsos-na.com/download/pr.aspx?id=10883.

21. See Helen Warrell, "Economists Urge Rethink on Immigration," in *Financial Times* (November 20, 2011).

22. See *European Report on Development 2009* (http://www.erd-report .eu/erd/report_2009/documents/volB/Backgrounds/ERD-Background _Paper-Nyarko.pdf).

23. The data was given to me in 2011 by Maria Asenius, who was head of cabinet for the European Commissioner for Home Affairs at the time. Italy, too, cannot afford to be too choosy about the color of its future work force. Without immigration, its population would have declined by 75,000 in 2009, the most recent year for which figures are available. With it, the population grew by a modest 295,000. See Benvenuto, "Up to a Point," in *The Economist* (June 9, 2011).

24. See Richard Ehrman, "The Power of Numbers: Why Europe Needs to Get Younger," in *Policy Exchange* (2009).

25. See "EU Moves to Attract Highly Skilled Migrant Workers," in *The New York Times* (September 25, 2008).

26. See James Surowiecki, "The Track-Star Economy," in *The New Yorker* (August 27, 2012).

27. Ibid.

28. Mass hysteria about the specter of Polish plumbers taking over local jobs following EU enlargement in 2004—when ten new Eastern European countries joined the European Union—led to several "old" members such as Germany, Belgium and Austria imposing long "transitional periods" before fully opening up their borders. Germany and Austria only ended theirs in 2011.With respect to the January 1, 2007, enlargement, which brought Romania and Bulgaria into the European Union, all EU-15 countries (Austria, Belgium, Denmark, Finland, France, Germany, Greece, Ireland, Italy, Luxembourg, the Netherlands, Portugal, Spain, Sweden and the United Kingdom), with the exception of Sweden and Finland, decided to impose restrictions on the access of Bulgarians and Romanians to their labor market.

29. See Fareed Zakaria, "To Become an American," in *The Daily Beast* (April 9, 2006); see "Germany Pushes Green Card but Indian IT Pros Ain't Playing Yet," in *Financial Express* (February 20, 2002).
30. See Kirk Semple, "Many U.S. Immigrants' Children Seek American Dream Abroad," in *The New York Times* (April 15, 2012).
31. See "Moving Out, On and Back," in *The Economist* (August 27, 2011).
32. See Pallavi Aiyar, "The New Indian Community in China," in *Chinese Cross Currents* 4:4 (Macau Ricci Institute, October 2007).
33. See "The New New World," in *The Economist* (April 6, 2013).

CHAPTER 3: THE VEILED THREAT

1. The six religions officially recognized in Belgium, which make them eligible for a degree of state support, are Catholicism, Protestantism, Anglicanism, Islam, Judaism and the (Greek and Russian) Orthodox Church.
2. In some countries, such as Austria, Islamic studies in public schools has been widespread from as far back as 1983. See http://www.euro-islam .info/key-issues/education/.
3. See Samuel P. Huntington, *The Clash of Civilizations and the Remaking of World Order* (Simon & Schuster, 1998).
4. See Christopher Caldwell, *Reflections on the Revolution in Europe, Immigration, Islam and the West* (Anchor, 2010).
5. A form of boules popular in France and Belgium.
6. See Tony Judt, *Post War: A History of Europe since 1945* (The Penguin Press, 2005), 8–9.
7. The Netherlands, which has the closest thing in Europe to an integration policy, adopted this policy only in 1981; in France and Germany, integration measures are piecemeal and often left to localities and/or intermediate institutions. See Randall Hansen, "Migration to Europe since 1945: Its History and Its Lessons" (http://homes.chass.utoronto .ca/~rhansen/Articles_files/20031.pdf).
8. See Christopher Caldwell, *Reflections on the Revolution in Europe, Immigration, Islam and the West* (Anchor, 2010), 30; see also Giovanni Di Lorenzo, "Drinnen vor der Tur," in *Die Zeit* (September 30, 2004).
9. See Seyla Benhabib, *Another Cosmopolitanism* (Oxford University Press, 2006).
10. See David Goodhart, "Do We Need More People in Europe?" in *The Observer* (May 17, 2009).
11. Bat Ye'or (or Gisèle Littman) are seen as the originators of the thesis, but the majority of supporters are Americans, including Mark Steyn, Bruce Bawer and Walter Lacquer. See Justin Vaisse, "Eurabian Follies," in *Foreign Policy* (January–February 2010).
12. See Simon Kuper, "Headcount Dispels Lurid Vision of 'Eurabia,'" in *Financial Times* (August 20, 2007).
13. See Mark Easton, "Why Have the White British Left London?" in BBC News, February 20, 2013 (http://www.bbc.co.uk/news/uk-21511904).
14. See Felici Dasseto, *Iris and the Crescent* (Presses universitaires de Louvain, 2011).
15. See Christopher Caldwell, *Reflections on the Revolution in Europe, Immigration, Islam and the West* (Anchor, 2010).

16. Towns where Muslim immigrants predominate are dubbed "dish cities" due to the ubiquity of satellite dishes permanently turned east. See Ian Buruma, "Death in Amsterdam," and Roger Cohen, "Dutch Virtue of Tolerance under Strain," in *The New York Times* (November 7, 2005).

17. See Simon Kuper, "The Crescent and the Cross," in *Financial Times* (November 10, 2007).

18. See Luc Sante, *The Factory of Facts* (Vintage Books, 1998), 80.

19. See "In Rapidly Modernising India, Caste Fatally Lurks," Reuters, May 7, 2010 (http://uk.reuters.com/article/2010/05/06/uk-india-caste-murder-idUKTRE64570Q20100506).

20. See Luc Sante, *The Factory of Facts* (Vintage Books, 1998), 144–45.

21. See Ian Buruma, *Murder in Amsterdam: Liberal Europe, Islam and the Limits of Tolerance* (Penguin Books, 2007), 9.

22. Van het Reve wrote that God was a donkey and he would make sweet love to the animal making sure it wouldn't get hurt when it climaxed. See Ian Buruma, *Murder in Amsterdam: Liberal Europe, Islam and the Limits of Tolerance* (Penguin Books, 2007), 97. The Netherland's "scornful blasphemy" law was drafted in 1932 in response to the argument by a communist newspaper for the abolition of Christmas. Van het Reve's case on anti-blasphemy grounds made it all the way to the Supreme Court before being dismissed. Most European countries retain some form of anti-blasphemy law, although most have fallen into disuse. See http://www.dw.de/dw/article/0,1894686,00.html. However, Germany's anti-blasphemy law dating from 1871 was successfully used as late as 1994 to ban a musical comedy that ridiculed the Catholic doctrine of immaculate conception by portraying crucified pigs.

23. For a decade-by-decade compilation of the censorship of books in India, see Nilanjana Roy, "Banning Books in India," September 30, 2012 (http://nilanjanaroy.com/2012/09/30/banned-books-week-banning-books-in-india).

24. See Praveen Swami, "Salman Rushdie & India's New Theocracy," in *The Hindu* (January 21, 2012); also see Srijana Misra Das, "A Trimmed Idea of India," in *The Times of India* (January 27, 2012).

25. See "Chetan Bhagat Attacks Rushdie, Says You Can't Hurt Feelings in India," in *The Indian Express* (January 22, 2012).

26. A study by the European Social Survey in 2008 found that upward of 50 percent of people in Britain, France, Belgium, Spain, the Netherlands and the Czech Republic *never* went to church (except on special occasions). See "Europe's irreligious," *The Economist Online*, August 9, 2010 (http://www.economist.com/blogs/dailychart/2010/08/religious_attendance).

27. For example, in Denmark, foreign spouses of citizens younger than 24 years of age cannot get citizenship.

28. See Simon Kuper, "Immigrant Muslims in Belleville," in *Financial Times* (October 2, 2009).

29. See Pallavi Aiyar, "Now Belgium Bans Burqa in Public Places," in *Business Standard* (May 1, 2010).

30. There is an association between the wearing of saffron robes and those with a Hindu nationalism bent. See, for example, the Wikipedia entry on Saffron Terror (http://en.wikipedia.org/wiki/Saffron_terror#cite_note-4).

31. See William Dalrymple's fascinating essay about an obscure corner of the Indian state of Kerala where local myth fuses the Hindu Goddess Bhagvati with the Virgin Mary into a single family. "Sisters of Mannarkad," in *Outlook* (August 11, 2008).

32. See Praveen Swami, "Salman Rushdie and India's New Theocracy," in *The Hindu* (January 21, 2012).

33. See Pankaj Mishra, "Beyond Boundaries," in *The National* (November 26, 2009).

34. See Josh Schrei, "The God Project: Hinduism as Open-Source Faith," in *Huffington Post,* March 4, 2010 (http://www.huffingtonpost.com/josh -schrei/ the-god-project-hinduism_b_486099.html).

35. The Carvakas are known to have reviled the Vedic texts. One proponent, Ajita Keshakambalin, went so far as to claim the Vedas to have been the work of "buffoons, knaves and demons." See Namit Arora, "Ancient Indian scepticism," in *Himal,* August 2009 (http://himalmag .com/component/content/article/70/594-Ancient-Indian-scepticism .html).

36. See Ian Buruma, *Murder in Amsterdam: Liberal Europe, Islam and the Limits of Tolerance* (Penguin Books, 2007), 94. Buruma also contextualizes Theo van Gogh's own polemics (which included calling Muslim immigrants in Europe a "fifth column" and likening Jesus to a "rotten fish," as part of a Dutch literary tradition of "abusive criticism" stretching back to the late nineteenth century whereby personal abuse was elevated to high style).

37. While exact numbers are disputed, thousands of people were killed in each of these incidents.

38. See Ian Buruma, *Murder in Amsterdam: Liberal Europe, Islam and the Limits of Tolerance* (Penguin Books, 2007), 7.

39. See Parag Khanna, "The Metrosexual Superpower," in *Foreign Policy* (July 1, 2004).

40. See Arundhati Roy, "Capitalism: A Ghost Story," in *Outlook* (March 26, 2012).

41. See Seyla Benhabib, *Another Cosmopolitanism* (Oxford University Press, 2006).

42. See Tony Judt, *Post War: A History of Europe since 1945* (The Penguin Press, 2005), 9.

43. All the details in this and the following paragraphs relating to the population transfers during and after the Second World War are taken from "The Legacy of War" chapter in Tony Judt, *Post War: A History of Europe since 1945* (The Penguin Press, 2005).

44. See Pamela Ballinger, *History in Exile: Memory and Identity at the Borders of the Balkans* (Princeton University Press, 2002).

45. In 1945, President Edouard Benes of Czechoslovakia said, "We have decided to eliminate the German problem in our republic once and for all." In the following months, Germans had their property placed under state control and were stripped of their Czech citizenship. Three million Germans were then expelled into Germany. Before the war, Germans had comprised 29 percent of the population of Bohemia and Moravia. By 1950, this was down to 1.8 percent.

46. See Tony Judt, *Post War: A History of Europe since 1945* (The Penguin Press, 2005), 9.

47. See Ariane Chebel d'Appollonia, *National Front and Anti-Semitism in France*, The Brookings Institution, 2002 (http://www.brookings.edu/fp /cusf/analysis/ chebel.pdf). Anti-Semitism played a major role in the creation of the National Front, which drew its inspiration from a variety of French far-right movements (e.g., Action Française, the Vichy regime, the Pujadiste movement, Organization de l'Armée Secrete, Occident, and Ordre Nouveau). "All of these previous political experiences were intimately connected with traditional French anti-Semitism. Because of its direct links to earlier far-right organizations, the National Front's initial recruitment efforts were confined to the traditional anti-Semitic, neo-militaristic margins of society (for example, former Waffen SS, former members of the Vichy Milice like François Brigneau and neo-Nazis like François Duprat)," 3.

48. See Valentina Pop, "EU Popularity Plunges Right across the Bloc," in *EU Observer*, July 26, 2010 (http://euobserver.com/social/30682). The turnout for the 2009 European elections was the lowest ever since direct elections for the European Parliament started 30 years earlier, with only 43 percent of those entitled to vote making the effort to go to the polls.

49. See Ian Buruma, *Murder in Amsterdam: Liberal Europe, Islam and the Limits of Tolerance* (Penguin Books, 2007), 181.

50. See Bhikhu Parekh, "European Liberalism and the 'Muslim' Question" (ISIM Papers, Amsterdam University Press, 2011).

51. Hoca is a Seljuk satirical Sufi figure who is believed to have lived around the thirteenth century and is considered a philosopher and wise man, remembered for his funny stories. He appears in thousands of stories, sometimes witty, sometimes wise, but often also as a fool or the butt of a joke.

52. See Anne Morelli, "A Walk through the History of Brussels," in *KVS Express* (December 2009–January 2010), 16–18.

53. See Bhikhu Parekh, "European Liberalism and the 'Muslim' Question" (ISIM Papers, Amsterdam University Press, 2011).

54. See Simon Kuper, "Immigrant Muslims in Belleville," in *Financial Times* (October 2, 2009).

55. See Ian Buruma, *Murder in Amsterdam: Liberal Europe, Islam and the Limits of Tolerance* (Penguin Books, 2007), 115.

56. See Bhikhu Parekh, "European Liberalism and the 'Muslim' Question" (ISIM Papers, Amsterdam University Press, 2011), 33.

57. See Ian Buruma, *Murder in Amsterdam: Liberal Europe, Islam and the Limits of Tolerance* (Penguin Books, 2007), chapter 6.

58. Ibid., 198.

59. See Dan Bilefsky, "Toulouse Killer's Path to Radicalism a Bitter Puzzle," in *The New York Times* (March 29, 2012).

60. See Pankaj Mishra, "A culture of fear," in *The Guardian* (August 15, 2009).

61. See Joan Wallach Scott, *The Politics of the Veil* (Princeton University Press, 2011); see also Linda S. Fair, *Muslims in Denmark: Discourse of the Veil*, Rutgers University, 2003 (http://geographyplanning.buffalo state.edu/MSG%202003/ 3_Fair.pdf), for a discussion of the veil in colonial discourse.

62. The term for a nation famously coined by Benedict Anderson. See his *Imagined Communities: Reflections on the Origin and Spread of Nationalism* (Verso, 1991).
63. See Swaminathan Aiyar, "My Family and Other Globalisers," *The Times of India* (April 2, 2005).

CHAPTER 4: TILTING AT WINDMILLS

1. See Margherita Stancati, "Almost 5,000 Indian Children Die Daily," *Wall Street Journal* blog, September 13, 2012 (http://blogs.wsj.com /indiarealtime/2012/09/13/almost-5000-indian-children-die-daily).
2. See Karl Gerth, *As China Goes, So Goes the World* (Hill and Wang, 2011), 25.
3. See Pallavi Aiyar, "Beijing on Overdrive to Curb Pollution," in *The Hindu* (August 2, 2008).
4. See Pallavi Aiyar, "Water Woes," in *Frontline* (June 29, 2007); see also David Barboza, "In China, Farming Fish in Toxic Waters," in *The New York Times* (December 15, 2007).
5. See *Excreta Matters* (Centre for Science and Environment, 2012).
6. Although the reason for this was that India lagged behind China in terms of its industrialization, some 2.7 million light vehicles (passenger cars and light commercial vehicles) were sold in India in 2010, as compared to some 16 million in China. See http://www.economist.com /blogs/dailychart/2010/12/car_sales.
7. The simultaneous accessions concerned the following countries: Cyprus, Czech Republic, Estonia, Hungary, Latvia, Lithuania, Malta, Poland, Slovakia and Slovenia.
8. See Dieter Helm, "A Critique of EU Climate-Change Policy," in *The Economics and Politics of Climate Change*, edited by Dieter Helm and Cameron Hepburn (Oxford University Press, 2009).
9. Communication from the European Commission to the European Parliament, the Council, the European Economic and Social Committee and the Committee of the Regions: Towards a Comprehensive Climate Change Agreement in Copenhagen, Brussels, January 28, 2009.
10. See V. K. Mishra, Robert Retherford and Kirk Smith, *Biomass Cooking Fuels and the Prevalence of Blindness in India* (http://ehs.sph.berkeley .edu/krsmith/publications/Mishra%20EM%20blindness%2099.pdf); see also Vinod Mishra, Robert Retherford and Kirk Smith, "Biomass Cooking Fuels and the Prevalence of Tuberculosis in India," in *International Journal of Infectious Diseases* 3:3, 1999.
11. See "Clean hands, stay healthy," in *The Hindu* (May 21, 2012).
12. Most bottled water is siphoned into PET (polyethylene terephthalate) bottles made out of petroleum feedstock. It takes 162 g of oil and seven liters of water (including power plant cooling water) just to manufacture a one-liter bottle, creating over 100 g of greenhouse gas emissions (10 balloons full of CO_2) per empty bottle. Extrapolate this for the developed world (2.4 million tons of plastic are used to bottle water each year), and it represents serious oil use for what is still essentially a single-use object. To make the 29 billion plastic bottles used annually in the United States, the world's biggest consumer of bottled water, requires

more than 17 million barrels of oil a year, enough to fuel more than a million cars for a year. See Lucy Siegle, "It's Just Water, Right? Wrong. Bottled Water Is Set to Be the Latest Battleground in the Eco War," in *The Observer* (February 10, 2008).

13. See James Garvey, *The Ethics of Climate: Right and Wrong in a Warming World* (Change Continuum International Publishing Group, 2008).

14. See *Navigating Numbers, Greenhouse Gas Data and International Climate Policy*, World Resources Institute, chapter 6 (http://pdf.wri.org /navigating_numbers_chapter6.pdf).

15. See Chris Buckley, "China Says Is World's Top Greenhouse Gas Emitter," Reuters, November 23, 2010 (http://af.reuters.com/article/energy OilNews/idAFTOE6AM02N20101123?sp=true).

16. See *Navigating Numbers, Greenhouse Gas Data and International Climate Policy*, World Resources Institute, chapter 6 (http://pdf.wri.org /navigating_numbers_chapter4.pdf).

17. For data on carbon emissions per person by country, see http:// www.guardian.co.uk/environment/datablog/2009/sep/02/carbon-em issions-per-person-capita.

18. See Michael Spence, *The Next Convergence: The Future of Economic Growth in a Multispeed World* (Farrar, Straus and Giroux, 2011), chapter 36.

19. See "Bjørn Lomborg on the Rio Green Summit: Poverty Pollutes," in *Newsweek*, May 28, 2012 (http://www.thedailybeast.com/newsweek /2012/05/27/bjorn-lomborg-on-the-rio-green-summit-poverty-pollutes .html).

20. See Radoslav S. Dimitrov, "Inside UN Climate Change Negotiations: The Copenhagen Conference," *Review of Policy Research* 27:6, 2010.

21. See Jeremy Kahn, "Why India Might Save the Planet," in *Newsweek* (March 13, 2011).

22. See Thomas Friedman, "The Copenhagen that Matters," in *The New York Times* (December 22, 2009).

23. See "Table: The World's Happiest Countries," in *Forbes* (http://www .forbes.com/2010/07/14/world-happiest-countries-lifestyle-realestate -gallup-table.html).

24. See "Livestock's Long Shadow" (Food and Agricultural Organization of the United Nations, 2006).

25. See Pallavi Aiyar, "Chewing the Cud Could Sink the Planet," in *Business Standard* (February 19, 2010).

26. For more on this stage in bilateral relations, see Pallavi Aiyar, *Smoke and Mirrors: An Experience of China* (HarperCollins India, 2008), chapter 4.

27. See Keith Bradsher and Matthew Wald, "A Measured Rebuttal to China over Solar Panels," in *The New York Times* (March 20, 2012).

28. According to Morgan Stanley, by 2020, the average Indian will be 29 years old compared to 37 for a one-child policy-shaped China. The argument is that while the world's richer nations and China confront the burden of caring for an army of retirees, India will continue to have more and more workers entering the highest producing/consuming phase of their lives, ostensibly representing a boon for the economy.

29. "Taking note" of the accord is a way for UNFCCC parties to formally acknowledge its existence without going so far as to endorse it.

30. In the report, it was shown that the economic crisis had reduced the cost of the 20 percent by 2020 cut from a 70 billion euro estimate made in 2008 to 48 billion euros. See http://ec.europa.eu/commission _2010-2014/hedegaard/ headlines/news/2010-05-26_01_en.htm.

31. In the post-Copenhagen years, Poland refused to endorse even vaguely worded EU strategies aimed at setting the 27 countries on track to meet a 2050 indicative goal of cutting CO_2 emissions by as much as 95 percent over the 1990 levels. Poland was dependent on coal for around 90 percent of its electricity generation. See "Poland Blocks EU Endorsement on Climate Change," in *Wall Street Journal* (June 15, 2012).

32. See Sonia van Gilder Cooke, "Will Austerity Derail Europe's Clean-Energy Movement?," in *Time* (February 10, 2012); see also Michael Birnbaum and Anthony Faiola, "Solar Industry Faces Subsidy Cuts in Europe," in *Washington Post* (March 19, 2012).

CHAPTER 5: THE AUSTERE NEW BOSS

1. Only 17 European countries share the euro currency: Austria, Belgium, Cyprus, Estonia, Finland, France, Germany, Greece, Ireland, Italy, Luxembourg, Malta, the Netherlands, Portugal, Slovakia, Slovenia and Spain.

2. See, for example, David Wessel, "For Europe, a Lehman Moment," in *Wall Street Journal*, December 11, 2011 (http://online.wsj.com/article /SB10001424052970204397704577069872430939482.html); see also Ed West, "Yet Another Catholic Country Needs a Bailout from the Protestant North," in *The Telegraph*, November 10, 2011 (http://blogs .telegraph.co.uk/news/edwest/100116846/yet-another-catholic-country -needs-a-bailout-from-the-protestant-north/).

3. See "Modell Deutschland, über alles," in *The Economist* (April 14, 2012); see also Norbert Walter, "Germany's Hidden Weaknesses," in *The New York Times* (February 8, 2012).

4. See Frederick Studemann, "Germany Swings to a Pragmatic Generation," in *Financial Times* (October 15, 2005).

5. See "Sikorski: German Inaction Scarier than Germans in Action," in *The Economist* blogs, November 29, 2011 (http://www.economist.com /blogs/easternapproaches/2011/11/polands-appeal-germany).

6. See Halik Kochanski, *The Eagle Unbowed: Poland and the Poles in the Second World War* (Allen Lane, 2012).

7. See "The ECB and OMT: OTT, OMG or WTF?" in *The Economist* (September 7, 2012).

8. See the EFSF website (http://www.efsf.europa.eu/about/index.htm).

9. German Federal Ministry of Finance data. See http://www.bundesfinanz ministerium.de/Content/EN/Standardartikel/Topics/Europe/Articles /Stabilising_the_euro/european-financial-stability-facility.html.

10. See Nico Itano, "Greece's Debt Crisis: Blaming Nazi Germany," in *The National Herald* (February 26, 2010).

11. See Anatole Kaletsky, "Can the Rest of Europe Stand up to Germany?" Reuters, June 20, 2012 (http://blogs.reuters.com/anatole-kaletsky/2012 /06/20/ can-the-rest-of-europe-stand-up-to-germany/).

12. See Wolfgang Münchau, "Berlin Has Dealt a Blow to European Unity," in *Financial Times* (July 12, 2009).

13. This put Germany in the company of Russia, Brazil, China and India. See Severin Weiland and Roland Nelles, "Germany Has Marginalised Itself over Libya," *Spiegel Online International* (March 18, 2011).

14. See Nicholas Kulish, "Greek-German Tensions over Finances Spill into Another Arena," in *The New York Times* (June 22, 2012).

15. The term "hidden champions" for the German mittelstand was coined by management guru Hermann Simon. See his *Hidden Champions of the Twenty-First Century: The Success Strategies of Unknown World Market Leaders* (Springer, 2009).

16. See http://www.ifm-bonn.org/index.php?id=889.

17. See Ken Bremer, "The German Mittelstand: A Glance at Germany's 'Hidden Champions,'" in *Germany Trade & Invest* (October 2012).

18. See Jack Ewing, "German Small Businesses Reflect Country's Strength," in *The New York Times* (August 13, 2012).

19. The Institute for Mittelstand Research in Bonn did a survey that found that even larger mittelstand reluctant to take on debt. Nearly all the said cash flow was the most important form of financing. However, 70 percent did take traditional bank loans, although less than 20 percent said capital market financing was an important source of cash. See www .ifm-bonn.org/.

20. Many mittelstand had, however, moved part of their manufacturing processes to China and elsewhere in Asia, in part to sell to the fast grow- ing local market, but also to gain access to lower-cost supplies and learn a thing or two about new production processes.

21. In 2012, despite the slump in demand within Europe, Germany was able to increase its exports by 4.3 percent due to rising sales outside the crisis-hit continent, in particular to China and the United States. See "Booming Sales beyond Europe: German Exports Seen Hitting New Record in 2012," in *Spiegel Online*, January 8, 2013 (http://www.spie gel.de/international/business/new-record-for-german-exports-expected -for-2012-despite-euro-crisis-a-876296.html). German exports to China in 2011 were worth 65 billion euros, double the amount in 2007. See also Ralph Atkins, "Germany: The Miraculous Machine," in *Financial Times* (April 19, 2012).

22. See Pallavi Aiyar, *Smoke and Mirrors: An Experience of China* (Harp- erCollins India, 2008), 145–49.

23. For example, 48 percent of Dutch "invisible earnings" before 1939 came from German trade passing through the harbors of the Netherlands. The French steel industry was also hugely dependent on coke and coal from Germany. See Tony Judt, *Post War: A History of Europe since 1945* (The Penguin Press, 2005), 155–56.

24. See "Why Doesn't France Have a Mittelstand?" in *The Economist* (Oc- tober 20, 2012). It's an excellent piece on the largely unsuccessful at- tempts in France to emulate the German mittelstand "model."

25. See Jana Randow and Aaron Kirchfeld, "German Mittelstand Still Thrives," in *Bloomberg Businessweek* (September 30, 2010).

26. "Mitbestimmung" literally translates as "co-determination" and refers to the joint role of workers and employers in formulating management decisions.

27. See "What Germany Offers the World," in *The Economist* (April 14, 2012).

28. In fact, the term "mittelstand" originally referred to artisans.
29. Thilo Sarrazin's previous book, *Germany Is Abolishing Itself* (Deutsche Verlags-Anstalt, 2010), criticized the impact of Muslim immigration on German society and had been equally combative, controversial and bestselling.
30. Data from the German Federal Ministry of Economics and Technology (www.bmwi.de/ . . . /facts-about-german-foreign-trade-in-2011).
31. See Michael Steen, "German Economy Slows Sharply," in *Financial Times* (January 15, 2013).
32. See Masa Serdarevic, "Greece, Portugal and Spain Really Have Benefitted Most from the Euro," in *FT Alphaville* (August 17, 2012); see also Alfred Steinherr, "Is Germany the Main Beneficiary of the Euro?" in *The Globalist* (October 18, 2012).
33. See Stephane Deo, Paul Donovan and Larry Hatheway, "Euro Break-up—The Consequences," *UBS Investment Research* (September 6, 2011).
34. See "The Limits of German Largess," in *The Wall Street Journal Online*, July 5, 2012 (http://online.wsj.com/article/SB10001424052702304 299704577500783720470896.html).
35. See Nicholas Kulish and Paul Geitner, "Merkel Stresses Limits to Germany's Strength," in *The New York Times* (June 14, 2012).

CHAPTER 6: CHATEAU CHONGQING

1. A short version of my reporting of this study group appeared in *Yale Global Online* on March 12, 2012 (http://yaleglobal.yale.edu/content /children-chinas-future-part-i).
2. See Evan Osnos, "The Grand Tour," in *The New Yorker* (April 18, 2011); see also "Chinese Tourists: A New Grand Tour," in *The Economist* (December 16, 2010).
3. "Chinese Tourists: A New Grand Tour," in *The Economist* (December 16, 2010).
4. The *China Daily* newspaper quoted a World Luxury Association report estimating that Chinese visitors accounted for 62 percent of Europe's luxury goods sales in January 2012, as millions headed abroad for holidays during the Chinese New Year festivities. The association put the total Chinese spending overseas during the holiday period that year at $7.2 billion. Another report by the School of Oriental and African Studies in London detailed how, as far back as 2009, Chinese tourists spent 158 million euros in duty-free shops in France alone. This was 48 million euros more than their notoriously big-spending Russian counterparts. In the same year, spending by Chinese travelers in Italy rose by 34 percent and in Sweden by 32 percent. The British luxury fashion house Burberry reported that 30 percent of the sales in its UK stores were to Chinese customers. London Luxury, a retailers' organization representing fashion boutiques in London's exclusive Bond Street area, revealed that in 2010, Chinese shoppers spent 230.7 million euros in this area itself, a figure that represented a 155 percent rise from the previous year.
5. See Dr. Kevin Latham, "How the Rise of Chinese Tourism Will Change the Face of the European Travel Industry," a report commissioned by Hilton Hotels & Resorts, October 2011.

6. See "China, EC Sign Milestone Tourism Memo," in Xinhua News Agency (February 13, 2004).

7. See Jean Pierre Lehman, "EU Seeks Chinese Eurozone Bailout—Oh the Ironies and Anomalies!" Fung Global Institute (October 3, 2022). According to IMF figures, China's per capita income of $4,382 ranks in the ninety-first position globally, just behind the Republic of Macedonia. Compare this with some of the eurozone countries: Luxembourg, $108,952 (1st), Netherlands, $46,986 (9th), Germany, $40,274 (19th), Italy, $34,059 (23rd), Spain, $30,639 and the "poor" Greeks, $27,311 (29th). In fact, the poorest eurozone country in GDP per capita is Slovakia at $16,104 (40th), thus about 3.5 times richer than China. The EU average is $32,537.

8. See Anderlini Jamil, "Bo Xilai: Power, Death and Politics,"" in *FT Magazine* (July 20, 2012).

9. See David Barboza and Sharon LaFraniere, "'Princelings' in China Use Family Ties to Gain Riches," in *The New York Times* (May 17, 2012); see also David Barboza, "Billions in Hidden Riches for Family of Chinese Leader," in *The New York Times* (October 26, 2012).

10. See Fareed Zakaria, "How China Can Help Europe Get out of Debt," in *The Washington Post* (September 15, 2011).

11. For an explanation of the breakdown of the Chinese character for crisis, *weiji*, see http://www.pinyin.info/chinese/crisis.htmland.

12. An erhu is a two-stringed traditional Chinese musical instrument.

13. See Harriet Alexander, "China's New Silk Road into Europe," in *The Daily Telegraph* (July 4, 2010).

14. See Amanda Mars and Miguel Gonzalez, "China se compromete a comprar 6.000 millones de deuda española," in *El Pais*, January 6, 2011 (http://elpais.com/elpais/2011/01/06/actualidad/1294305420_850215 .html).

15. See François Godement and Jonas Parello-Plesner with Alice Richard, "The Scramble for Europe," European Council on Foreign Relations Policy Brief, July 2011 (http://www.ecfr.eu/page/-/ECFR37_Scramble_For _Europe_ AW_v4.pdf).

16. See Thilo Hanemann and Daniel Rosen, "China Invests in Europe: Patterns, Impacts and Policy Implications," Rhodium Group, June 2012 (http://download.www.arte.tv/permanent/u1/Quand-la-Chine/RHG _ChinaInvestsInEurope_June2012%5B1%5D.pdf).

17. See Hans Kundnani and Jonas Parello-Plesner, "Beware the New Beijing-Berlin Bond," in *Financial Times* (May 14, 2012).

18. See Kenneth Dyson and Stephen Padgett, *The Politics of Economic Reform in Germany: Global, Rhineland or Hybrid Capitalism?* (Anglo-German Foundation, May 2005).

19. See Hans Kundnani and Jonas Parello-Plesner, "Beware the New Beijing-Berlin Bond," in *Financial Times* (May 14, 2012).

20. Sino-German trade increased by 400 percent between 2000 and 2010, touching 144 billion euros in 2011. German investments in China were worth 26 billion euros by mid-2012. According to the *China Daily* newspaper, Germany is Europe's biggest technology exporter to China. By April 2011, contracts worth $52.2 billion, covering a total of 15,448 transfers to China, had been signed between the two countries. See Li

Xiaokun and Fu Jing, "China, Germany Sign $15 billion deals," in *China Daily* (June 29, 2011); see also "China: Good Economic Cooperation," Federal Government of Germany, August 31, 2012 (http://www.bundesregierung.de/Content/EN/Reiseberichte/2012/china-2012-08-29-regierungskonsultationen.html).

21. See Sanjaya Baru, "Merkel in China," in Project Syndicate, August 27 2012 (http://www.project-syndicate.org/commentary/merkel-in-china-by-sanjaya-baru); see also Judy Dempsey, "German Business Moves Beyond Russia to China," in *The New York Times* (July 13, 2010).

22. Merkel eventually visited Greece in October 2012, almost two years after the crisis first came to light.

23. See Hans Kundnani and Jonas Parello-Plesner, "China and Germany: A New Special Relationship?" European Council on Foreign Relations Policy Brief, 2012 (http://ecfr.eu/page/-/ECFR55_CHINA_GERMANY_BRIEF_AW.pdf).

24. See Nils Klawitter and Wieland Wagner, "Buying Germany's Hidden Champions: Takeover Could Signal New Strategy for China," in *Spiegel Online*, February 9, 2012 (http://www.spiegel.de/international/business/buying-germany-s-hidden-champions-takeover-could-signal-new-strategy-for-china-a-813907.html).

25. Ibid.

26. See "China's Sany Acquires Germany's Truck Mixer Maker Intermix," in Xinhua news agency (July27, 2012).

27. Figures sourced from Germany Trade and Invest agency; see also "China Becomes Top Foreign Investor in Germany," in Xinhua News Agency (March 15, 2012).

28. See Francois Godement and Jonas Parello-Plesner with Alice Richard, "The Scramble for Europe," European Council on Foreign Relations Policy Brief (July 2011).

29. See "Rising to the China Challenge," in *Business Europe*, October 2011 (http://www.businesseurope.eu/content/default.asp?PageID=568&DocID=29298).

30. See Andrew Willis, "EU Industry Chief Voices Need to Block Chinese Takeovers," December 28, 2010 (http://euobserver.com/china/31579).

31. Data provided to me in an e-mail exchange with José Luis Hermoso, Senior Analyst and Head of Research of IWSR (International Wine and Spirits Research).

32. See Jane Anson, "Bordeaux and China," *Wine Business International* (May 2011).

33. The French word for "late" is "*retarde*."

34. Abridged version of this story appeared in *Yale Global Online*. See Pallavi Aiyar, "The New Barons of Bordeaux," September 12, 2012 (http://yaleglobal.yale.edu/content/new-barons-bordeaux).

35. See Li Xiang, "Reds' Star Rises in the East," in *China Daily* (August 3, 2012).

36. See Gaurav Anand, "Bordeaux's Wine, China, and Négociants," *Wine Forays* (December 9, 2011).

37. See "India-EU Bilateral Trade and Trade with the World," DG Trade (http://trade.ec.europa.eu/doclib/docs/2006/september/tradoc_113390.pdf).

38. Chen Zhimin, Dai Bingran, Pan Zhongqi and Ding Chun, "China's Priorities and Strategy in the China-EU Relations," in *Serie Unión Europea* 38 (2011).

39. See Guy de Jonquières, "Wanted: A European China Policy," CNN, September 4, 2012 (http://globalpublicsquare.blogs.cnn.com/2012/09/04/wanted-a-european-china-policy/).

40. See "Jin Liqun: Europe Induces 'Sloth, Indolence,'" Al Jazeera, December 27, 2011 (http://www.aljazeera.com/programmes/talktojazeera/2011/11/2011114434664695.html).

41. See Antoaneta Becker, "China Looks at Life after Euro," in *Asia Times Online*, November 10, 2011 (http://www.atimes.com/atimes/China_Business/MK10Cb01.html).

42. See Joshua Chaffin and Gerrit Weismann, "EU Trade Officials Face China Dilemma," in *Financial Times* (September 2, 2012).

43. See Guy de Jonquières, "Wanted: A European China Policy," CNN, September 4, 2012 (http://globalpublicsquare.blogs.cnn.com/2012/09/04/wanted-a-european-china-policy/).

44. The case was finally settled in July 2013 in which a minimum price for solar panels from China was set, in exchange for which the European Union agreed not to impose any punitive tariffs. However, the ceiling set was less than 0.56 euro a watt, a price that was about 25 percent lower even than when the case began. The deal was widely seen as a European capitulation to the Chinese. See Keith Bradsher, "Weak Finish from Europe on Chinese Solar Panels," in *The New York Times* (July 28, 2013).

45. See Guy de Jonquières, "Wanted: A European China Policy," CNN, September 4, 2012 (http://globalpublicsquare.blogs.cnn.com/2012/09/04/wanted-a-european-china-policy/); see also Philip Blenkinsop, "EU Holds Fire on ZTE, Huawei Telecom Trade Case," Reuters (October 10, 2012).

CHAPTER 7: THE GLOBAL GHERKIN

1. Data is for 2011 from official EU sources. See http://ec.europa.eu/trade/creating-opportunities/bilateral-relations/countries/united-states/.

2. All data is for 2009, taken from the report: "Europe 2020, Competitive or Complacent?" by Daniel S. Hamilton (Brookings Institution Press, 2010).

3. The numbers may not have been particularly impressive but economic ties between India and the European Union had shown a sharp upward trajectory over the first decade of the twenty-first century. The value of EU-India trade grew from 28.6 billion euros in 2003 to 75 billion euros in 2012. EU investment in India more than tripled between 2003 and 2010, going from 759 million euros in 2003 to 3 billion euros in 2010. Trade in commercial services tripled during the same period, going from 5.2 billion euros in 2002 to 17.9 billion euros in 2010. All data is from the EU website http://ec.europa.eu/trade/creating-opportunities/bilateral-relations/countries/india/. Crucially, the European Union was India's largest trading partner. Nonetheless, the European Union's market share is declining fast (from 45 percent in 1960 to 28 percent in the early 1990s to 15 percent today) and nowadays represents less than one-sixth of total Indian trade. Conversely, in the past few years, China has become the largest trading partner of India if one includes the indirect

trade through Hong Kong and the Middle East. See Jean-Joseph Boillot, "The EU and India: Reinvigorating a Tired Partnership," in G. Grevi and T. Renard (eds.), *Partners in Crisis: EU Strategic Partnerships and the Global Economic Downturn* (European Strategic Partnerships Observatory Report, November 2012).

4. See Pallavi Aiyar, "Belgian Crystals to Make a Comeback in India," in *Business Standard* (March 10, 2010). The exterior of the new city museum in Antwerp uses red sandstone from India. Inside the museum there is an entire section devoted to the city's Jain community.

5. See Pallavi Aiyar, "Changing the Toothpaste Tube Market in China, the Essel Way," in *The Hindu Business Line* (March 24, 2008).

6. For more details on the Aalst carnival, see Katrien Lindemans, "Hit Parade," in *Flanders Today* (February 8, 2012).

7. Accounting for about 35 percent of gherkin exports from India, the company produced 65,000 tons of the vegetable in 2008, 55,000 tons of which were grown in India alone. By 2012, it was manufacturing 80 million jars of vegetables a year, 90 percent of which were grown in India. Ninety-five percent of Global Green's sales revenues were generated outside of India by 2012.

8. The base year for the figures is 2009.

9. See "Crompton's Sudhir Trehan Is BS CEO of the Year," in *Business Standard* (February 11, 2010).

10. When I visited a year later, the name had officially been changed to CG and all signs of Pauwels had been taken down. The locals, however, still referred to the place as Pauwels and my taxi driver had no clue where "the CG plant" was. But he was able to take me to "Pauwels" without a problem.

11. See "Don't Touch Taittinger," in *The Economist* (June 1, 2006). Arcelor was the world's largest steel producer in terms of turnover and the second largest in terms of steel output in 2004. The company was created by a merger of the former companies Aceralia (Spain), Usinor (France) and Arbed (Luxembourg) in 2002. See "Cast-iron," in *The Economist* (June 15, 2006). In 2006, Mittal Steel made a bid to acquire Arcelor, leading to opposition from the company's board of directors as well as the governments of France, Luxembourg and Spain. Interestingly, only Belgium, where several Arcelor plants were located, declared a neutral stance. The European Union backed the bid as well. Mittal was finally successful in his bid in late June 2006. The resulting company, Arcelor-Mittal, became by far the world's largest steelmaker in terms of market value, revenue and output. See "Little Love Lost," in *The Economist* (June 29, 2006).

12. See Khozem Merchant in "Partner or Protectionist? India's View of Europe," European Business Forum Debate, Issue 26, Autumn 2006.

13. I met with Avantha Group Chairman and CEO Gautam Thapar in late 2010 and asked him about the special challenges of acceptance that an Indian company faces when buying a European one. His answer: "There is always tension. If I come and buy you and you've been around for 40–50 years, the uncertainty and fear factor is huge. People feel you've bought the company but you have not bought my mind, my loyalty. So you need to earn that right. If it was GE that had bought Pauwels, it would be a very different reaction, because it is already an

established global name. But when a CG comes in we have to earn our spurs, so there is an extra mile or three we have to walk to get to the same place. But if you do it right and start showing results, then the initial fears that these people have come here to buy us and move all the jobs to India disappears. In fact, we have created new jobs in the locality. So after that hurdle is crossed, the coalescing is very quick." For the full interview see http://www.business-standard.com/india/news/qa -gautam-thapar-chairmanceo-avantha-group/408456/.

14. Suzlon boasted global manufacturing centers in Germany and Portugal as well as R&D centers in Germany, Denmark and the Netherlands. In December 2009, Suzlon beat French heavyweight Arvea to take over German wind energy manufacturer RE Power, which was Europe's second-largest company in the sector.

15. According to the European Wind Energy Association, the market for offshore wind in Europe by 2020 will be worth in excess of 88 billion euros. Moreover, by 2030, offshore wind farms may provide nearly one-fifth of the European Union's electricity, making a huge jump from the 1.5 GW they generate today to a mighty 150 GW. See "Offshore Wind in Europe: 2010 Market Report," KPMG.

16. But while acquisitions in western Europe might not have been focused on market share given that these were usually perceived as saturated and offering little growth opportunity, the same was not true of the European Union's new, eastern European member states. Jean-Josef Boillot lists the following examples of Indian acquisitions to prove this point: Romania (Mahindra Tractors), Hungary/Poland (Videocon, Escorts, Strides Arcolab, Reliance Industries, Ranbaxy, Essel Propack, Zensar Technologies, Tata Consultancy Services, HCL Technologies and Infosys). See Jean-Joseph Boillot, "The EU and India: Reinvigorating a Tired Partnership," in G. Grevi and T. Renard (eds.), *Partners in Crisis: EU Strategic Partnerships and the Global Economic Downturn* (European Strategic Partnerships Observatory Report, November 2012).

17. See "Mittalic Magic," in *The Economist* (February 14, 2008). Mittal might have been an Indian national, but his Mittal Steel (the company that predated ArcelorMittal) had been headquartered in Rotterdam and managed from London. Mittal's iron-and-steel career has spanned mills in Indonesia, Trinidad, Mexico and Algeria, to mention a few. But he has no active investments in India itself, despite attempts in recent years to set up facilities.

18. See Stanley Reed, "A Global Steel Giant Scales Back," in *The New York Times* (July 25, 2012). In 2012, European demand for steel was 25 percent below 2007 levels.

19. Ibid. I was, however, relieved to read that the Ghent plant was to be kept alive, having formed an odd attachment to the place, perhaps for its having taken my heavy industrial processes-virginity in such visceral style.

20. "French Min: No Solution than Closing Peugeot's Aulnay Plant," in *The Wall Street Journal* (http://online.wsj.com/article/BT-CO-20130205-70 1144.html?mod=WSJ_qtoverview_wsjlatest).

21. Matters were made worse by the withdrawal of subsidies to the wind energy market in many countries. Plans to lay off nearly a third of its work force in Belgium were announced by CG, and some operations were being relocated to lower-cost Hungary.

22. See http://www.sayouitofrance-innovation.com/why-say-oui-to-france/a -competitive-open-leader.
23. TCS is one of India's largest IT services companies and among the top ten technology firms in the world.
24. See "Mahindra Satyam Inks Deal with BASF IT Services," in *Economic Times* (May 4, 2010).
25. See Shruti Sabharwal, "CSC Outplays HCL, Bags ArcelorMittal deal for $600 mn," in *Economic Times* (January 13, 2011).
26. These statistics were for 2010. By 2012, the number of Capgemini employees in India had grown to over 40,000 and almost half of the company's total staff were now on offshore locations. See Karl Flinders, "Capgemini Will Be a Mainly Offshore Based Supplier by 2015," ComputerWeekly.com, November 8, 2012 (http://www.computerweekly.com /blogs/inside-outsourcing/2012/11/capgemini-will-be-a-mainly-offshore -based-supplier-by-2015.html).
27. See Amitav Ghosh, "Europe and the Fate of the Earth, Part I" (http:// amitavghosh.com/blog/?p=4860).
28. See Chapter Two for a detailed discussion of the proposal.
29. See EBF (European Business Forum) Debate, Issue 26, Autumn 2006.
30. See James Slack, "Secret EU Deal Forces Britain to Take in 12,000 Indian Workers Despite Soaring Unemployment," in *Daily Mail* (March 2, 2012).
31. One of the UPA's main coalition partners, the Trinamool Congress, withdrew support from the government over its opposition to FDI in retail, in September 2012.
32. See, for example, Krista Mahr, "The Underachiever," in *Time* (July 16, 2012).

CHAPTER 8: DISUNITY IN DIVERSITY

1. "Time to call it a day," in *The Economist* (September 6, 2007).
2. See Harry Pearson, *A Tall Man in a Low Land: Some Time among the Belgians*, (Abacus, 1999), 1–2.
3. Ibid., 127.
4. Ibid., 105.
5. Robert Mnookin and Alain Verbeke, "Persistent Nonviolent Conflict with No Reconciliation: The Flemish and Walloons in Belgium," in *Law and Contemporary Problems* (Spring 2009), 151–86 (http://scholarship .law.duke.edu/lcp/vol72/ iss2/14).
6. Anti-German sentiment during the First World War caused the British king George V to change the name of his family branch, from Saxe-Coburg and Gotha to Windsor, in 1917.
7. For a look at the role of Indian troops who died fighting in Flanders during World War I, see Pallavi Aiyar, "Lost Cause?" in *Business Standard* (April 3, 2010).
8. The linguistic terms "Dutch" and "Flemish" are often used interchangeably in the Belgian context. In Flanders, standardized Dutch is taught in schools and used in government and media. However, several dialects of Dutch, including Brabantian, Limburgish and West Flemish, are also included under the term "Flemish," in addition to standardized Dutch.

9. Unfortunately, the ancient Brussels patois, an almost fifty-fifty mixture of French and Dutch with some Spanish thrown in, has itself been allowed to die out.

10. See "Only "Politically Neutral" Music in Brussels Metro," in Flanders news.be, May 25, 2011 (http://www.deredactie.be/cm/vrtnieuws.english /news/1.1031697).

11. Quentin Langley, "Putting Belgium on eBay?" in *The Globalist,* October 26, 2007 (http://www.theglobalist.com/storyid.aspx?StoryId=6488).

12. In Belgium, wage increases were automatically tied to inflation. It was one of the factors that many economists felt kept the country from achieving its competitive potential.

13. See Harry Pearson, *A Tall Man in a Low Land: Some Time among the Belgians,* (Abacus, 1999), 137.

14. See Robert Mnookin and Alain Verbeke, "Persistent Nonviolent Conflict with No Reconciliation: The Flemish and Walloons in Belgium," in *Law and Contemporary Problems* (Spring 2009), 151–86 (http:// scholarship.law.duke.edu/ lcp/vol72/iss2/14).

15. See Luc Sante, *The Factory of Facts* (Vintage Books, 1998), 157.

16. An example of a Herman haiku:

   In a nearby ditch
   toads mating passionately
   inaugurate spring.

17. See Bruno Waterfield, "Children at Flemish School in Brussels Punished for Speaking French," in *The Telegraph* (February 15, 2012).

18. For more on these Western predictions, see Ramachandra Guha, *India after Gandhi: The History of the World's Largest Democracy* (Pan Macmillan, 2008).

19. See Diana L. Eck, *India: A Sacred Geography* (Harmony, 2012).

20. See Luc Sante, *The Factory of Facts* (Vintage Books, 1998), 160.

21. See Robert Mnookin and Alain Verbeke, "Persistent Nonviolent Conflict with No Reconciliation: The Flemish and Walloons in Belgium," *Law and Contemporary Problems* (Spring 2009), 151–86.

22. Ibid., 175.

23. These numbers have been contested by Belgian historians. But Hochschild is upfront that the figures are not only about deaths resulting from murder but also from starvation, exhaustion and disease. See Adam Hochschild, *King Leopold's Ghost* (Houghton Mifflin, 1998).

24. See "Congo Free State, 1885–1908," Yale University's Genocide Studies Program (http://www.yale.edu/gsp/colonial/belgian_congo/index.html).

25. In 2013, the museum will shut down for a three-year-long renovation, which is in part aimed at reframing the manner in which Belgium's colonial history in the Congo is presented along more "modern" lines. This process was already underway when I last visited the museum in 2012. By then the hall where the names of all the Belgians who had died in the service of the country in the Congo were listed was now superimposed by a series of projected "x"s, that symbolically represented the missing names of the Congolese who had died during the colonial period.

26. The Belgians, however, had a much better track record when it came to primary education, one that was favorable when compared to that of the other colonial powers in Africa.

27. See Luc Sante, *The Factory of Facts* (Vintage Books, 1998), 218.

28. See Adam Hochschild, *King Leopold's Ghost* (Houghton Mifflin, 1998), 311.

29. Finally in 2001, a Belgian parliamentary commission admitted that the country had a "moral responsibility" in Lumumba's assassination. Although the government apologized, it did not mention any names and no legal action was taken. The parliamentary investigation was undertaken following the publication of a book by Belgian researcher Ludo de Witt called *Assassination of Lumumba* (Verso, 2002), which detailed the Belgian role in the murder.

CHAPTER 9: CELEBRATING THE DECLINE OF EUROPE?

1. See Pallavi Aiyar, "Celebrating the Decline of Europe," in *Business Standard* (May 23, 2010).

2. See Arvind Subramanian, "This Is a Golden Age of Global Growth (Yes, You Read That Right)," in *Financial Times* (April 7, 2013).

3. See Suzanne Daley, "Spain Recoils as Its Hungry Forage Trash Bins for a Next Meal," in *The New York Times* (September 24, 2012).

4. See Pallavi Aiyar, "Ugly Vegetables Gain Acceptance in European Union," in *Business Standard* (July 2, 2009).

5. See Ramachandra Guha, "A Nation Consumed by the State," in *Outlook* (January 31, 2011).

6. SAARC includes the countries of India, Nepal, Pakistan, Bhutan, Bangladesh, Sri Lanka, Maldives and Afghanistan.

7. See Indermit Gill, "Demolishing Five Myths about Europe's Decline," in *Europe's World* (Autumn 2012).

8. Ibid.

9. See Pallavi Aiyar, "The Idea of Asia," in *Business Standard* (August 21, 2010).

10. ASEAN, or the Association of Southeast Asian Nations, comprises the ten countries of Brunei, Cambodia, Indonesia, Laos, Vietnam, Singapore, Thailand, Malaysia, Myanmar and Philippines.

11. See Ruth Le Pla, "China–Southeast Asia Trade Links Expanding Rapidly," Asia New Zealand Foundation, February 12, 2013 (http://www.asianz.org.nz/node/5658).

12. The Shanghai Cooperation Organisation is a security grouping founded in 2001 by the leaders of China, Russia, Kazakhstan, Kyrgystan, Tajikistan and Uzbekistan. India, Afghanistan, Mongolia, Iran and Pakistan have observer status. The East Asia Summit was founded in 2005 and includes all the ten members of ASEAN as well as China, Japan, South Korea, India, Australia and New Zealand. Later, the United States and Russia were also inducted as members.

13. See K. Subrahmanyan, "Why SARRC Cannot Be an EU or ASEAN," in *The Times of India* (January 8, 2002).